YOU
ALONE
MAY LIVE

YOU ALONE MAY LIVE

ONE WOMAN'S JOURNEY THROUGH THE AFTERMATH OF THE RWANDAN GENOCIDE

MARY K. BLEWITT OBE

dialogue< >

First published in Great Britain in 2010 by
Dialogue, an imprint of
Biteback Publishing Ltd
Heal House
375 Kennington Lane
London
SE11 5QY

ISBN 978-1-906447-06-9

1 3 5 7 9 10 8 6 4 2

A CIP catalogue record for this book is available from the British Library.

Set in Sabon by SoapBox

Printed and bound in Great Britain by
TJ Internnational Ltd, Padstow, Cornwall

THIS BOOK IS dedicated to the silent victims who are not here to tell their story, to my father, my mother and my brother, and to all the victims of the Rwandan genocide.

To my beloved mother Epiphania, who lived a silent, troubled life, and whose genes I have inherited: thank you for nicknaming me 'United Nations'; in so doing you made me a global citizen. I have lived in many countries as a refugee, eventually taking citizenship in Britain and dedicating my life to supporting the survivors of the Rwandan genocide. You gave me the values that you yourself practised: above all, respect for humanity.

To my brother Jean Baptiste, my hero, who sacrificed his young life to stay in Rwanda, the country he loved: I can't imagine how much pain you felt, and the fear that engulfed you as men wielding machetes murdered you in cold blood. I will never forget you.

I also dedicate this book to the family I left behind, who kept me going and gave me unconditional love.

I have been blessed to have a wonderful husband, Richard. He loved me and backed me unconditionally. We gave each other support to grow and achieve our potential, sometimes sacrificing being together to reach our goals. Without his understanding I doubt whether I could have made it through the hard times.

My son, also Richard, brings hope into my life; he has inherited my mother's sense of humanity and, like me, is not content to have just one good friend but wants to make friends with everyone. He is hard-working and motivates me to stay focused. He is the only person who can judge my changes of mood no matter how I disguise them to protect my family. If I am really feeling down he hugs me without saying anything, which comforts me greatly. He is witty and can always make me smile.

Christine, my beautiful daughter, is an inspiration, although she pushes the boundaries. Like her brother, she is acutely aware of other people's pain. She is extremely kind and compassionate. She is also smart and a good judge of character, but above all she is a fighter, even when it's not entirely necessary. She is a survivor of the genocide and this book is dedicated to the memory of her parents, whom we never met.

Life would be meaningless without my children and devoid of their support I could not have achieved what I have so far.

Most importantly, I am blessed still to have eight siblings who were outside Rwanda at the time of the genocide. Although we live in different countries, the love and security our mother gave us when growing up keeps us together. She would be proud of us. I dedicate this book to them; their contributions will help us all remember past events.

Finally, the book is dedicated to the survivors of the Rwandan genocide and to the many friends who have touched my life, and to everyone working with victims of torture.

CONTENTS

Acknowledgements

You Alone May Live is an expression of my personal journey. It consists entirely of my own views and reflections on the legacy of war, displacement, separation and genocide, events that changed my life forever.

My first debt is to Margaret Parsons, a dear friend who over the years has not only seen me through the toughest times, but also encouraged me to write my story.

In spring 2009, I met Katherine Dykstra, a writer, editor and teacher at Gotham Writers' Workshop and New York University (NYU). I missed my first class with her and arrived late for the second, because I couldn't find the lecture theatre. I interrupted Katherine as she was telling the class, 'We all have a story to tell, and we can write.' That sentence was all I needed to conquer the world of writers and authors. Katherine speaks softly, but is reassuring and firm in her teaching. She helped transform me into a creative writer after nine lessons. I credit every chapter of my book to her persistence, her feedback and her encouragement. Her support has been invaluable.

So, based at the Robert F. Wagner School for Public Service at NYU as a visiting scholar, I began my extraordinary journey. It truly has been an experience, involving many agreeable hours writing everything that jumped out of my memory, going through my diaries and heaps of survivors' testimonies, presenting lectures and meeting extraordinarily energetic and creative people. They helped me decompress from years with the Survivors Fund (SURF), but also reminded me that there was life after SURF. Their friendship, acceptance and drive gave me the energy I needed to face my past, revisit and reflect on my work over the last fifteen years and help put my life in perspective. Thank you to Dean Ellen Schall for that opportunity, and all her team, who made the transition so easy for me, and to my roommate, Chris Robinson, for putting me up and putting up with me.

There are some people without whom this book could not have been written: my son Richard, daughter Christine, nieces Marian, Louise, Aline, Danielle Mary, Françoise, Yvonne, Danielle and Georgia, and nephews John Paul, John Baptist, Christopher, Daniel, Isaac, Leonard, Alain, Denis and Jordan. They were the only audience that had the time to listen to my story, their family story. Although sometimes I had to bribe them to stay focused and interested! They lived this book as I did. I must also add the latest edition to the family: my niece Epiphania, named after my mother and born the day before this book went to press.

The story of my life could not be complete without the colleagues who supported and believed in my vision and the survivors whose stories motivated me to set up SURF. In particular, I want to thank Gabo Wilson, Sam Munderere, Liam Dempsey, Andrew Sutton and David Russell, without whom SURF would not have been a successful charity, and all the trustees that have served on the SURF board over the years. Also, I continue to be grateful to Alex Sklan at the Medical Foundation for all his support, and to all the many patrons and donors that make SURF's work possible.

I am extremely grateful to all SURF's supporters and volunteers and everyone who has touched my life in the last fifteen years working with survivors of the Rwandan genocide.

The final days of putting together the chapters of this jigsaw were the toughest times, deciding what remained in my memory and what became part of my book. I spent those days at Mosa Courts Apartments in Kampala, locked away in my room with my laptop, mobile and scraps of paper everywhere. The welcoming family setting at Mosa Courts Apartments gave me the stability, friendship and the security to pull the book together. I am eternally thankful to the Mosa Courts staff and management for the support they gave me.

Lastly, for all those whose names are too many to mention here, who showed interest and enthusiasm in my book, I owe you my sanity. You made me believe that there is nothing I can't do if I have the will to do it. You are my inspiration. I wouldn't like to forget to thank particularly Dino Rozman and Dennis Couprie, my personal trainers, for keeping me mentally and physically balanced.

I could not finish without mentioning the survivors who have touched my life. Our journey has been bumpy at times, and the recovery has been slow but sure. You will always be in my heart and I will continue to support you in any capacity I can. God bless you all.

ONE

Mind the gap

I ARRIVED IN the UK in October 1986. It was a daunting journey. I hardly closed my eyes on the plane, longing to be home with my family. I had lived as a refugee all my life, in three different countries, and had no place to call home. I was relieved to be starting anew in the UK, far from my troubled past, with friends of my family, even though I had never met them before. I didn't stop to wonder what they were like, whether they had children or not. I knew they were old, but didn't know much about their background.

My departure was abrupt; I had spent years, like many other Rwandan refugees in Uganda, being targeted by different regimes. An opportunity to start my life away from the troubled past was one worth taking, albeit in a country I had no knowledge of and although it meant leaving my family behind. I had so much to do: talk to my family, sort out my secondhand clothes business, pack the few possessions I had and get a visa. By the time I left I was feeling exhausted and uncertain of what I would do in the future.

All my family came to see me off at the airport. We arrived early and with every moment that passed I felt more anxious and afraid, but I have always been the strongest in the family, so I tried to hide my feelings by making jokes. The goodbyes were tense but no tears were shed: Mother always told us that crying when one was leaving was bad luck, so we all smiled and hugged.

I had an uncomfortable flight, sandwiched between an overweight snoring man and a boy whose parents were sitting nearby. He moved up and down the plane and his parents kept making a fuss about his food and making him swap places with another sibling every few minutes. Strange disturbing sounds kept me awake, and the turbulence almost made me reach for the sick bag.

A little under nine hours later we landed at Gatwick Airport, and my nerves gave way. I felt far from the safety net of my family and the Africanness that I was familiar with. I had never been to an airport this big; there was so much to take in. I quietly asked a female African passenger who had been on the plane with me, 'How do I get out to meet my host family?'

'Follow everyone. We are all going out,' she replied, raising her voice so that I felt ashamed and looked around to see if anyone heard. No one seemed bothered, nor did anyone seem interested to help me.

I followed everyone through customs and immigration, noticing that I had broken into a sweat. I was filled with anxiety. My uneasiness worsened as I waited at the baggage reclaim, where there were so many black suitcases that I wondered if I would recognise mine. 'I'll wait for everyone else to pick up their luggage. That way, I won't take someone's suitcase,' I thought.

'I hate airports,' an elderly man grumbled, as he pushed his way past me through the crowd that surrounded the carousel. My eyes followed him, and secretly I agreed with him, wondering if he too was anxious like me. We waited for a while, all eyes fixed on the empty conveyer belt. The elderly man began tapping his feet on the floor in irritation and mumbling something I could not hear.

Eventually the luggage appeared. Some of it fell off and occasionally someone picked up a wrong bag. I was so absorbed in the action I didn't see my two brown boxes of avocados and bananas until they were trundling away from me on the opposite side of the carousel. I ran towards them, negotiating my way through the trolleys and the people, only to see them disappear. I kept my composure, eyes now wide open, and before long they reappeared on the side where I had been standing earlier. I picked them up and waited to identify my suitcase. A medium-sized black case made a few trips round; no one had taken it, and by now nearly everyone was gone. I picked it up and opened the zip and, yes, it was mine.

As I made my way out, my eyes were drawn to two signs: 'Goods to declare', indicating a red exit, and 'Nothing to declare', indicating a green one. I wondered which exit I should take, or what it was that one declared, so I asked a tall man in a smart navy blue uniform.

'Where have you come from, Madam?' he asked me in a gravelly voice.

'Uganda,' I replied.

'What are you carrying in those boxes?'

'Avocados and sweet bananas for my host family.'

'Please open the boxes and your suitcase,' he commanded firmly.

I rummaged for my keys in my handbag and unlocked the suitcase. But the sisal strings holding the boxes would not open. I tried undoing them with my teeth, but they cut through my lips. The man in uniform handed me a penknife and I cut them loose and exposed the contents, my hands sweating, my heart thumping.

I thought I was in trouble. Otherwise why was I the only one opening my luggage? And how was I to find my way out of here? All the other passengers on my plane had left. Martin and Shirley, my hosts, would have been waiting for a while now. They didn't know what I looked like nor me them.

'Is someone picking you up?' the man in uniform asked. I handed him a piece of paper with the address and phone number.

Suddenly I heard an announcement. 'Calling Mary Kayitesi arriving from Entebbe, please report to the information desk where Martin and Shirley are waiting for you.'

'That's my name!' I said, jumping with excitement.

'You may go now.' The man showed me the way out.

I felt relieved as I packed my clothes and tightened the sisal on the boxes. I made my way out to where hundreds of people were waiting for arrivals. I could not find the information desk, which was hidden away. There was too much to take in, so I asked someone to show me the desk. All I knew was that Martin was black and Shirley white, but as I approached the information desk, looking out for them, Martin hurried towards me and gave me a huge hug. I wondered how he recognised me, but didn't ask.

Martin and Shirley were in their late sixties. Martin had a light complexion and pink lips as if they had been burnt. He was wearing a light brown suit, his coat slung messily over his shoulder, his shirt buttoned in the wrong holes, and he had a cowboy hat on his head. He walked with a sideways swagger, in a manner that showed his carefree attitude. He introduced himself and Shirley.

Shirley was slightly shorter, with puffy eyes and greying hair, looking rather frail in a striped black and white dress. Wrong choice of colour for her complexion, I thought, but elegant. She was smoking a cigarette, her eyes moving from my feet to my head as if she was measuring my personality through my body language.

'Welcome to London,' she said, kissing me on both cheeks in the French style. 'We've been waiting for nearly four hours, so we had a little to drink.'

Martin was a perfect gentleman, and took the luggage trolley off me and led us to the train. Steering the trolley appeared hard for him; he nearly collided with a man in a phone booth. He explained the train would take us to Victoria station, where we were to take a taxi to their home in Barnes.

I found Gatwick daunting, a large railway station teeming with people, some boarding and others disembarking. The flow was endless. As we sat on the train, I had my first shock: two people in this carriage were lovers and they were openly displaying affection. I had never seen anyone kissing in public. I tried to look away. A woman sitting beside them gave a good-natured jealous smile; they winked at her. An old couple sitting opposite them mumbled something in disgust. 'Couldn't they wait until they get home?' I thought, rather bothered by this unacceptable behaviour.

I turned my attention to a smartly dressed young woman opposite me, no doubt a professional, maybe a lawyer, or perhaps even a fashion designer, I thought, as she was lost in a fashion magazine. From time to time she nibbled on a chocolate bar that she took from her handbag. That couldn't be right; surely she can't be eating on the train. In Africa people don't eat on buses or in public places except in designated areas.

At the end of the carriage, two children were playing under the silent gaze of their mother, straying a little away from their seats, stumbling as the train moved. Nothing was adding up to my expectations. Where I come from children are seen and not heard; how can these children act in a manner that their mother will not correct? I could feel a culture shock coming. I had been in the UK only a few hours, with no guidance, no tourist book on cultures, what to do and what not to do.

Martin and Shirley were busy telling me all about London. They chatted as though we had met before, asking me how my family was, and saying that they were happy to host me. I was feeling tired and struggled to keep up with the conversation; there was so much to take in. Martin pulled out a small flask of whisky from

5

his jacket pocket and offered me a sip. 'I don't take alcohol, thank you,' I said. Shirley reached for hers, which contained vodka, from a worn-out maroon leather handbag. I felt something was not right, but I ignored the thought.

'We bought this pair of his-and-hers liquor flasks in Harrods,' Martin told me.

'Tomorrow we will take you to Harrods to buy you winter boots – soon the weather will be cold, so you need the right shoes. We have Harrods store cards,' Shirley said.

Harrods? What is Harrods? But I wouldn't ask, because they spoke to me in a manner that suggested I should know. 'Thank you,' I replied.

The train snaked away and I got lost in its movement, as it created the illusion of a river of lights flowing away far as my eyes could see. The lights soon gave way to tall glass buildings, clusters of brick houses, high-rise blocks, television antennae sticking like spikes from balconies and roofs. In a little under thirty minutes the train stopped.

Victoria station was even further beyond my comprehension. People were in such a hurry, bumping into each other, moving this way and that as if they would never stop. I wondered if I could ever be part of this world that was sending my head dizzy with the endless flow of movement in all directions.

Outside the station we joined a long queue for taxis. Now this was impressive, even for my tired head; no one was jumping the queue, unlike back home, where everyone was so used to pushing their way to the front, regardless of who was there first. Before long we got a taxi, which negotiated its way between buses, cars and traffic lights, passing more tall glass buildings and eventually crossing what Shirley told me was 'the river Thames'. Martin was quick to show me their local pub just before it disappeared from view under Hammersmith Bridge. 'We will get you a job there when you are settled; the manager is our old friend,' he told me.

'A job in a pub,' I thought. I have a degree in international relations and political science. Surely the pub is not the right place to work. But I kept my opinion to myself.

Martin and Shirley's home in Barnes was a three-bedroom flat in a beautiful block just across Hammersmith Bridge, a short distance from the Thames. There were no lifts, so we carried my boxes and suitcase up the stairs to the fourth floor, Martin and Shirley visibly straining their muscles as they climbed slowly but surely. I offered to take the luggage, thinking they would fall with a crash all the way down to the lobby, but they held onto the banisters. Shirley tripped on the last step. 'Blimey,' she exclaimed. They both laughed, coughing and panting breathlessly. I found myself laughing too.

The flat was modest, subdued. I had expected it to be more luxurious given the posh area and the fine building. Martin pushed the door open, which rubbed against a thick grey carpet and led to a spacious living room whose large windows were hung with dusty net curtains. There were two shabby leather sofas with several multi-coloured cushions. In the far corner I could see a round black and chrome glass table, an armchair with a scarf slung across it and a sideboard. There was a unmissable statue of the crucifixion, pictures of Christ dotted all over the walls, woven prayer tapestries and other religious objects on the mantelpiece.

Shirley gave me a tour of the flat, showing me the open-plan kitchen and their master bedroom. At the foot of the bed was an armchair drowning under a heap of jeans, jumpers and other clothes that were waiting to be washed or hung up.

Then she showed me my room. It was small and plain, with a bed that squeaked when I sat on it, a wardrobe and a side table. I noticed the large windows that made the room look bigger, overlooking the trees that hid the Thames from view. At the back of the flat, past the kitchen, was another small room, which they rented to a student from Botswana. He was out when I arrived.

While Shirley was busy making dinner, I put my family photo on the side table and my clothes in the wardrobe. I had all my possessions in one medium-sized suitcase. I was starving.

'Dinner's ready,' Shirley called out.

'Not cheese on toast again,' grumbled Martin.

'That's what you're having, I'm afraid; it's too late to cook anything.'

I joined Martin and Shirley in the kitchen. I sat down and stared at two slices of bread for my dinner. I went through them very fast and was still left hungry. That was not a familiar dinner for me, and I couldn't even ask for more. I remembered reading Charles Dickens's *Oliver Twist*: 'Please, Sir, I want some more.' I tried picturing Oliver lost in London, but that wouldn't happen to me, so I stopped entertaining the thought. I politely thanked Shirley for dinner.

I couldn't wait to go to bed. I must have been so tired because when I awoke, I felt like my life had been displaced. I pulled the curtains back to let in the light. The sky was a crisp blue. I opened the window and a cold, moist wind rushed in, dampening me. Instantly I shivered, reached for the duvet and wrapped myself up. Through the window, everything was neat and orderly. I craved something familiar, like the boisterous African markets, full of people in bright multi-coloured clothes, and with the smell of *nyama choma* – roast goat – everywhere.

I was surprised at what I missed – such little things. Like vehicles stretching for miles at filling stations, the smell of raw petrol lingering in the air, the glittering beads of sunlight reflecting off corrugated iron rooftops, familiar voices of people speaking the many dialects in the neighbourhood, the voices of my siblings.

I couldn't imagine how I would rebuild my life. I had been displaced in Sudan before, when I had just turned seventeen, and here I was again, seven years later, totally alone with a family I didn't know. I coped by hanging onto good memories from my childhood. I missed my elder sister Riisa, nine months older than me. I called her the memory box, as she never forgot details or events. She would always remind me of the times when our mother took my side if we had a fight, which was often. I also had flashbacks to Jeanne d'Arc, the fourth born. She rarely smiled and kept herself to herself. I could see her walking, her heels hardly touching the ground; she seemed to walk on springs, as if she was about to pounce on somebody. She did pounce on people, especially later when she joined the army.

The next days and weeks increased my sense of culture shock. Shirley and Martin took me to Harrods and bought me a pair of blue knee-high boots. Shirley also gave me a thick jumper and a warm coat. I spent hours with Shirley passing shops covered in red signs for the Christmas sales, shoppers falling over each other to catch a bargain, while I felt invisible, in the middle of a white snow-covered city, unbearably cold, so that I had to wear layers of clothes and heavy boots that made it so hard for me to walk or breathe normally. Nonetheless I wasn't about to let the cold touch my soul except through my stiff nostrils.

Being poor and from a large family, we didn't celebrate birthdays, New Year or Easter. Our special time was Christmas. Now, in London, Christmas would be upon us in a few days. I remembered how on Christmas Day, my sister Jolly, the second last born, would be busy patching up our clothes, mending and adding embroidery to our dresses, so that her additional touch would make our one 'Sunday best' outfit look even better. She was very kind but always let her attitude get the better of her. My sister Lois, seventh in the family, was skilful at helping our mother prepare beef stew and organise the menu on this special occasion, one of the few days we could afford to eat meat or chicken. Lois was laid back; she laughed a lot and brought sunshine into our lives. She was always in trouble for starting a giggle; she would set us all laughing, and sometimes even our mother gave up and joined in too.

'Christmas has come early; nobody told me,' my brother Joseph would complain if Mother treated us to meat at any other time of the year, normally if we had visitors staying and Mother didn't want anyone to know we were poor; otherwise it was beans and cabbage for us all year round. Joseph, the third youngest, was streetwise and always busy; he would sell all sorts of things to raise a little money for the family. He was easy-going and generous, and always had his feet on the ground. He was also quite incapable of thinking about tomorrow. If any significant amount of money came his way, and it seldom did, he immediately bought food and anything else that came to mind until he had spent it all.

My brother Louis, fifth in the family, always acted older than his age. He was very thoughtful and extremely polite, even when he was a toddler. He was good at making catapults from inner tubes that he salvaged from the bicycle tyre repairers, and he used them to shoot birds in the trees. Once or twice he missed the birds and accidentally caught another target, a bully that had been tormenting his siblings. Then he would leg it home so fast that the culprit never found out what had hit him. Even so, he was the most responsible in the family, very protective. He remembered everyone's special day and always wanted them to feel good about themselves.

Being alone in London, far from my siblings, made me appreciate the family comedian and magician, my brother Francis. Slightly younger than Louis, he was a gifted mathematician, his head full of calculations. He was very handsome, a golden boy, and he knew it. Although he was clever, he was rather lazy, but he had a good sense of humour and could charm his way out of any sticky situation.

Every morning in Shirley and Martin's flat I would gaze through the wide windows that I dared not open because it was too cold. I could picture my younger siblings spinning a wheel down the street with a stick while the older ones played a card game called *matatu*. Our last-born baby, Rose, was too young to join in most games. She loved to stay close to Mother; she was the 'queen of the castle'. She was the most beautiful of us all, quite shy and reserved, unlike me, and sixteen years younger than me. She cried whenever she didn't get her way, but silently, not in a spoilt manner. We wouldn't notice for hours that she had been crying, and sometimes she couldn't even remember why.

Sunday in London was the most torturous day. Well-dressed families gracefully made their way to church, sitting together, nudging and squeezing each other to fit on one pew, young children and babies straying off or occasionally crying from boredom. Sometimes tears escaped my eyes when I watched them. I would remember Sunday with my family, walking to church together, our mother looking at all of us with such pride in her eyes. Mother was a quiet, religious woman who had come from a family of practising Christians. She would wear her hair natural and short. She dressed modestly, but she always looked beautiful to me.

We always prayed for my brother Jean Baptiste, a year younger than me, who had stayed in Rwanda. Jean Baptiste and Jeanne d'Arc had been separated from us when my father died in exile in Burundi. My grandfather went to bury my father and then, to ease my mother's economic burden, took my two siblings back to Rwanda with him. We grew up apart; only later did I make a trip to Rwanda to find them and reunite them with the family. Jean Baptiste preferred to live with our grandparents, who had brought him up, but he visited us in Uganda often. I remembered his kind, gentle nature with fondness.

Away from everyone, I had only my good memories to keep me hopeful. I remembered the ease with which my siblings crowded the air with words, tugging each other along, emphasising a point, always interrupting each other; I remembered the scrabbles and rivalries, but also the quickness to laugh. There had been so many happy days and nights, but now the enormity of my slow separation was stealing the happiness I had enjoyed growing up.

Over the next months, Uganda slowly became a distant memory, like a place I had once imagined, the dry heat, dusty roads and the amicable noises of people. Everything familiar was replaced by white snow, in a cold dark winter that slowly froze my emotions. I had no friends, but I kept busy. I discovered a love of books and I would borrow them from the local library, where I would also read the papers.

Martin and Shirley were very friendly and helpful, and we got on well, when they remembered I was staying with them. They lived in a world of their own, steeped in vodka and whisky. Once a week, and on special occasions such as Halloween, they took me to a pub in Barnes called the Bridge. They were well known there and they chatted with the barman.

'The usual for you, and what does the young lady drink?' the bartender would ask. 'Where are you sitting? I'll bring your drinks.'

'You're very kind,' Shirley and Martin would say. They would stop to speak to the locals, introducing me to everyone.

'Vodka, whisky and Coke! Enjoy your drinks.'

'Let's drink to that,' Martin would reply, raising his glass to the bartender.

Four hours later the pub would announce last orders, and Martin and Shirley would invariably have one for the road. I would help them make their way home, pushing them onto the bus, and getting them up the stairs to the fourth floor.

Martin and Shirley were intelligent. They read a lot – or rather, they borrowed books that they unintentionally never got round to reading. I never found out for certain, but I think they held good jobs before they retired. I had asked Martin how he recognised me when I arrived at Gatwick for the first time. He teased me for weeks, claiming he was psychic. I nearly believed him until he pointed out that my boxes of fruit were printed with 'Uganda OMO' in large letters. Omo is a washing powder brand. Then I thought, he is not so clever after all.

Life was so lonely. All I did was work in the flat and do the shopping, always stocking up enough supplies for Martin and Shirley. Sometimes they would stagger downstairs in the middle of the night to knock at the local kiosk for more. The shopkeeper knew them well, and I suppose he wanted their business, so he would even give them vodka on credit if they had spent all their money. I would make them a proper meal every day, even introducing fried plantains, sweet potatoes and spinach in groundnut sauce, which Shirley loved. I immersed myself in household chores, cleaning the flat, washing the dusty curtains and the greasy kitchen surfaces, and painting the fading walls.

Shirley would give me a small amount of pocket money. If I had any spare, I would call home and speak to my family and friends. Mother would sometimes go to the post office and speak to me; she missed me too, but she was proud I was getting on in London.

Martin had bought me an A–Z, which I read like a bible, a page every day. I discovered the joy of riding on the Underground, which I found fascinating – the way people exchanged places with one another, hastily hopping on and hopping off. At every stop I would wait to hear 'Mind the gap between the train and the platform' from a person I couldn't see. And for days the announcement would ring in my head. Sometimes I would mumble it repeatedly to myself while getting on with my chores: 'Mind the gap between the train and the platform.'

'Stand clear of the doors, stand clear of the doors,' then passengers diving through the closing doors, rucksacks getting jammed and people aggressively clinging onto the handles. The drama and entertainment were endless, and observing what everyone was doing was almost the only amusement I got. I would see the odd person sitting opposite me talking to himself, face buried behind a large newspaper.

The most interesting passengers were the ones who fell asleep. In every carriage there would be someone with their eyes closed, occasionally nodding off and then looking up to see if anyone had noticed. And they would close their eyes again as if it was acceptable to take a nap from time to time. How did they know when they arrived at their destination, I always wondered. Sometimes a passenger awoke at a stop, checked the route map and quickly jumped up, pushing everyone out of their way to get off the train before the doors closed.

Then there were the escalators, constantly going up and down. I always hoped to see a familiar face on them, and I would look attentively at everyone on the opposite side. Being in the Underground felt like another world. I had never been underground before, except maybe into the basement of a house. Otherwise, I associated it with the space where the human body rested after death. Here I was experiencing the beauty of the underworld before I was laid to rest.

Within a few months I knew how to get around in London, which became handy when I was looking for a job. After being interviewed and turned down again and again, apparently because I was either overqualified or lacking work experience, I became frustrated that no one would hire me. I left my degree qualification off my CV and landed my first job, as a part-time chambermaid at a hotel in Bayswater. The pay was poor, the work back-breaking, especially on Sunday, when new guests arrived and the rooms had to be thoroughly cleaned. Sometimes the departing guests left some coins in the room for the chambermaids – if the supervisor didn't get to them before we did. She was a pain in the backside. We were not allowed to go into the rooms before eight o'clock, but the supervisor would arrive before us and rush through all the rooms picking up all the pound coins and silver, leaving just a few coppers for us.

I couldn't be fussy about my job, because I needed to help Mother with expenses at home. Soon I was sending money home for school fees and food, and I sent clothes which I bought from secondhand shops, or the wholesalers at Liverpool Street. I even managed to save enough to buy a plot of land and start building my mother a house.

With a good reference I was offered several part-time jobs as a sales assistant with the Co-op, Underwoods and Marks & Spencer. Shirley wanted to rent my room so I moved to an international hostel; I visited her and Martin a few times, when they were able to open the door for me, which wasn't often. Eventually social services moved them to a care home as they had become a danger to themselves, and they both died there four years later. Not being the next of kin I never got to know what really happened to them. All the time I stayed with them I never saw any relatives visit them, and they never spoke of their children. There were no photos from the past. I often wondered how they had met and whether with their heavy drinking and smoking they would survive long.

At an early age, I started questioning what the meaning of moral obligation is and how it relates to human values. Humanitarians prize human rights. In simple terms, this is what I understood. They mean well and do good – intervening to save the most vulnerable and focusing their efforts on the most in need. So, to take this further, once I left the hotel I enrolled part time on an African development studies course at the School of

Oriental and African Studies (SOAS) and life began to take on a kind of normality.

We were seven students on the course, which was held in our professor's small office. It had fading brown woodchip wallpaper; the ceiling, once white, had turned nearly black from the professor's heavy smoking; there was a bookcase neatly stacked with heavy volumes that had collected dust over the years. The professor would sit on his desk, which was covered with all sorts of documents, stationery, ashtrays and photos from his past.

The professor had taught at Makerere University in Uganda, where I had obtained my first degree. With his thick glasses covering half of his eyes, he would look up and ask for my opinion of his lectures, most of which questioned in a controversial but truth-seeking way why the West bothered to develop Africa. 'Africans are different, corrupt, not capable of learning from the West,' he would say. He used to refer to Makerere University and ask me if it was still the same after twenty-five years. Of course a lot had changed except his perceptions of African development, a point I referred to frequently but which he dismissed. He was out of touch with reality, and too often we got into long debates on what I thought was good for the Third World to get itself out of poverty. 'What about focusing on education and healthcare to grow a generation of learned Africans who could replace expatriates who often come to Africa with good intentions but with no understanding of the dynamics and backgrounds of the states they work in? "Teach a man how to fish and he will be hungry no more. Give a man bread and he will depend on you for decades to come." Ever heard this expression?'

'I've heard that nonsense before alright,' he would tell me.

I made a number of friends while on the course, particularly Richard, who had joined during my final year. A very active young man, he had just completed a marathon in three hours and that was his selling point, apart from being cynical and funny.

Richard joining the course didn't make my task easy; like the professor he saw corruption as the cause of African problems, without considering debt and trade controls. He had introduced himself as having a good knowledge of Sudan, which would be his contribution to the course. No disrespect – he had been an English teacher for four months in Darfur – but I wondered how much he really knew; no doubt he had seen poverty at first hand, but how much of that had any bearing on the politics and the people of Sudan? To be fair to him, though, his heart was in the right place and he had passion.

After lectures, we would sometimes continue our heated arguments in the university cafeteria over a cup of coffee. Richard would ask me questions about Africa that I answered with amusement as most of what he asked was common sense. He would talk constantly and tell jokes, most of which I didn't understand. We didn't have many opportunities for these discussions, as I was normally in a rush to go to work, but Richard thought I was avoiding him. I wasn't; I had to earn money to pay my tuition. 'I'm not lucky like you. You've been sponsored to do this course; you don't have to pay a dime.' I would leave knowing that I didn't have just my tuition to think of, but I was also the primary bread earner for my family and my mother counted on me.

Richard would passionately defend humanitarian aid, which he said was making a difference to the Third World. Though we were both studying African development studies, I begged to disagree with his belief in aid, which did no harm but had limited impact on people's lives. I would remind Richard of the poverty that continued to engulf many Africans who live on very little, in dire conditions, with no running water, and few economic opportunities despite the millions of pounds being poured into Africa. I was on this course to find ways in which development aid could be repackaged to bring real benefits to the poorest.

I told him about the first time I met humanitarian failure face to face. When I was a young teenager, living as a refugee in Uganda, if things were really tight my mother sent me to the United Nations High Commissioner for Refugees (UNHCR) to ask for help with money or food for the family. That was when we were really desperate. One day I sat there from nine o'clock. I had no appointment, so everyone who came was seen before me. As the team left for lunch they apologised, saying that I would be seen somehow, at some time, when a slot became available. At about four o'clock, two ladies invited me in and listened to my story for a little less than five minutes. I was told to sit outside and wait while they discussed how to help me. How kind I thought they were. I would return home with help at last.

I was called back in. They sat me down. I was told that I did not qualify for the food rations, or money, but that they would instead give me a single mattress to take back to my mother. I was eternally grateful and returned home with the mattress. The look on my mother's face has never left me. Our dignity and humanity were tested to the limit that day.

Richard and I had a lot in common. He was Catholic, although he admitted he had not been to church for many years, and he believed that many aid workers were driven by morality and not so much the money and the prestigious jobs available in Africa.

Of course as an African and a Catholic, my values were religious. I told Richard of the white missionaries, dressed in white short-sleeved shirts and khaki shorts, who learnt to speak the local language in our homes. I saw development in practice in schools and hospitals – and of course, not forgetting church, where I spent many memorable years at Sunday school.

I remember one Sunday vividly, when I must have been about eight years old. A white missionary visited our parish, I can't remember where from. My school prepared songs and plays to welcome him. I was made to sing a verse from 'Amazing Grace', after which the missionary got up and lifted me up in the air, and said, 'She is so beautiful and blessed.' And there were cries of 'Alleluia'. My parents and all the adults got up and clapped, and for a moment I felt so beautiful that I was touching the clouds, as if I was in Heaven. The missionary then gave me a coloured flag as a present, which sat proudly in our sitting room on the mantelpiece for a long time. No doubt everyone who visited my house was told of my brave encounter with the white missionary. In those days, white missionaries seemed to bring harmony to our community.

Later, when I was about sixteen and at convent school, I decided to ask for support from my history teacher, who was British. I had been told that she knew sponsors in the UK willing to support Rwandan refugees, and that she was running a charity that supported education. She was a Catholic, so surely the least she could do would be to help one of her faith in need. She gave me nearly an hour of her time. I told her everything my mother had warned me never to tell a stranger: the days we went with no food, my mother's long-term illness, which doctors could not diagnose.

She came back to me a few weeks later. Donors in UK would not help. 'Why?' I asked her. Because I did not live in a refugee camp. My mother was very proud and would rather work than live on handouts in a refugee camp. I thought humanitarian aid was supposed to help us to be self-sustaining. But my mother's pursuit of her profession, which didn't generate enough money for the family, cost her the humanitarian aid she was entitled to. She chose not to give up midwifery and return to the camp so we could be registered as vulnerable enough to deserve humanitarian aid. The measure of vulnerability was dressing in rags, with bare feet, and looking unwashed and homeless. The standard housing in the refugee camps could not be described as standard in any other context. It was crowded, you slept on straw instead of mattresses, and went without food except for the rations, because there was no land to cultivate your own food. It was then, aged sixteen, that I gave up on humanitarian aid. Even the Church had developed stringent criteria and red tape.

Richard and I spoke of how humanitarianism had changed its face over the years. Aid workers started living in compounds, they were paid great sums of money, they drove large four-wheel-drive Land Cruisers and ate out in restaurants. The closest they got to their beneficiaries was through their Third World staff, who earned a fraction of their wage, even though better qualified, and did most of the work.

Being with Richard always made me secure. It must have been the fact that I didn't understand him well, that he was a bit mysterious, that had attracted me to him. By now I felt a little more settled, and I had made friends at work, university and at the hostel. I wasn't so lonely now; it was time to rebuild my life, or so I thought. But I couldn't escape my troubles.

TWO

Memories never fade

IT WAS ON 11 November 1988, around three in the morning, when the dreaded news came. I had been in the UK for two years.

A fortnight before, my mother had been given only a few days to live. All my siblings gathered, including Jean Baptiste, who had come from Rwanda, but two weeks passed and she was still fighting. Meanwhile, for months I had been sending my mother yet more suggested cancer medication to relieve her of her pain, but the last batch arrived late and in any case her body could take no more medication.

I was still living in the international students' hostel in Bayswater, and any telephone calls would come into the communal phone booth on the ground floor – there were no phones in the rooms. For those particular two weeks, I wouldn't sleep in my room, on the third floor. I would bring a blanket and sit in the communal television room. The other students would be talking about trivia and flicking through the channels, watching crappy TV, which distracted my attention. I felt frightened and anxious. I lost my appetite and I stopped going to lectures. Every day, from what my sister Riisa told me, I became less and less convinced that my mother would pull through. I was just waiting for that last phone call.

In the early hours of that morning, the phone rang. I jumped and ran to pick it up, fear and emptiness hitting me hard. I didn't want to think things through: that my mother was no longer at home in Lukaya, that she would never live in the house I was building for her, a place where I would drop in as if I had never gone away. She never saw the house completed; she spent the last five months of her life in the cancer ward in Mulago hospital in Uganda, her last home.

The voice at the other end was Emmanuel, my childhood sweetheart. 'Hallo, Maria, what are you doing up late?'

'Never mind that, what about you?' I replied.

'You have to be strong.' He paused and I held my breath. Then he quietly unburdened himself: 'Your mother died a few hours ago. She passed away at one in the morning. The whole family is by her bedside. She died peacefully in her sleep,' he told me.

'Thank you, Emmanuel.'

After he hung up, I felt a taut heaviness settle in my heart. I desperately clung to images of my mother alive. Although I expected her death sooner rather than later, I wanted to stay awake another day, to wait for that phone call one more day. I desperately wanted my mother to beat the odds. She had managed weeks and months – why not years more? She was the only person who made me feel attached to something. And now I had lost her.

I revisited the last five months, from the time when my sister called to tell me that Mother had been diagnosed with leukaemia. I clutched the phone in silence, wishing it wasn't true. They must have got it wrong. She is a midwife; she would have found out long before. My feelings slowly began to freeze.

'Maria, are you listening?' My sister's voice sounded ghostly.

I wanted to wake up from this nightmare. The most graceful and hard-working woman I knew, my mother was beginning her life's final journey. I couldn't accept it. I wanted my sister to stop talking. I can't explain the grief; I wanted to die, to stop breathing so that I couldn't feel anything.

My sister, still on the phone in a post office booth in Kampala, was running out of money. 'Sis, are you there?' But I couldn't speak, my tongue was twisted. 'The phone will cut off soon. Be strong. I will let you know what's going on.' Silence, then peep, peep, peep. . . and she was gone. I clung onto the phone, thinking I would wake up and could tell someone about my horrible dream. I don't know how long I stayed standing by the hostel telephone booth.

I pulled my jumper over my face and sobbed quietly, the news of my mother's illness stabbing away at me. After a while I managed to compose myself. 'Who do I tell or call now?' I thought. 'What next?' Mother might pull through, she is a fighter. I needed to think how to help her practically, but first I needed to get all the facts from my sister. I tried calling her and left messages for her to call me back. When I eventually reached her, she told me Mother's leukaemia was advanced. The doctors were saying that she had a slim chance of survival, but nonetheless they had recommended all sorts of drugs which were not available in Uganda.

I pulled my thoughts together and tried to stay calm and strong for my sister. 'How has Mum taken the news?'

'She is very frightened and shaken.'

'Don't worry; you know Mother is a fighter.' We arranged to speak every day and she would update me on Mother's progress. 'Tell Mother I love her and I will send medication in the next few days,' I said.

There were so many questions and I had little time to think. I was getting more anxious by the minute, partly because I was living in the UK, separated from my mother by thousands of miles. I was a student working part time. To buy mother's expensive medication I would have to take out a bank loan and find another part-time job to pay it off. I managed to borrow £5,000 from Barclays Bank and sent the first batch of cancer drugs to Uganda. Within weeks of treatment Mother seemed to show signs of progress.

My sister told me Mother was in capable hands. An old friend, Dr Nzaro, diagnosed the cancer and spent days visiting Mother and undertaking more tests. Thank God, my sister was a midwife at Mulago hospital, and most of the doctors were known to her and my mother. They were as shocked as we were and wanted to do their best to save her. But Uganda's hospitals, like most African healthcare centres, were not equipped to give patients a chance to fight. The cancer ward at Mulago was swamped with row upon row of patients lying in shattering anguish, hoping their turn for treatment might come faster than death.

A few days later Mother sent me a message asking me to buy some perfume that she could give to Dr Nzaro's wife to thank him for diagnosing an illness that no one had identified for years. I bought her a bottle of Poison, not thinking of the irony that the cancer was poisoning my mother's blood.

My sister described the following months as the toughest time of her life. She had no money to support my siblings and take care of Mother in hospital. I had diverted all my money to buying cancer drugs. With tears in her voice, she described how once, on her usual morning trip to visit my mother, she walked into a park and found a place to stand protected by trees and flowery bushes. She made sure there was no one nearby and let out a loud scream: 'Please, God, what did this woman do to you? What kind of punishment is this? Hasn't she been through enough? Why make her suffer?'

My heart bled with every word from her. I wished I was there to help, but it was either being there seeing my mother through the toughest times or working to pay for her medication. I kept remembering Mother's messages – 'Tell Maria to come home tomorrow.' Then the next morning she would ask my sister to tell me to hang in there, she was going to be alright. Besides by this time I had no money to pay for a ticket to Uganda. So I waited, hoping for a miracle.

God heard my sister's lament. Mother survived a few more months, and the doctors kept raising the stakes. My sister had to manage her work, in between checking on my mother and also looking after all our teenage siblings who had come to live with her. I wanted Mother to get another chance to fight, as she had fought and for years struggled to bring us up in a foreign country after the revolution of 1959 which killed part of her family and led her into exile.

She was among the rising stars in Rwanda, educated and going places. She struggled to bring us up and would not let anything get in the way of her family. She had no airs and graces, just good manners and a striving for success. She held a job, paid her bills despite difficulties – she was a new age woman, independent long before many Rwandan women of her generation.

Throughout my life, I had looked upon my mother as more resilient than anybody else's. She always picked herself up whatever the circumstances. Part of me believed she still had the fire to fight back this time. She had been newly diagnosed; I hoped the medicines were going to make her better. After everything else my mother had been through, she didn't deserve to die of leukaemia in her early fifties.

I called my sister every day. She gave all she could, but it wasn't enough. She watched as Mother lived out her last days on earth, helpless, in too much pain, waiting for the inevitable death. She would describe Mother as being confused sometimes, saying, 'Are all my children here? Riisa, Maria, Louis? Is Jean here? Lois, come and sit next to me.' She would call our names in no particular order. At other times she made sense. She would say to my sister,

25

'Tell Maria and Louis I love them. I know Maria will look after you; tell her not to bother coming home.'

Once she said to Lois, 'I don't want to die without seeing a grandchild.'

'Mother, if you hadn't been strict, I would have brought you grandchildren a long time ago,' Lois replied, whereupon Mother cried. But there were also moments when jokes were made and she tried to force a smile.

Towards the last days of her life, the news from home was desperate: blood was seeping through Mother's skin, possibly a side-effect of the medication. I was emotionally numb; I knew I couldn't go home to bury her. I needed to work and pay for the funeral and the loan. By the time she died, I had debts of over £5,000.

That early morning in November, my mother's fight was over, but my agony was just beginning. She had told my siblings that I would look after them. I tried to suppress my feelings and focus on protecting and rebuilding their lives without our mother.

For days, I stayed in a state of denial, visualising the last memories of my mother, walking to my school, bringing me whatever she had – bananas, bread or milk. I saw her mending and making our dresses or knitting a cardigan. I remembered the scar that covered the left side of her face, from a terrible accident when an overloaded truck she and Riisa were travelling on veered off the road and tumbled thousands of feet down a hillside. More than ten people died, but my mother and my sister survived.

I remembered Mother teaching us to pray, at night kneeling down to thank God for the day. My siblings prayed for ridiculous things that made us all giggle, then she would say, 'Dear God, give mercy to these children who are laughing while praying,' which made it even worse. I remembered how she would make a cross on our forehead and a little pat on the cheek as a blessing. Her relief was her children.

I could hear her lovely lilting voice that made me stop to listen as she sang her favourite Rwandan songs, the soft sweet notes drifting through the open window to the garden outside where I would be playing. I slowly dug into my memory box, hanging onto the goodness Mother brought into my life.

Mother to me was timelessness and permanence itself, the centre of my emotional journey, which had proved more constant than anything or anyone else. I could never imagine that one day I would go home and she would no longer be alive. I was in my twenties, and her death brought my world crashing down, nearly turning me into a nervous and physical wreck. For months I lived with insomnia, a waste of energy, which drove me close to a state of frenzy.

Eventually I had to face the world outside my hostel. My journey to work from the Underground station to Brent Cross shopping centre became difficult. I would sob deeply and want to scream out loud. Sometimes I would see my mother walk by or feel her touch my face or even sense her presence on a windy winter's day. Then I would close my eyes and connect with her. A shadow hung over the life I had led, the responsibility that had stopped me from doing the decent thing, being there for my mother when she was dying. But I'd had to earn money to buy the medication that gave her a chance to fight.

I had periods of depression that lasted for weeks, where I didn't want to see or speak to anyone. Mother was gone and what was left was the space where I had grown around her, like a tree growing around a fence. For a long time, the tree remained hollow and if it hadn't been for my love of dancing, like my mother, I doubt if I would have pulled through.

I can't remember what it was that triggered my love of dancing again or when it was, but it was the only thing that healed my soul. I would look forward to it every weekend. With alcohol lightening my head and that wild music wailing away, it didn't take long to loosen up the dancing instincts from my African heritage. From then hardly a party took place without me turning up, inviting myself if I had to and dancing my life away. If I wasn't dancing I would be listening to music. I managed to rebuild my life; the depression returned only occasionally but then, I would allow myself to cry for as long as I felt like. I felt bad for not having been there for my mother and that guilt would remain with me over the course of my life.

THREE

No sanctuary

I LOST ALMOST everything when my mother died. The only thing I hung onto was her resilience in a world I came to know through her tales, her resolve to give me a better upbringing in a world without sanctuary – a world where I was always reminded of my foreignness, where her accent was always different and where she worked hard to overcome prejudice.

One hot sunny morning in January 1971, just after we'd settled into our classroom, the headmaster summoned the school to the assembly hall. Many of the teachers were also present. I was used to such short-notice emergency meetings; being head of the disciplinary committee there were often calls to discuss exclusion or to supervise a student on a punishment. But this time the mood was sombre, the expression on the teachers' faces was unusual, the sort of expression that preceded the news of a death in one of the student's families or a pupil's expulsion.

The headmaster asked us to remain calm. The radio had announced that Idi Amin Dada had staged a coup and toppled Dr Milton Obote. 'Who is Idi Amin?' I wondered, 'and what has this got to do with us?' I was old enough to know that Obote was our president. The radio news would always start with what he had been doing: 'He was visiting Korea' (where the hell was Korea?) or 'He was planting a tree at a new seminary.'

We didn't have access to newspapers, I don't know if they didn't exist in the rural area where I lived, or whether my mother could not afford them. But occasionally, especially on market days, we got hold of old newspapers, which the vendors used to wrap goods for customers. I would get a chance to see pictures of Obote and other people. He was a round-faced, very dark-skinned man, with a natural Afro hairstyle and an blank expression.

We lived in a quiet village hundreds of miles away from Uganda's capital, Kampala, where the coup had taken place. I had never been there, but some of our classmates whose fathers served in Obote's government told us fascinating tales about the vibrant, busy city, with clean roads, where someone had to hold your hand to cross the road, lest you get run over by the traffic flowing in both directions. In some places there were lights that changed colour automatically to stop the cars, so that you could cross. I always wondered why anyone would want to cross to the other side if it was such a hassle. Our village had only one bus, one pick-up and one saloon car. Sometimes other vehicles brought visiting relatives. On market days too, pick-ups would deliver merchandise. Even then there would be fewer than ten vehicles. People relied on bicycles and a few motorbikes. I don't remember two vehicles on the road at the same time. Why couldn't they stay on the same side of the road? But I never asked anyone for fear of being embarrassed.

This man, Idi Amin, had staged a coup, but what was a coup? I couldn't understand the relevance, or why we had to keep the school calm. Some students seemed excited and they chuckled quietly to each other. It was not until later that I learnt that Amin was the new president; he had forcibly replaced Obote. I also learnt that some of our classmates would be affected as their parents were ministers or close to the Uganda People's Congress (UPC), the party that Obote belonged to. It wasn't clear to me then that our school was privileged and some of our benefactors were in the UPC, and our local parish, as I came to learn, supported the ruling party.

That afternoon, the parish priest called for a service at a local church, adults and children joining in to pray for Uganda. He gave a long sermon asking God to bring peace, understanding and comfort to the people of Uganda. I closed my eyes like everyone else and prayed for the country. The reverend called for everyone to share and give something back to God. Young and old had a duty to share their talents with God. This always meant money rather than skills. The reverend would often say, 'Give every penny to God, because God will always fill the purses of those who share,' sometimes adding, 'God knows you have something you need to share with him.' This service was no different. I had a coin that mother had given me to buy fruit for lunch, and I put it in the collection box and went hungry, hoping that God would give me blessings. Indeed, later I was rewarded in the form of a mango and some sugar cane that a school friend gave me for free.

The tension surrounding the coup lasted for a few weeks, then we seemed to get back to normal. Soon Amin was the most talked-about President of Uganda, and he would be featured on the radio. I heard more about him through classroom gossip. People said Amin was brutal, that he had set up an intelligence bureau which terrorised and hunted down his enemies. A number of students left school because their parents were connected with Obote, and Amin had some of their fathers murdered after the coup. The school's mood changed as we began to hear quite often that someone in the community had disappeared. It was always quietly murmured and never openly discussed.

Sometimes, people said that Idi Amin's State Research Bureau was penetrating the village and planting spies to ensure no enemy of his was operating in it. Our village was not far from the border with Tanzania, where Obote and his government had been exiled. Although all this was going on, the school ran normally and our lives continued more or less as usual.

At first my family was not affected. Plenty of people continued to attend my mother's private clinic, but sometimes they would speak about Amin and his terror. Mother started to worry about the so-called spies; she had been warned that Amin was accusing foreigners, the Asians and Rwandan refugees, for supporting Obote. She told Riisa and me to stay out of any rumours about Amin at school. She explained that we were refugees and second-class citizens. This shattered my confidence in the world I was looking forward to enjoying. I felt a need to prove myself all the time, either at school or in anything I did.

Rwandans and other foreigners were the first targets of the state machinery, and our lives changed. We became isolated in the village, rumours circulating that mother was aiding Obote's return. Every patient that visited the clinic was a potential Amin spy. As news intensified of the torture and killing of Amin's enemies, my mother became protective of us. I remember fearing that one day she would disappear, and we always ran home from school worried deep down that she would not be at home.

Mother was brave; she never showed us her fear although I knew from the way she warned us not to get involved in circulating rumours that she was anxious for our lives. She saw patients from local towns and from all walks of life. She had built a reputation as a leading private midwife so that everyone nearby who wanted private treatment would come to her clinic. She even had Amin's generals based at the Simba Mechanised Battalion Barracks bringing their families to her practice. Perhaps because of this, before long someone warned Mother that she was seen as a spy for Amin. The villagers stopped attending the clinic and she became paranoid.

One day in August 1972, eighteen months after the new government came to power, Idi Amin declared an economic war, expelling all Asians from Uganda. Many lost their entire savings and businesses. Asians dominated Uganda's trade and manufacturing sectors, as well as forming a significant proportion of the civil service. The abandoned businesses were handed over to Amin's supporters.

Around the same time, Obote launched a war against Amin from his base in Tanzania, staging a return to power. The insurgents came through our village; I remember hearing bombs in the distance but every day the sound got gradually closer and closer. At school we were told to report anyone, any stranger, who acted suspiciously to the head teacher or anyone hiding in the school or in the shrubs and bushes on the way home. I remember being told Obote was staging a return to Uganda.

It was a frightening time. Shrapnel and bomb fragments lined the road to school. We would walk to school in a group in case a stranger pounced on us. My sense of hearing was sharpened; I could hear crickets chirping and birdsong which I had never noticed before. Sometimes the bigger children would call for an alert. 'Shh. . . I think I can hear something. Stand still.' Then we would huddle together ready to let out a scream at the top of our voices if someone appeared. A few minutes later they laughed and told us they were joking.

In fact one man was captured in the village and after that, terror reigned. Rumours from 'Radio Katwe' (literally 'radio in your head') became popular. If anything was reported, it was said to have come from Radio Katwe. It was a time of uncertainty, but also for me a time of excitement. I felt like a news reporter always eager to hear more and sitting with other classmates comparing our latest Radio Katwe version of events. Even our teachers got involved in the debates and discussions. Politics was then introduced into my vocabulary and my life took on a new meaning. I knew what a coup d'état was, but why was it in French, I always wondered. What was the equivalent in English?

I understood the different political parties and what they stood for. I understood the power of the president, so I thought, because Idi Amin seemed to make all decisions. I was confused about the army's involvement, and whether the army was more powerful than the president. I could not imagine the power this man had; it seemed beyond human imagination.

We'd heard about Amin's hunt for people linked with or suspected of working with the British, Obote and Yoweri Museveni, one of Obote's generals, against his government. Our parish reverend's two adult sons were taken from their home, never to be seen again. Radio Katwe blamed the reverend; apparently he had aided arms smuggling, hidden guerrillas at the church and, when Obote's uprising failed, helped them escape. If anyone disappeared, and many did, people would say they were killed by the State Research Bureau. It turned out later, after Amin's regime fell, that some people believed to be dead, as per Radio Katwe, had escaped to Tanzania to join Obote and Museveni's internal guerrilla war. They returned safely years later.

For years, Amin ruled in terror but at the same time the Ugandans went on with business as usual. My mother became increasingly insecure, being a refugee, unable to bring up her children in a safe environment. Now for the first time she explained why she had fled Rwanda following the revolution of 1959, and why we were refugees.

At the end of my primary education, my mother moved her practice from our village to a trading centre 12 miles away, on the main road from Kampala to Rwanda. We abandoned the house she had built for us, because she was getting harassed both by the villagers, for her supposed activity as one of Amin's spies, and by Amin's state bureau, which suspected her of helping Obote and Museveni's exiled army in Tanzania, and started life in rented accommodation. Mother seemed to settle down quickly, as did we all. She wasn't known to people here so she could treat patients from all walks of life without being accused. More clients from Amin's military came to her clinic, especially those who had complicated pregnancies. Mother had a magic touch. I don't remember her having complications with any patient. She visited them at home and some became friends of the family.

I slowly started seeing my mother's resilience come into play. She would make abrupt decisions to protect her family and she was always right. I think this must have been the time I began to build my own defence mechanisms. I accepted that I was different from my peers. I was more careful of how I related to people outside my family circle. I also became aware of Mother's difficulties bringing us up and started to take on more responsibility.

Meanwhile, I had managed to enrol in Maryhill High School, a Catholic secondary school, and the next four years, 1974 to 1978, were the best time of my adolescence. An all-girls' boarding school run by mainly Irish nuns, it was about 8 miles from my new home. It was one of the best schools in Uganda. The school did not distinguish or discriminate on the grounds of being a refugee, as long as you made the grades and you were a Catholic. So as a refugee in Uganda, I was blessed to make it in. This school shaped my values and helped define and influence the human being I later became.

At the school, my Christian ethos and values found room to grow. The school protected the girls from the outside world; we were not allowed to leave, except during emergencies such as a death in the family. Our sick bay was well equipped, probably better than the local hospital, so we didn't need to leave school if we fell ill. Our families and friends were permitted to visit twice per month.

I heard less of Amin's politics and concentrated on strengthening my Catholic upbringing and my studies. Limited numbers of students from other faiths were also admitted to the school. There was a good number of other Rwandan refugee students, some of whom I had met at a Rwandan refugee school I had attended in primary education. The school was a safe environment for me, and my fear and anxiety of my mother's safety seemed to fade with time.

I became a prefect and took on other responsibilities: I was chair of the Girl Guides, led the rosary group, and became head of the reading group, which you were nominated for if you read and wrote the most book reviews. I went through a book a day. I was a fast reader, but sometimes if the book wasn't interesting I just flicked through it and made up the review. After lessons I managed the school shop, selling women's essentials, soap, sweets, handkerchiefs, bread and biscuits.

The most exciting responsibility was managing the dance floor. Sister Moran, our music teacher, had put me in charge because I was good at the Irish folk dances which she taught. I had also trained in health and safety and first aid in the Guides. I would open the school hall on Friday and Saturday nights. We had no DJ, just records. I would coach the girls in dancing; I don't know where I learnt the moves, possibly from years dancing with my mother, but everyone thought they were cool. I would take girls through waltzes, breakdancing, and winding up and down to Bob Marley and the Wailers. With patience, I got everyone to a level where they felt able to dance with boys at the next opportunity. Girls in senior four, aged around sixteen, had the chance to dance at two boys' schools in the locality.

My first time dancing at the boys' school must have been when I was turning fifteen. As soon as the dance date was confirmed, I asked the rich kids to lend me something, blue, pink, any colour. I borrowed an armlet, a watch, shoes, ribbons, everything short of underwear. I came from a poor family; I had two Sunday best dresses and one pair of shoes. I tended to wear our school uniform most of the time.

The dress rules for the dance ran like this: no hemline above the knees, chest and arms decently covered. Strictly no makeup allowed, except a bit of eyeliner and lip gloss, or Vaseline in many cases. Perfume was tolerated, but it didn't matter because not many people had any, although those that did were generous, so we all had a squirt of what then was an exotic smell. In the end everyone smelt the same.

Days before the big event, I was excitedly trying on other people's clothes, choosing what was most up to date and curvaceous. My culture inhibited me from wearing seductive clothes. Being in a strictly Catholic school didn't help either. Despite all this, I felt like Cinderella and didn't want the Ugly Sisters to fit into the beautiful tiny glass slipper and marry Prince Charming. I dressed to impress.

The sisterly comradeship was wonderful. We shared hair straightener and body moisturiser. There was no bullying, bitching or nasty gossip. Everyone in my dormitory wanted me to look my best. They suggested how to comb my hair, helped with dressing up, covered me in powder that made my face pale and kept my underarms dry. It was the most exciting moment of my life. The preparations, anticipation and rising hormones were as good as the actual dance.

The bus ride to the boys' school was filled with excitement. Everyone was talking at the same time, adjusting their belts, earrings or necklaces. The nuns gave out their list of dos and don'ts, and a last reminder to keep the 'school's honour'.

The dance was held in the school dining hall, which had large windows, and boys who couldn't attend stood and watched from a distance, gaining their initiation in adolescent encounters. If the boys came to the girls' school, the nuns ensured all the girls not invited were locked well away in their dormitories, so they could only share in the event through gossip from the attendees. This is probably why the girls were always more excited by the dance than the boys.

We were accompanied by three nuns, Sister Moran, Sister Elizabeth and the headmistress, Sister Josephine. Sister Moran was too busy dancing with another teacher to notice that we were cheek to cheek with whomever. Sister Elizabeth paced back and forth, holding onto her Hail Mary rosary, possibly praying for the sinful thoughts in the girls' heads and making sure we were observing the rules. Sister Josephine, a graceful black woman, didn't have to turn her head to check on the girls. She had eyes in the back of her head and her presence was so powerful that no one would dare do anything.

The girls were supposed to reassemble on one side of the hall every time the music stopped. It took a minute or so to replace one record with another and the nuns would not leave it to chance for the girls to stand and chat with the boys. My gaze drifted around; I eyed boys from across the hall, in sight of the godly watchful nuns, not daring to wink or smile, only communicating with my eyes to boys I liked. I had no problems finding a partner. Word had gone around that I was a very good dancer, for some of our girls had brothers in the local boys' schools, and I was often complimented by boys who visited our school.

I waited in anticipation as the head girl, the head boy and their assistants opened the dance floor. Then everyone joined in. The boys rushed and pounced at the girls, hoping they wouldn't get turned down. I convinced myself one of them would be Prince Charming and sweep me away. The lights were slightly dimmed and everyone moved to the centre. The boys pulled the girls towards them, forming a curtain that concealed me from the nuns' policing as my partner got closer and closer. Then the record stopped and I rushed back to join the others across the hall.

When it was the girls' turn to pick boys, they were shy. I moved ahead of everyone, picking the best dancer, who I had spotted earlier. I loved dancing and didn't need to be prompted. It was second nature. Many girls openly told me they envied me during the school dance, because I was enjoying myself immensely and I didn't worry about the nuns' religious policing. Other people's opinion wasn't a problem for me at all.

During the course of the night, the dance got less formal and boys and girls formed a bond. It was not allowed to hold hands, or dance too closely. Despite this, love was in the air, my mind was floating in the clouds, and occasionally I closed my eyes, allowing myself to be led, but ensuring we were not too close. From time to time the music would stop, but my heart didn't; I continued dancing, captured by the vibe and the aura of adolescent love.

After the dance I had a brief encounter, or my first infatuation, with a high school boy called Emmanuel, who had watched me dance at his school. He was two years my junior and lived in my home village. I noticed him on the way home, at a distance. Our eyes met; he smiled and winked at me. For a moment I forgot my dance partner, who was escorting me to the school bus.

Many days later, I was on a bus and spotted Emmanuel on his bicycle, his black complexion radiating under the hot sun. He looked gorgeous. My heart missed a beat as I watched him ride on the opposite side of the road, unaware that I could see him. I remembered his wink and his warm smile; I was sure he had been watching me dance all night and possibly liked me. I entertained the thought that I was in love with him. I was fifteen and had never felt so absorbed by someone whom I hadn't even spoken too. I had a crush on him, but for months I couldn't tell anyone. I would stand in my mother's bedroom gazing through her window, hoping Emmanuel would ride past on his bicycle.

As he was younger than me, I knew we had a slim chance of ever meeting, but I could not get him out of my mind.

I couldn't speak to anyone about it, but at school we were constantly reminded that God could read our minds. I decided to confess to our school's reverend father. He suggested sending me to a silent retreat over the weekend to find God and forget about this boy. This was a disastrous solution. I spent my silent hours trying to speak to God but instead Emmanuel's image intruded, so that I thought of him even more.

The reverend father was not forgiving. He told me to recite a Hail Mary every time I thought of Emmanuel. So I wore my rosary around my neck, and when those panicky warm moments came I quickly pulled it off and followed the cross. It didn't work either; I felt like a sinner, for I couldn't control my feelings. I would lose track of how many Hail Marys and Our Fathers I was reciting, and repeated each bead. Time to visit the priest again; I didn't want to go to purgatory.

The reverend father looked at me with a bemused expression. 'Maria, I will pray for you, my child. But remember the Ten Commandments.' So I went back to the dormitory, wrote out the Ten Commandments and hung them on my wall. As long as I didn't break them I would be safe.

One afternoon, in a school athletics competition, I was representing my school at the high jump, and Emmanuel was representing his. He cheered me and I him; it all seemed innocent – we came from the same village and we were looking out for each other. After the event I ran into him and panicked in case I gave away my feelings for him. He was standing opposite the gate which was the only exit from the stadium. His eyes lit up and he crossed the road to talk to me. I couldn't believe it.

'Well done. You're obviously a better high jumper than me,' he said.

I modestly complimented him on his style. 'You're not so bad yourself,' I said, looking away to avoid his eyes.

'Are you going home on a coach or should I walk you to school?' he politely asked me.

'I don't mind – either.' I knew that was a wrong answer but I didn't want him to know I was in love with him.

'It would be my pleasure to walk you to school.' He offered to carry my athletics kit, and we strolled all the way as if we both didn't want this moment to end. I can't remember what our conversation was about; I know we didn't speak about feelings, but it was obvious the atmosphere was electric.

A group of laughing and squirming schoolchildren appeared walking in the opposite direction. Emmanuel moved me to one side as if to protect me from an oncoming stampede as he gently slipped his hands in mine. The sensation almost knocked the breath out of me. With a tightening feeling, every nerve in my body caught fire. The whole experience must have lasted less than a minute and yet when it was over, I'd been initiated into a mystery – the beginning of the end of the age of childhood. I pulled my hand away although I didn't want to. Sensing a strange feeling, a hollow in my stomach, I reached into my pocket for my rosary, made of glass beads with a touch of blue and purple. I put it around my neck and recited a Hail Mary in my head. He too was now quiet, as if silence could speak the words between us. At the school gate, he reached for my hand, squeezed it silently and left.

I giggled all the way to my dormitory. I flashed a smile at anyone who looked my way, and burst into song. That night I went to sleep full of joy and love, and became completely obsessed with Emmanuel.

Emmanuel came to visit me on the next visitors' day and brought me an orange drink called Tree Top. I kept that bottle for a long time, taking little sips. I didn't want to finish it, this symbol of

Emmanuel's presence in my life. This was the first personal decision I had made, to love someone, that wasn't influenced by anyone else, my mother or my Catholic upbringing – my own discovery.

I saw Emmanuel almost every visitors' day. We sat under a hibiscus tree looking across a valley towards a row of beautiful eucalyptus trees that ran alongside a river. We would watch the traffic pass by and talk about all sorts of things, but we never spoke of our love for each other. We wrote letters each week in between school visits. Once he sent me a book inscribed with his love for me: 'Please wait for me, whatever our paths, one day we will be together. Every moment in your presence is forever treasured.' I learnt every single line in that book by heart. It was my secret book; I hid it from my friends and read it before I went to sleep, under my bedcover, using a torch.

I shared a room with a highly morally driven girl who despised boys. 'In a million years I will never fall for a boy,' she would swear.

During the holidays I saw Emmanuel a lot; he would ride his bike past my house. I took a bold step and invited him home. I told Mother I had invited a friend to meet her. I had now been with Emmanuel for two years, but we'd had no physical contact. Being a good Catholic girl, I believed God disapproved of my relationship and I wanted a blessing from my mother. I had never before said anything like it, and Mother covered up her surprise.

I laughed to myself a long time afterwards about how Mother's mouth flew open when Emmanuel showed up at the front door. A well-bred young man, he was small, a little shorter than me. I introduced him and Mother was warm and sincere. They sat and talked while I made tea. They were like old friends; you wouldn't have thought Mother was closing in on a son-in-law. I knew that Mother would have already extracted Emmanuel's entire life story and would be all but discussing wedding plans.

42

When Emmanuel left Mother grinned with excitement. 'He is a fine young man, a little bit younger,' she commented. She could read my mind; I was in love and there was nothing she could do.

At school I was busy studying for my O-level exams and looking forward to spending time with Emmanuel afterwards. By the end of term I was exhausted and couldn't wait to go home. Meanwhile a friend of my mother's, a Rwandan woman married to a Major General Taf from Idi Amin's army, had just had a baby and was at my house being nursed by my mother. News came that Major General Taf was being transferred to Kampala and they wanted a babysitter. I had been looking forward to the long summer holiday, but they would pay me for the work and we needed the money at home. I left home to live with the Tafs in the capital. This was the first time I would get to see the city.

I didn't want to leave Emmanuel, but I went along with the job. It would be only a few months before I returned home. On the other hand, I looked forward to seeing the city. Riisa had been at school there and came home with photos of big tall buildings. She told me of theatres and concerts, the buzzing nightlife and famous people that she had met. Although I wanted to experience it all, I said goodbye to Emmanuel reluctantly. We were to remain separated for a long time.

FOUR

Living with Idi Amin's tribe

I WAS NERVOUS about moving to Kampala to live with people I didn't know very well. It was my first time in the city, a very big contrast to my home town. I was comforted by the thought that in four months I would be back home, with my family, with extra money for Mother. I was also anxiously expecting my exam results. I needed good grades to enrol for A-levels, and I was aiming to go to Makerere University. Major General Taf's nephew was studying at Makerere and told me all about it.

I settled in with Major General Taf's Kakwa tribe. There were always so many people around. Fleets of cars, lots of food, and so much love and togetherness in this family, Major General Taf was a Muslim and shared the same compound with his three wives.

I missed my family and above all I missed Emmanuel. I spoke to my mother on the phone every so often and even managed to speak to Emmanuel a few times. I spent my days nursing the new baby; there were many helpers, but I bonded with this child. Major General Taf's wives had all gone to my mother to have their babies, so I felt like part of the family.

Major General Taf, a high-ranking officer, offered a contrast to what I had heard about Idi Amin's regime. Often Amin was referred to as a butcher who ordered his opponents' heads cut off, or did it himself. Taf was 7 feet tall, dark, lean and muscular. He had the look of a footballer, and a no-nonsense air about him if you didn't know him well. But at home he was very kind, he laughed a lot and always made time for his many children. He talked to them about school, about what they wanted to do, and he would eat with them.

The family lived in a very spacious compound of two-storey buildings. Each wife had a five-bedroomed house for herself and her children, and there was another large house used for leisure, fully furnished with a large-screen television and music system, with speakers wired everywhere. There was a large kitchen and an adjoining dining room which gave onto a balcony with a view of Lake Victoria in the distance.

In the compound there were two large gazebos with barbecues, used during the day when the sun was too hot. Adults sat in one and young people and children occupied the other. When the Tafs entertained visitors, which happened most weekends, both gazebos would be full of adults, and the children would take refuge under the large mango and avocado trees. Beautiful scented flower beds, sheltered by hibiscus trees and bougainvilleas, gave the feeling of a little village. Paved sidewalks separated the car park from a lush green carpet of grass.

Many people lived in this compound and there was a great deal of interaction and movement. It was a job to learn everyone's name and get to know them. Everyone was friendly and the children were polite, but Shamim above all made an impression on me.

Major General Taf's first wife's stepdaughter, Shamim, was about my age; she was a mixed-race Arab and Nubian. She was very withdrawn and said little to me or to anyone else. Everyone in the house would call for her: 'Shamim, clear this. Shamim, where is my book? Shamim, the children are hungry.' She didn't go to school; she was always at home helping with household chores. I felt sorry for poor Shamim but she never complained.

She came across as shy sometimes or even mean, depending on the circumstances. Occasionally, though, when we were alone, her eyes shone and she spoke to me as though we were good friends. Later she was to be my confidante and best friend. The rest of the children were vibrant, lively, secure and loving. Just like any normal household.

There was a turn in events at the end of 1978, a few weeks before I was due to return home. Idi Amin launched a military exercise called Operation Magurugur on the Ugandan–Tanzanian border. Uganda Radio announced that the country had pushed its border with Tanzania to the Kagera River, annexing 710 square miles of Tanzanian territory in retaliation for the recent alleged Tanzanian invasion of Uganda. Major General Taf announced that Amin was a patriotic president, that he was restoring land that had been given to Tanzania during the European scramble for Africa, he had crowned himself the conqueror of the British Empire, and now he was claiming what foreigners had taken from Uganda. I didn't think this would be an all-out war.

Tanzania responded by invading southern Uganda and in a matter of weeks occupying my home town. I could not go home. Within three months of the war starting, the frontline was close to Kampala. Phones were cut off, roads closed; I lost communication with my family. Once again I would be caught up in a war, but this time there was only one version of events: Idi Amin was winning the war and there was no reason to panic. Major General Taf, being a top army officer, didn't come home every day, and when he did he showed no sign of fear, resignation or panic.

I was anxious about my family. Major General Taf assured me that everything was under control, that he had been able to speak to my mother and that he would look after me and return me home safely when the war was over, which he said would be soon. I also had siblings living with my stepfather, near the Uganda–Tanzania border, and I was worried about them. My stepfather had remarried and had apparently taken his new family to Tanzania, where he was working, leaving my siblings with his mother. Major General Taf proudly informed me that he had sent an army escort to rescue my siblings and that they were at home safely, reunited with my mother after six years of separation. This was fantastic news, the last I heard from my family. I never stopped to wonder how my stepfather could rescue his new family and leave my siblings, his own flesh and blood, to fend for themselves with relatives.

Knowing my mother, despite the drama, I had no doubt she was keeping her head high and looking after the rest of my siblings despite the fact I was now away from home, as if there was nothing wrong.

Idi Amin left Kampala in April 1979. The country was falling to Obote's rebel forces, supported by the Tanzanian army. That was when Major General Taf's family panicked, packing up all their belongings, even looting cars to escape Kampala. We were woken in the middle of the night to find the compound filled with gleaming jeeps and flashy sports cars. The women had tied their hijabs messily, the children were in pyjamas and I was in a pink track suit; people were throwing suitcases with all of their belongings into empty cars, contents spilling out. We were herded into the waiting convoy, under the nervous watch of men patrolling up and down, dripping with bullets, hiding their faces behind heavy sunglasses although it was dark. I had no choice but to go with them; Major General Taf said he had promised my mother to keep me safe and would not leave me in Kampala.

A dusty convoy of lorries, pick-ups, Mercedes and Land Cruisers wound its way towards northern Uganda, heading for the West Nile area. It was a day's journey and the traffic up north was so heavy that dust trails covered the skyline. Brand new cars with no registration plates, 'borrowed' from showrooms, were evidence of the chaos left behind. We drove through a national park, and our escorts stopped to shoot deer for dinner. They killed seven; there was not enough room for them in the cars. They waved down oncoming traffic and gave the drivers meat to take home. It felt like I was an extra on a movie set, looking and listening but not saying much.

The retreat and escape was like a story from an exciting adventure; everyone was upbeat. People were waving at one another, the younger drivers overtaking each other to show off their skills behind the wheel. They were either unaware of the situation or, like myself, had no idea of its gravity. The older people possibly worried about the escape, but were in partial denial. I heard them say, 'It's a temporary evacuation. Amin will retake Uganda; he is in Libya to get reinforcements from Gadaffi.'

We arrived late at night at Major General Taf's house at Koboko, a district bordering Zaire (now the Democratic Republic of Congo) and southern Sudan. It was a modest village house with about twelve rooms, which the family used as a getaway from the stresses of the capital. Every inch of the house was occupied, the Kampala people mingling with their local relatives. They switched from English to Kakwa, a language I didn't understand. It was if English was a banned language. People spoke as though I wasn't there or supposed to hear their conversation. It was an isolating experience. I felt like a stranger; although the family didn't deliberately ignore me, there was no doubt that no one cared whether I was there or not.

Shamim was the only one who spoke to me. She introduced me to her Nubian cousins, another large family with a brown Arab complexion, most of them well educated – doctors, lawyers, entrepreneurs. Their mannerisms were very different from those of their darker cousins. They visited every day, bringing me books to keep myself busy, and Shamim and I would chat with them while getting on with the chores, cooking, washing and cleaning. Shamim taught me a few basic words and phrases – *talin* 'come here', *nyereku* 'children', 'What's the time?', 'My name is'. Soon I was beginning to pick up and understand a little of what was being said. I could even string a few basic sentences together.

For nearly two months, people crossed the border into southern Sudan, trading and returning to West Nile. They made money selling looted goods, cars, machinery, clothes, odd merchandise that they had no idea how to use. Soldiers in plain clothes mingled with civilians and turned into salesmen. There was a lot of money around, plenty of food and, strangely, a warm relationship between everyone. Although most people were related, outsiders like myself felt welcome.

During this time there were conflicting stories of what was happening in Kampala. No one seemed to know where Idi Amin was, but no one seemed worried either. Some people said he had fled; others believed he was regrouping and would retake Uganda. I heard that the frontline had shifted past Kampala, heading our way. We didn't see Major General Taf at all during this period, as he was commanding a battalion somewhere. One night he arrived covered in dust; I believe he mentioned being stationed at Soroti, in eastern Uganda, where Amin continued to broadcast his hold on power. At dawn the next morning we were woken, packed into a convey of Mercedes and driven across the Sudanese border to Kaya, near the customs posts on Sudan's frontiers with Uganda and Zaire. Well over 20,000 people crossed the border into Sudan during this time, but the exodus of Ugandan refugees seemed highly selective, consisting mainly of people who had reason to believe their lives would be in danger, business associates who had looted the country with the support of Idi Amin's regime, high-ranking officers and anyone deemed important and associated with the regime.

After clearing the Sudanese border, less than a mile away we entered a no man's land, where the border zone was shared between Uganda, Sudan and Zaire. It was crawling with a mixture of people – locals, Sudanese, Ugandans and Zaireans – sharing streets and homes. It was a hub for illegal trade and everyone was buying or selling something.

The northern Uganda border was now closed and Obote's forces established a new government and pursued Amin's men. Meanwhile the no man's land was filling with pimps, hustlers, prostitutes, bootleggers and other colourful characters, mixing with both Sudanese and Zairean police and protection agents, each one of them naming their bribe and exchanging favours for protection.

We moved further inland, about 5 miles from the border, to a place known as Poki. This was Major General Taf's home town, where he was welcomed back. Initially we took up residence in a compound of small huts, built on Major General Taf's traditional land to accommodate all his returning family. There were about ninety people in the compound. The women and children lived there, while the men always returned to a makeshift camp in the town for the night. There was not enough accommodation to rent, so many refugees built new homes. Poki and another town in south Sudan, Yei, became an explosion of energy, construction taking over most business.

Major General Taf built a big house with many rooms. All his male relatives worked on the building site, leaving in the morning after breakfast and returning for dinner. Meanwhile the bigger girls and I spent the days cooking, washing up, and going to the market to get more food. I sometimes spent a good six hours peeling and chopping onions and garlic. The food was delicious, there was always meat, and every sauce would have tons of garlic and onions. Breakfast would consist of fresh doughnuts, pancakes, eggs, plenty of fresh fruit and sometimes leftovers from the previous day.

Every day Shamim and I would take a trip to the market. As we passed the stalls we would be hustled to buy jewels and other stolen goods, and men would wink at us and call us all sorts of names – 'Angel', 'Goddess', 'Princess' or 'African Queen'. We would smile as if flattered and walk on. When we got to know them better they turned out to be harmless and quite friendly. I enjoyed going to the market; it was a sort of escape from the routine.

Every day I went to bed exhausted and thought about my family. I worried how I would get back home, but no one seemed to notice this. Major General Taf was not around for the first four months, so I couldn't leave. He had gone to the Sudanese capital, Khartoum, promising to book a flight for me to return to Uganda. There was no chance of returning by road, and the only other option would be to cross into Zaire and take a boat across Lake Albert into Uganda, which was a dangerous route for a woman to take alone. When Major General Taf eventually returned he promised to get me back home safely when things had settled down in Uganda. A few people were beginning to go back home, although the situation was described as volatile. Major General Taf told me to be patient; he would find a trustworthy person to escort me back home. He was trying to get me travel documents so I could fly from Khartoum to Entebbe, a much safer route than across Lake Albert.

Months passed. I learnt that my O-level results were out, but I could not get hold of them. Everyone here was preoccupied with their new existence. I had no one to speak to about my anxiety. Despite my good treatment, I missed my family and friends, and the lack of news from home was getting tougher every day. I stopped being so chatty and focused on my jobs to keep my fear hidden, in case the family thought I wasn't appreciative of their kindness. I would volunteer to do more chores, especially if they accorded me time away from the family.

I started going to the market more often, sometimes more than four times a day, depending on when supplies ran out. We only carried enough groceries for the day, and if visitors popped in, which was often, I would be sent to the market for more supplies. I made sure I ran there and back, returning in no time at all. Shamim hated running, she was more ladylike. That suited me well, as it gave me a chance to be alone.

At the market I would listen to customers and vendors exchanging news about the war in Uganda. Many refugees were grasping for news and twisting it, so that by the time you got to hear the latest it would have been changed many times. 'Obote's men have been pushed back, his days are numbered,' they said. 'Amin is getting more reinforcements and training ex-soldiers to stage a comeback.' I often wondered what the soldiers were doing at the border if training was in progress to recapture Uganda. I couldn't bring myself to ask in case I was seen as less supportive of Amin's return. I don't know if they believed this hearsay, but I think many of the soldiers were illiterate and had no real idea what was going on.

A new school term had begun back in Uganda, and I knew my friends would be preparing to start their A-level courses. Two months into the term, I became completely depressed. I lost my appetite, I couldn't focus on any work and I was tearful, but I managed to cry only when on the way to the market or in the toilet. The family started to notice the change in me. I could see them speaking about me, and I became increasingly paranoid.

I felt like an imposter when the older men and women fussed over me or showed me any attention at all. I started noticing them talking about me. I would hear my name and see them look at me in the special way people use while talking about you in a language they know you don't understand very well, as if you were dead or not there. All I could do is smile politely.

'Maria loves going to the market,' the women would say, looking in my direction, so that they knew I could hear them. 'Don't you, Maria?'

'You're extremely quick – you run like a cheetah and return before the kettle boils,' Shamim's mother would say.

'It must be her long legs. But be careful: at your age a woman should walk gracefully. Didn't your mother teach you anything?' another woman commented.

I was tall and lanky, my legs long and thin as needles. I felt less beautiful, as if the woman were sarcastically complimenting me while at the same time disapproving of me.

'Hajji has his eyes set on marrying Maria,' Shamim's mother would say shyly. Hajji was Mama Shamim's nephew on her mother's side, from the Kakwa tribe. He was always at home for breakfast and dinner, he was pleasant to me and sometimes he talked to me about my mother and my family. Soon all the family was talking about Hajji's bride to be. 'You would have to convert to Islam. Hajji is a generous man; he will take you on a pilgrimage to Mecca,' they would tease me.

I didn't take it seriously except when Shamim teased me and asked me if I loved Hajji. 'Hmm, I can see a big wedding, my black cousins and Arab relatives lavishing expensive presents on you,' she would say, jealously, as though she wanted to be me.

Hajji was far from my thoughts. I missed Emmanuel, but I had never discussed him with anyone, least of all now when I felt so anxious about getting back to Uganda. I continued my chores, going three times to the market, seeing people on their long, wild spending spree. Expensive cars would be parked near the market. Amin's people opened exclusive cafes where men sat on the veranda, with their pistols in full view on the table, and eyed up any woman passing by. There was no crime; even the police knew not to mess with Amin's men. A myth had followed them from Uganda to Sudan: 'It's known that if upset, they break open your head and think nothing of it,' a Sudanese woman once told me while plaiting my hair.

Every day would be the same, except Fridays. On Fridays, all the refugees would attend the mosque, the men wearing white gowns and the women in black, covering their heads with hijabs and sitting separate from men. After prayers they met at home for dinner which lasted till late in the evening. I would not have a chance to go to the market. I would be in front of the stove cooking and clearing dishes. I hated Fridays as there were more mouths to feed.

Every day I listened out for any news, my ears soaking up information like a sponge. One day a hairdresser who I used to visit to have my hair plaited mentioned in passing that she was waiting for Ugandan traders to deliver extensions and hair products for her salon. She had nearly run out of the black thread which she used for plaiting.

'I'm not here to have my hair done,' I replied on one occasion when I visited. I had made friends with this market woman, a Congolese, and I was planning an escape. 'I want to send a letter.' I said it was my best friend's birthday and I missed her.

She told me traders were coming to Poki from Uganda across Lake Albert. I asked her to introduce me to them. For weeks I waited, but no one she knew came. She would tell me that the traders were still selling their wares and would soon return.

The seasons were changing. Soon the heavens opened and in the storms birds and bees hummed in harmony, feeding on the beautiful wild flowers that covered the landscape. But the air was thick with mosquitoes, and tens of thousands of refugees caught malaria. Some sorcerers said it was a curse, and in the absence of a clinic, they charged huge amounts of money to lift the curse. Not long afterwards I began to feel under the weather; I came down with a fever and headaches and felt generally unwell. One minute I was shivering and shaking like a leaf and the next I would be too hot and felt as though I was sweating blood.

'You need a sorcerer's portion,' Shamim teased.

It was no joke any more; I felt nauseous and couldn't keep anything down. I knew from my experience, seeing people with malaria visit my mother's clinic, that it could be severe and even affect your brain – or, if undetected, kill you. I was given chloroquine tables, which made the vomiting more severe and gave me an upset stomach. But I reminded myself that I was a fighter and this bout of malaria would take up to seven days on chloroquine to lift. I put it down to the emotional turmoil and anxiety that I was going through.

One hot sunny day I was lying under a heavy blanket, trying to make myself sweat to accelerate my recovery. I can't remember who advised me to do this but I always felt better after sweating. Shamim's mother returned from the market and summoned me to a hut. She wanted to speak to me. Her eyes flashed and she was almost breathless when she spoke to me.

'How can you bring shame to this family?'

She took one look at me, moved towards me, lifted her arm and slapped me hard across the face. I gasped as her rings and bangles grazed my skin and staggered back, nearly falling on the floor, blood dripping from my nose. I screamed from the shock as much as from pain.

'Why did you do it? How dare you! How dare you!'

I felt dizzy and ill. Visibly agitated, her face rigid with hate, she paced rapidly up and down. I hadn't done anything wrong and so I couldn't make sense of her explosive body language. I had barely sat down when she slapped me again. I lost balance.

'How dare you, you spoilt tart! You think you could plan an escape and get away with it?'

I didn't cry or react. I was too sick to think.

The hairdresser at the market had sent a message that a trader had arrived and would be returning to Uganda soon, and she wanted me to come and meet him. I hadn't been to the market for days and I don't remember who gave me the message, but I was told later that when I didn't get back to the market woman, she sent a second message with one of the boys living with us at home. He innocently told Shamim's mother to pass the message onto me. She was livid and stormed over to the market to find the woman. Without giving her a chance to explain, she told her to stay away from me.

'So tell me, when did you start seeing this man?' Shamim's mother asked. 'What did you expect us to tell your mother? She entrusted you to us. Wait until everyone hears what you have been up to.'

I stayed silent, feeling like I was going to throw up. Unable to bear it any longer, I turned around, opened the door and staggered outside. She followed me.

'I should have known from your latest change of mood, the nausea, vomiting, loss of appetite. Here you are, pretending to be ill. Are you pregnant?'

I didn't answer; I had no energy to explain myself. Shamim's mother had presumed that the man I was supposed to go and meet was an acquaintance. I didn't even know him.

Shamim overheard her mother screaming at me and came to my rescue. 'Mother, leave her alone. You destroyed my life; I will not stand by and see you mistreat Maria.'

She tried to say something to her, but Shamim wouldn't have it. 'Go away now, Mother,' she shouted. She sat next to me and for the first time told me how her mother had locked her up in the house all these years. She would not send her to school for fear of men finding her. She didn't know her real father, who seems to have been a Nubian her mother met on a one-night stand, hence the reason she was of mixed race.

'Look, Mama is wrong, she shouldn't have—'

I tried to interrupt Shamim; I wanted to forget the past few moments. I didn't want her to apologise for her mother, but she carried on. 'I don't approve of her behaviour. She has such bad friends; they spend hours gossiping about other women, despising everyone and meddling in other people's affairs.'

I could see she was ashamed and hurt by her mother's behaviour. I told her not to worry. I tried to smile and reassure her that it was a misunderstanding I preferred to forget about. I still lived with the family, so I wasn't about to show the fear and anger I was feeling. I was also too weak to make sense of the whole episode.

I told Shamim I was worried about my family and wanted to get news from traders coming from Uganda. I was depressed because all my friends were now in school and I was losing time. It had been almost nine months and an opportunity to be accepted at any school was slipping away. I didn't know whether I had passed my exams, whether I had a place waiting for me or not. There was no sign or hope of getting back home. Shamim was so kind and comforted me, but I didn't tell her about the slap. A few days later, I felt better and resumed my normal chores. Shamim was happy to have help at last.

I saw the market woman every day; I told her my family wasn't happy so I wouldn't be sending any letters home. I had spent sixteen months away from home and I had abandoned any hope of returning.

One afternoon, in the middle of the market, full of people in a hurry, jostling and pushing each other, I heard a voice which I thought sounded familiar. I turned around, but the speaker had his back to me. What were the chances of seeing anyone I knew in this part of the world? Nevertheless I paused and listened carefully. The man was haggling with the trader for a price of a bag of sugar. There could be no doubt: it was Mamdan.

Mamdan used to be a driver for Major General Taf. The last

time I had seen him was when we left for the north. He had refused to go with Major General Taf's family. He had a wife and children behind enemy lines, and he decided to stay in Kampala and wait until the roads were open to the south of Uganda so that he could go to find them.

He started to move. I called his name. He turned his head around slowly.

'Maria. . . Thank goodness you're alive!' he exclaimed, excited to see me. 'Your mother has been worried sick since you left. She will be happy to hear from you.' He told me that my mother hoped I would return soon – and that I had passed my exams. He didn't remember details of my grades, but I was excited anyway, because I knew it would only be a matter of time before I went back home.

Mamdan came with me to meet the Tafs. Everyone was happy to see him again. I wanted desperately to go back with him but Major General Taf was away and the others wouldn't let me go without his permission.

However, Mamdan returned the next month, and this time he did take me back to Uganda. It was June 1980. Major General Taf's big family hosted a lavish party for me. Everyone turned up to say goodbye, eager to show how much they would miss me. The boys surprised me with a disco after dinner. It was a moving farewell, and I felt quite sad to leave. I got on well with nearly everyone, and without realising they had become my family. I promised to look out for them when they returned to Uganda, and I kept that promise years later.

My journey took me to Bunia, a city in the Democratic Republic of Congo. It lies west of Lake Albert, separated from it by the Rift Valley, and about 40 kilometres from the Ugandan border. There was no connecting road to Uganda, and the only way we could get there was across the lake in a local fisherman's wooden boat. I was escorted by five people, including Hajji and some of his brothers, who had family in Bunia. The journey to the lake took a day in a Land Rover, negotiating swamps and waterlogged roads. We arrived just before dawn to find that Hajji and his brothers had prepared another party for me. It was another emotional farewell, but I didn't have much time to think about it. It was time to drive to a small port which was bustling with traders, some coming to Bunia, others going to Fort Portal in Uganda.

The family waved me off as the boat pulled away from its mooring. Mamdan told me to hold onto the side. It was powered by a motor which took a few minutes to fire up but soon we were on our way. We crossed the waters of the Nile, which leave their distinctive reddish-brown trail as they pass through Lake Albert. I dipped my hands into the water, scooped up a handful and washed my face, amazed by how a river can cross a lake.

The journey took almost another whole day – it was very slow but sure. We reached Uganda in the late afternoon, and the next day Mamdan and I left for Mbarara, where my family lived. They knew Mamdan was bringing me home, but had no idea what state I would be in. My mother was delighted to see me, but her joy was lessened because our time together was to be so short.

The next day Mother packed whatever she could lay her hands on and we took a bus to my school. The school had reserved me a place and I enrolled on my A-level course. I turned up to find my old friends from the convent school had just offered a mass to pray for my soul, believing I was dead. For the next six months, my old friends spent their free time helping me to catch up. With their assistance I just scraped into university. I had set my sights on studying law, but it wasn't to be. I went to Makerere University and studied political science and sociology.

Many years later I was in London, separated from my family again. I had just completed my master's degree. Life had been unkind to me, and I had just lost my dear mother, who I missed terribly. But, taking a leaf from her book, I was determined that life must go on. I had my siblings to take care of and I promised not to disappoint my mother. I felt I could celebrate survival once more and look forward to a better future. Surely nothing could be worse than the experiences I had encountered in the past!

FIVE

A *pinnacle* of my life

AFTER MY MASTER'S degree I searched for jobs, but with my only experience as a sales assistant for Marks & Spencer, I couldn't get into development work. I volunteered for a charity and enrolled on an IT course. I had stayed away from relationships and concentrated on dealing with my own life. I had my mother's children to support after her death. So, as ever, work took over my life.

It was on the IT course that I met the man who would later be the father of my son. He was very gentle and patient, and he made feel valued. He didn't really say much about his personal life, keeping his cards close to his chest. This didn't bother me, as I too had a history behind me. I was working as well as finishing my dissertation, and he was studying for his Bar exams, so our lives were busy, but we found time to be together and we had a lot to talk about, mainly legal matters. We grew close and, as with all couples, our first days were bliss. I worshipped him; he seemed to replace the hollow in my life. I commuted from my flat in south London almost every day to be with him in the East End.

After a while, though, I began to question his commitment. He spoke about taking me to meet his parents, although he never did. We considered living together, but even that didn't materialise. He could always find an excuse for this or that. 'We can't meet my brother, because he's away on business,' he would say. Sometimes, I admit, he would be busy reading for his exams, but I never got to meet any of his friends or his family.

We had been together for nearly a year when I found out I was eight weeks pregnant. We both wanted a child, or so I thought. I was over the moon, but I couldn't say the same for him. He now decided he didn't want to have a child after all, but he said he would support it when it was born. That was the last I heard from him.

The separation from my boyfriend was painful, but after my mother's death, nothing would ever hurt me as much again. When my son was born, four years after my mother had died, I finally felt a little relief from the pain and guilt of not saying my last goodbye.

I was still in touch with my friend Richard, who I had met while studying at SOAS. He became my pillar; he was always there for me. He took me to Devon on holiday before my son was born. In fact I named the baby after him and later he became his stepfather.

Richard's ambition was to work in Africa and soon he landed a job in Sudan, but we stayed in touch. Every week I received a letter from him full of stories of how he was saving the world. I too would write every week about my baby: names, scans, hospital appointments and my cravings for carrots, lettuce and mayonnaise. This was the happiest time of my life. My pregnancy and the birth of Richard junior sealed off the many painful years.

Very early one morning, around the time when young Richard was turning one, Richard senior, still working in Sudan, rang up and said, 'I'm coming home to marry you!' He was always joking, so I didn't take him seriously. We chatted and after I'd hung up the phone I didn't think any more of marriage until I received another phone call a little while later, at about 6.30 a.m.

'Hello, is this Mary?'

'Yes,' I replied.

'This is Richard Blewitt's mother.' The voice on the phone sounded very angry. 'I don't know whether to congratulate you or not. Did you put him up to marrying you?'

'Hello,' I replied. 'I thought he was joking when he called me.'

'So are you going to marry him or not?' she asked firmly.

I hadn't given it a thought until this phone call. 'I guess so,' I said.

She slammed the phone down.

I could understand why she was livid; she didn't know me well. I had a young child, not a good start for a marriage, at least from a mother's point of view. After the phone call, I realised I had committed myself, and this was not one of Richard's jokes.

The phone rang again. 'It's me. I'm sorry, I'm in shock. Can't you postpone until I return from my holiday?' Mrs Blewitt asked.

'I guess so, but I can't reach Richard. I'll tell him when he calls next.'

Richard would not reschedule the dates. Over the next few days, I told my family and a couple of friends the news, but I can't say anyone was thrilled. Just 'Congratulations' and 'We'll try to take time off'. The wedding was on a weekday morning, when everyone would be at work. I borrowed African boutique shorts and a shirt from my best friend. I didn't buy anything new or go mad in a traditional white dress.

Richard arrived only two days before the wedding. He ran around buying a few things for himself and then surprised me with a wedding ring, which didn't fit. We had to force it even half way. There were only five of us at Hammersmith Town Hall. When the registrar recited the vows, my son repeated them before we did. He had just started speaking, aged fourteen months, and had turned into a chatterbox. He would entertain himself, speaking and repeating every word on TV.

Richard's best friend brought a camera which he forgot to put a film in. To this day I believe he deliberately forgot the film. After the marriage ceremony, we piled into my secondhand car and stopped at a McDonald's for a takeaway lunch, which we washed down with a glass of champagne. In the evening we had dinner with a few friends at Dino's restaurant by Gloucester Road station. The next day we went to the Lake District for a three-day honeymoon. Richard was in London for only three weeks before returning to Sudan; our marriage had started with a separation that would characterise the rest of our married life. Despite this, though, I felt I was leaving my troubled world behind me once again. Time to rebuild my life and move on.

Three months after Richard and I married, Richard junior and I prepared to move to Nairobi to join him. He had been transferred from Sudan and had already started his new job as a regional development programme officer for a charity, overseeing projects in Kenya and Sudan. He was waiting anxiously for his new family to join him in Nairobi. He had been in Nairobi for nearly three months.

I cleared my flat ready to rent it out while I was away, carefully ensuring all my expensive mantel ornaments were safely stored away. I shipped baby supplies, unsure whether I would be able to buy them in Kenya.

Richard was waiting for us at Jomo Kenyatta airport in Nairobi. He couldn't control his excitement as we appeared in the arrivals lounge, me pushing a trolley full of our suitcases and Richard junior sitting on top of them, enjoying the ride. He jumped over the barrier and ran towards us. Richard junior leapt off the luggage and fell on the tiled floor, screaming with excitement. It was an emotional reunion; we hugged and made our way to the car park.

Richard drove us through the capital. The ride took under thirty minutes. He took us through a bustling, vibrant city, with vendors, markets, music buzzing, restaurants and ultra-modern high rise buildings. Along the way I saw overcrowded slums, run down and neglected – a poverty-stricken neighbourhood in contrast with the city. Richard was driving carefully, dodging and zigzagging around the local transport called matatu, Nissan minibuses that pick up and drop off passengers wherever and whenever they choose, collecting as many passengers as possible en route.

It was a gorgeous sunny day, a light breeze whipping through the leaves of the jacaranda trees. As we approached the house, the car halted and Richard hooted the horn, excited to show us our new home. The house was surrounded by a high iron fence. I peered through the bars; even the gravel paths were beautiful. The gate had a large sign that read 'Protected by INTERSEC'.

Since when do we need high level security and protection? I thought of my flat in South Kensington, my cosy one-bedroom flat which I had occupied for many years – charming, spacious and bright, with its own private patio, overlooking a secluded garden. It was conveniently located in a secure area, with Sloane Square, Harrods, the King's Road and Hyde Park all within a short walk. I thought of the freedom to come and go. Intersec protection didn't make sense until I was told stories of local armed bandits, attacking foreigners and stealing their property.

A guard peeped through a small sliding window at the gate and slowly released the main gate to allow us into the compound. Behind, a large whitewashed house came into view, nestling between purple-flowered jacaranda trees, in the heart of the Nairobi suburb of Westlands. 'Its location avoids the noise and bustle of the city. Yet it is still within easy reach of the centre, a nice walk to the all the major shopping malls,' my husband told me.

We were greeted by a guard, a gardener and a cook. They unloaded our luggage as Richard led us inside the house and gave us a tour of our new home. There was a cushioned lounge with a cosy fireplace, an intimate dining room and a private garden at the back. Three spacious bedrooms opened onto a large veranda, a place for private relaxation. Paths led from the lounge into a tangled garden, and there was a beautiful view towards rolling hills covered with fabulous trees, giving canopies of colourful foliage. The garden had been planted with hibiscus and bougainvillea. To the south, the house gave onto two terraces. On the second, my husband built a large Wendy house for Richard junior.

The whole setting felt excessive and extravagant. 'Why do we need three people to run the house? It's just the two of us and Richard junior,' I said to Richard.

'Kenyans need jobs and this is a way to put bread on their families' tables,' he explained. 'Otherwise they would have no job and no income.'

The next two days were packed. We visited the city market and afterwards we went for lunch at the fascinating Carnivore Restaurant, which served a range of charcoal-barbecued game including zebra, ostrich, buffalo and crocodile, expertly carved onto your sizzling plate until you said 'No!' Then we took a trip to see some local handicrafts: wood carvings, belts, jewellery, key rings, bangles and all sorts of items made from colourful Masai beads. There were many places to visit, including the Karen Blixen Museum, the elephant orphanage and the giraffe manor, where Richard junior was delighted to feed a giant giraffe from his hands and stroke it.

After a week introducing us to Nairobi, Richard senior left on fieldwork. He would be gone for two weeks. I didn't notice the trend of separation: I was starting a new life with my husband away, just my son and me; unemployed, surrounded by helpers, with absolutely nothing to do with myself. I felt isolated, I had no friends to speak to, no relatives and nothing to keep me busy.

I had followed Richard to Kenya with the hope of starting a new life with him, and was assured I would find a job that was challenging. I didn't want to be a 'yummy mummy', a housewife waiting on her husband. From the start something was missing, my husband. To pass the time, manicure, pedicure, coffee shops and salons became the options. I could afford them; Richard was earning a good salary. But I felt so uncomfortable because I was living on aid. We lived a luxurious life compared to the local staff. I would challenge Richard, to the extent that I refused to drive the organisation's cars and bought a small secondhand car of my own.

I focused on looking after Richard junior. My husband had arranged a nursery place for him, where all the expats sent their children to school. The school was just five minutes from the house, but everyone drove there.

On the first day at school, I felt anxious for Richard junior. Until now, he had always been with me. It was wonderful to have him. So much of the meaning of my days, my daily routine, revolved around him. I would spend evenings reading stories for him, until he fell asleep, and I would put him in his bed. Sometimes he entertained himself with his Power Rangers figurines or swords, pretending he was a brave worrier. He was self-sufficient, but I kept an eye on him; he had been known to post anything, including his shoe, into the fireplace. Our worlds had been inseparable; it was difficult for me to let him go – until now he was my company when my husband was away. My son being at nursery left a big gap for me to fill during the day, alone until he came home.

I asked the teachers if I could stay for the first couple of days, until my son settled in and was comfortable in the new environment. I am not sure if it was Richard I was worried about or my own feeling of isolation. I became increasingly insecure. A world that I had imagined for the three of us when I moved to Kenya was somehow fragile right from the beginning. I suppose I built a balance that rested upon putting myself second and hoping Richard senior would eventually settle down and spend some time with me.

I met the expats' wives; like me, they had accompanied their husbands, most of whom were at work while they stayed at home and entertained themselves. They were friendly and had been expecting me. They took me to their favourite ice cream and coffee shop. 'We meet here after dropping the children,' they told me. The friendly staff, who were given big tips, knew their names and their favourite morning drinks.

'We have a tennis tournament tomorrow. Would you like to help with catering?' an expat's wife asked me. 'We need volunteers.' There was a dinner and dance to raise funds for some charity, I can't remember which. I spent the next days meeting other expat wives, talking about the tournament. I would be in charge of the raffle tickets, for which the prize was a car, apparently donated by Uchumi supermarket. I think it was won by one of the expat wives in the end.

The conservation was filled with who was coming to the various events, gossip in the expat world, who had been seen with whom, what to wear to impress, and booking the salon. There was always something happening, but the talk was basically the same, day in, day out.

I settled into a new routine: driving my son to school, passing by Uchumi to pick up groceries, then on to the butcher, delicatessen, and the main market to buy fresh fruit and vegetables. I just about managed to avoid the gossip-fuelled coffee mornings. Dropping the shopping home, I made a cup of tea and retired to the veranda to read a book, buying time until lunch, when I collected Richard junior. He was a blessing; he kept me busy for another hour, telling me, in a way that only a toddler can, all about his teachers, his friends, the horses he rode on and what an expert he was at everything. After lunch he would be exhausted and take his afternoon nap.

The life that had seemed blissful changed within a few months. I began to feel the separation from my husband. Without Richard junior, I was totally bored. Meanwhile Richard senior would return for two or three days at a time, mainly at weekends, and then head back to the field.

When he was around he took us on safari trips and to Mombasa beach. I don't know if they come much cleaner than this – Nyali Beach, my favourite, was spotlessly white and had no tangling seaweed. It offered activities galore during the daytime for people into water-sports: kite-surfing, windsurfing, snorkelling, diving and boating.

At night we hired a baby sitter and went for dinner under the stars, listening to karaoke, singing along to Shirley Bassey's 'Diamonds are Forever'. If we felt adventurous, we would hit the discotheque until the early hours of the morning.

There were many weekend places to chill out, but my favourite was the three-day trips to the Aberdare safari lodge, a hidden world of wildlife. Elephant and buffalo moved almost silently through the undergrowth, while overhead noisy birds and Columbus monkeys dominated the canopy, and there were beautiful gardens, with peacocks stalking the lush green lawns. My husband enjoyed their small golf course, which tested even the best player. I followed him on the golf course retrieving stray golf balls, with Richard junior strapped on my back securely with an African cloth. I still have the best memories of a wonderful setting, delicious food and friendly staff. We visited so many times that the staff knew my son's name, and his favourite meal, chips with plenty of ketchup.

I should have been having the time of my life, with both Richards really happy, but I was not fulfilled. The separation was mentally and physically disruptive to our marriage. Richard's work came first and he didn't seem to notice that I was tired of waiting for him. 'Sorry, darling, there's an emergency in Eritrea. I'm leaving for Asmara tonight.' There was always an emergency meeting, a long night preparing or typing reports, conferences and seminars that seemed endless. I had lived alone for years and managed my life. I knew what I was doing, when and where. Marriage seemed to wipe my slate clean; I was only responding to my husband's work and schedule, like a good, understanding housewife.

Four months on I was totally fed up. I had applied to many organisations for work and had had no luck. I told Richard, 'I'm thinking of going back to the UK. I have no purpose in Nairobi except to wait for you and take care of my son.' But Richard junior was happy in school, and I was stuck between using my return ticket to the UK before it expired, disrupting Richard junior's and senior's lives, and settling down unhappily, continuing to try and find some meaningful things to do.

Until now, I had always worked and never had a dull moment. I am naturally a hyperactive person and idleness was getting to me. I needed a challenge, a meaningful routine. I began to question why I was here. I missed London, my lifestyle, my friends and family, and my flat, which I had reluctantly said goodbye to.

Kenya turned out to be very competitive. There were many foreigners and getting a job depended on who you knew. Richard was never around enough to keep his ear to the ground in case there was a short consultancy job coming up. It was up to me to go from organisation to organisation looking for any job that could keep me busy. I took a voluntary job helping children learn how to read at my son's nursery school, but this was not enough. I put the word around that I was available for work, through parents at the school, and tried to create networks.

I proactively placed my CV everywhere, and after nearly six months, I landed my first consultancy job. It didn't pay well but it was better than nothing and raised my profile in the world of humanitarian experts. After successfully organising a fundraising workshop for a charity, more work came my way. Richard continued to travel. I missed him, and we tried to catch up when he was around.

Despite the separation and constant travel Richard turned out to be a wonderful dad for my son. They played games, climbed trees, swam together. He would get involved in any chores at home as well, helping in the kitchen and cleaning. I gradually let him be, allowing him to take all the decisions when he was around.

The jobs I got were all short term and irregular, so in the end I settled to seeing both Richards happy. I tried to lead a normal life, accommodating my frustrations in Nairobi, especially when we hosted dinners at home for the many foreigners and Richard's friends that passed through Kenya, either on holiday or working with Richard.

'So what do you do while Richard is working?' they would ask.

'I breed horses,' I would say confidently, to get their attention. I didn't know anything about horses, but if I mentioned cows, which I was familiar with, that would not interest them.

'How fascinating. Commercially or for a hobby?' they asked with amused interest.

'For business. I supply hotels with game and horsemeat is exotic, a favourite on the menu when barbecued,' I would reply.

'I would never eat horsemeat. I may try zebra or crocodile but certainly not horsemeat.'

Sometimes I would say, 'I am a housewife looking after my husband and my son.'

'Really? That's wonderful. Richard is a lucky man,' male contemporaries would reply, pointing out that Richard always spoke about me. But the women avoided me. I didn't have a British accent; I wasn't working. Richard was an intelligent young man, bursting with energy and enthusiasm about his work, passionately full of positive stories about the different projects he was overseeing. Sometimes I felt like a imposter, as if I wasn't really there.

I would find myself falling into feminist discussions. 'Should mothers work and take their children to nurseries or childminders? Or take time out of work to nurture their children while giving up their career and dreams?'

Everyone focused on Richard junior, who was such a show-off and got all the attention he needed. I would be lucky to gain attention from anyone for more than five minutes. So I settled for explaining the dishes that the wonderful cook and I had prepared, their names, the spices and all the traditional ingredients.

As for family and friends, they had a guidebook of the must-see places. I drove them everywhere when Richard was working, and at the weekend he joined and took over as if our life was bliss.

From the outset of our marriage, Richard's work was paramount; he wanted to change the world and I shared his vision, and as time passed this became the reality. Our relationship became secondary, and work consumed my husband's time and passion. If ever I was brave enough to raise the issue of being away from home, he would always say, 'I am working for my family.'

I wasn't working so I could not argue.

Sometimes he would become irritable if I mentioned his job taking over our lives. 'I am a good husband,' he would say, 'and I love you. Why are you making a big fuss?'

I immersed myself in bringing up Richard junior, as Richard senior focused on saving the world and devoted less time to our marriage. At first I was mad at him for being absent, but in order to cope I made excuses for him. I stopped noticing him leave or getting excited when he returned. I wanted to have peace of mind, because he didn't seem to try to reduce the number of his trips away from us.

'I will be a good wife. It's only early days, and maybe he needs time to appreciate me!' I consoled myself. 'Things will get better with time.'

SIX

Where there is no hope

The UN Blue Berets are here; no harm will come to us.
                                    Jean Baptiste (March 1994)

I WAS BADLY mistaken if I thought that I had left hard times behind. As I began to settle down, towards the end of the 1993, stories of human rights abuses against Tutsis by the government of Rwanda began to emerge in my home country.

Ethnic conflict was not new to Rwanda, often called 'the land of a thousand hills' or 'the Switzerland of Africa' due to its rolling hills and folded mountains to the north. It had been locked in ethnic strife for three decades.

One of my earliest memories of Rwanda is from when my parents were in exile. I must have been about five years old. I later learnt that they had fled to Burundi during the 1959 revolution that foreshadowed the genocide that was to come thirty-five years later. My maternal grandparents, as well as other relatives, lost their lives in this massacre.

Mother always reminded us of our heritage. She even sent us to study at a Rwandan refugee school to ground us in our culture. From her I learnt that Rwanda had three ethnic groups, Twa, Hutu and Tutsi, who had coexisted peacefully. They all shared a culture and a language. Traditionally the differences between the groups

74

were a matter of occupation: Twa were hunters, Hutu farmers and Tutsi cattle keepers. They intermarried over the years. Mother never said anything against the Hutus to us, but she explained that the relationship between them and the Tutsi took a new turn when the European colonisers arrived at the end of the nineteenth century.

During the 1885 Berlin Conference, which carved up Africa between the European empires, Rwanda fell under German rule. But after Germany's defeat in the First World War, Rwanda was transferred to Belgian control in 1919. The Belgians introduced identity cards and a policy of divide and rule. Abetted by the Catholic Church, the colonialists exploited and exaggerated the hierarchical differences to facilitate their indirect administration of the country. They promoted the interest of the Tutsi ruling elite at the expense of the Hutus, institutionalising their power in a way that transformed what had previously been a reciprocal relationship into an entrenched system of Tutsi domination.

The end of the Second World War provided an impetus for anti-colonial struggle and the Belgians betrayed their Tutsi allies and switched support to the majority Hutu to protect their trade in Rwanda. The widespread discontent engendered by these divisions eventually resulted in a revolt in 1959, which left 20,000 Tutsis dead.

This conflict shattered my mother's life. She lived with unimaginable pain and loneliness. She liked to sing, and some of her songs were painful. Sometimes when she sang, you could see the grief in her eyes and hear her deep sorrow reflected in her voice. There is one song I remember, 'Nashatse Mama Ndamubura' ('I have been searching for my mother and cannot find her'). Her own mother had long since died, alongside most of her family.

Mother told us how thousands who survived the massacres were forced to flee as refugees, to Uganda, Tanzania and Burundi.

Sometimes, as in our case, people had gone to all these countries looking for asylum. Mother told us how the Hutus continued to kill and suppress Tutsis who remained in Rwanda, that thousands of Tutsis were butchered with machetes and dumped in rivers, and that violence, arrests, intimidation and abuse increased during President Habyarimana's Second Republic, which claimed to be sympathetic to Tutsis.

Meanwhile Rwandan refugees, forced into exile, and their children suffered persistent discrimination in neighbouring countries. In Uganda I witnessed Amin's targeting of Rwandan refugees. His expulsion of Ugandan-born Asians left the Rwandan refugees and other foreigners in a vulnerable position. I also lived to see Obote's counter-insurgency campaign, which threatened to drive my family and other Tutsi refugees back to Rwanda. My family managed to escape the repatriation, but many were returned and denied the right of citizenship despite being Rwandans. Repeat appeals to Habyarimana to allow refugees to return as recognised citizens came to nothing despite the involvement of the UNHCR in the negotiations. In 1982 many Rwandan refugees, rather than wait for Obote's regime to harass them, joined Yoweri Museveni's National Resistance Army (NRA), which eventually won control of Uganda in 1986.

Having gained experience in the NRA, Rwandan refugees subsequently formed the Rwanda Patriotic Front (RPF), led by the youthful Fred Rwigema, which took up arms against the Rwanda government in 1990, leading to the international community's recognition of the refugee crisis. My younger sister Jeanne d'Arc was among the first recruits to join the RPF. She had grown up in Rwanda with my brother Jean Baptiste, and both witnessed the discrimination against Tutsis in schools and communities. She often told us stories about how teachers asked Tutsi children to stand while they took the roll call in the morning, or about how children were sometimes denied places in higher education or on an athletic team because they were Tutsis. Jeanne d'Arc in later years came to live with us in Uganda, but Jean Baptiste refused because he was fond of our ageing grandparents, who had brought him up.

The 1990 RPF invasion gave Habyarimana's government a pretext for imprisoning thousands of Tutsis and Hutus who dared criticise the regime. In 1992, hundreds of Tutsis were massacred in Bugesera and the killing did not stop there. These killings were essentially political crimes with ethnic overtones. President Habyarimana could not tolerate the sharing of power with Tutsis.

During this time, a series of agreements backed by the international community were being signed between the RPF and the government of Rwanda to ensure a peaceful settlement of the Rwandan crisis. In August 1993 the Arusha Peace Accords, negotiated between the RPF, the exiled Tutsi-led army in Uganda and the government of Rwanda, delivered the promise of democratic power-sharing and the eventual integration of the RPF into the national armed forces. The UN dispatched peacekeepers shortly after the accords were signed to help ensure the country's security, establishing a transitional government and elections. Ironically, in the months before the 1994 genocide, the accords generated much optimism and the arrangements were seen as a model that offered the prospect of peace and democracy. Little did we know that all the while the government was planning the killing lists.

During this period I was wrapped up in finding a job and settling with my husband in Kenya, the headquarters of the UN in Africa. From what I could learn, the meetings led by the UN were becoming speculative, and no one had any idea how the government of Rwanda would react to letting the refugees return home, or how it would share political power with the rebels

77

demanding to be accepted back to Rwanda from exile. Everybody was hoping for a smooth transition somehow.

Reports claimed that 'the United Nations peacekeepers have been dispatched to Rwanda to oversee the peaceful transition of power-sharing between the RPF and the government of Rwanda and therefore there is no cause for alarm'. This was despite stories of atrocities and reprisals against Tutsis inside Rwanda, which I heard were becoming more and more common every day. Jean Baptiste was in Rwanda and I was concerned for him.

Nine months into his job, in the midst of my anxiety about Rwanda, my husband was planning a transfer to Ethiopia. We needed to pack and ship our belongings to Addis Ababa. But first we had to take our annual leave and we planned to return to the UK. I was still thinking about Rwanda, but I was distracted by the move. Remembering how long it took me to settle in Kenya, I was not keen to restart my life in Addis Ababa.

Back in the UK for two weeks we were busy meeting friends and relatives and catching up with life away from the unfolding disaster. There was hardly any news reporting on events in Rwanda.

One morning, a Tanzanian aid worker I had met in Kenya at the UN's Rwanda debriefings phoned. I had told him I didn't work for the UN but I was attending all the meetings to find out what was going on, as I had family in Rwanda.

'Mary, I wanted to let you know that the situation in Rwanda is fast becoming explosive,' he said.

'What's happening?' I asked anxiously.

'A Hutu extremist has been assassinated, and the government has responded with reprisal attacks on Tutsis across Rwanda.'

'Are you recalling your staff from Rwanda?' I asked.

'There is talk of being cautious but foreign staff are on standby in case the country erupts into further chaos.'

I felt extreme fear sweep through my body. What if Jean Baptiste was killed in these reprisals? He was already targeted, because my sister was in the RPF and he had siblings abroad. I called him to warn him and to ask him to leave Rwanda; being a Tutsi he would not escape. But as always, he warned me to stop playing the protective big sister.

'The UN Blue Berets are here, no harm will come to us' he said.

Nevertheless, I became so worried that I called a British charity which worked in Rwanda to ask if there was any news. The charity invited me to a briefing. It was preoccupied with the logistics of extending aid to areas under the control of the RPF. It couldn't afford to ignore the RPF, since it was due to sign the peace accords that morning and become legitimate.

During the meeting, two people mentioned their unease about the pending crisis, citing the underlying tension in Kigali and escalating human rights abuses by the government of Rwanda. Unfortunately, no one read the signs. I left the meeting fearful for my brother's life.

SEVEN

Darkness falls

I have not lost faith in God. I have moments of anger and protest. Sometimes I've been closer to him for that reason.

Elie Wiesel

ON THE EVENING of Wednesday 6 April 1994, a plane carrying President Habyarimana from Dar es Salaam, where he had supposedly finally consented to put in place a broad-based transitional government, was shot down on its approach to Kanombe airport in Kigali.

I awoke the next morning in London to phone calls from friends. I had missed the BBC News, which was claiming that the Rwandan president had been killed. Horrific events were unfolding in Rwanda, and I heard that roadblocks had been erected on all roads. The city was crawling with soldiers, and an armed militia group known as Interahamwe ('those who attack together') were killing anyone holding a Tutsi identification card.

There was total confusion, and in the tension of what was happening, the messages I was receiving from everyone were too difficult to comprehend. Who were the Interahamwe, and why were they killing everyone? The numbers and concentration of deaths, the intensity of the killings, the extensive use of rape and physical violence, the massive involvement of Hutu neighbours in butchering Tutsi – all this was simply astounding. It was just not believable that ordinary people, once neighbours and friends, were now turning against Tutsi, calling them cockroaches and beating them to death! The scale of massacres in such a short time sent me frantic with fear for Jean Baptiste's life. Until this moment I had been concerned only for him, because he was in the capital. I hadn't thought the rest of my family would be in danger.

I called Richard, who was now in Addis Ababa. He promised to speak to colleagues and get back to me. I waited for his call anxiously. At least he was close to Rwanda, and someone at the African Union headquarters would have information about the country.

Meanwhile, the phone stopped ringing. I crawled up on the sofa that was once my comfort zone, but I was tense and shaking, terror ripping through my body. The major news channels, BBC, CNN and Sky, were all continually broadcasting messages coming from RTLM radio in Rwanda of the president's death, with details of how his plane crash-landed in the grounds of his palace. Everyone on board was dead, including the president of Burundi. I flicked from channel to channel, hoping this wasn't happening. Surely someone will intervene to stop the killings, I consoled myself.

By the end of this beautiful spring day, the dark clouds of evil had descended on Rwanda. Pictures emerged of men wielding machetes, roadblocks packed with refugees, dead Tutsis lying by the roadside where the Interahamwe had killed them, women and children being beaten to death. I could only hang onto Jean Baptiste's last words, and hope that the UN would protect my family. But I couldn't help but feel anxious. Tutsi men had been a target for many years and Jean Baptiste was not new to the dangers. But I still hoped for a miracle. For weeks I had no news about my brother.

In the middle of the mayhem I joined my husband in Addis Ababa. Events were now becoming clearer. The scale of the massacres was alarming and numbing. News was leaking out of Rwanda that was truly beyond comprehension. Within hours of President Habyarimana's death, the first wave of killings was unleashed. Opposition leaders and moderate Hutus advocating peace were hunted down by the Presidential Guard and were among the first murdered. A list of Tutsis was circulated, urging the Hutus to not rest until they were tracked down. In the days that followed, the stories got tenser, with reports that the Interahamwe were carrying out massacres across the country.

'The UN Blue Berets are here; no harm will come to us.' I wanted to believe my brother. But soon after the genocidal terror took over the country, the deaths of ten soldiers from Belgium led its government to call for the immediate withdrawal of UN peacekeepers. The UN withdrew most of its forces and all foreigners were evacuated to safety, giving the killers a clear signal that they could continue unfettered. I knew then that Jean Baptiste's hope and security were shattered.

I wanted to fly to Rwanda, but all the borders were closed. All I could think about is when I would be able to get into the country. I spent anxious days tied to the radio, calling the Rwandan community at the UN headquarters in Addis Ababa to find out any news. Every time the phone rang I jumped with fright. As the situation worsened in Rwanda, I waited helplessly to hear if my family was safe. Then I heard that women and children were being killed. Soon I prayed that I'd be able to find someone, anyone, still alive.

My nightmare began in June. It was a nice sunny day. I had just returned from collecting Richard junior from nursery. After lunch he always fed a rabbit he called Peter. I opened the door of Peter's hutch and Richard shoved carrot leaves towards him. 'There you are, be a good boy and eat all your food,' he told the rabbit, which happily munched away as though it hadn't had a meal in ages.

Then the phone rang. I quickly closed the rabbit hutch in case

Peter escaped and fell into the hands, or should I say the mouth, of our dog, Mimi. I told Richard to stay put while I got the phone.

There was a woman's voice at the other end of the line. 'Is this Maria?'

'Yes,' I replied.

'It's Riisa. I have bad news about our brother Jean Baptiste.'

I took a deep breath, and slowly walked out of the house to keep an eye on Richard, who was calling me to give Peter more carrot leaves.

'Jean Baptiste is dead.'

My body froze, and a sharp dagger sliced through my heart. I didn't interrupt.

'He was killed in the first week of the genocide.'

'No!' I screamed out loud.

'Jean Baptiste was among the first people killed in the genocide, in the first week of the cold-blooded massacres.' Riisa sounded calm and collected, as if death was inevitable and an expected occurrence.

I remembered a similar call: 'Your mother died a few hours ago. She passed away at one in the morning. The whole family is by her bedside. She died peacefully in her sleep.'

We both fell silent. I thought I could hear Riisa's heartbeat through the phone, or maybe it was my own bleeding heart that I was feeling. I was holding back tears. I didn't want Richard to see me upset or crying, although he was still occupied feeding Peter Rabbit.

'Jean Baptiste is dead? Maybe this is a mistake.' My mind wandered to Rwanda; perhaps it was the wrong Jean Baptiste.

Riisa didn't wait for me to ask her how Jean Baptiste died. 'I'm sorry, Maria,' she said. 'A female refugee who was escaping the massacre was asked by Jeanne d'Arc to find me and let me know.'

'So how did this woman escape?' I asked her.

'Maria, I hear from refugees that many people are dead, butchered with *pangas* (machetes), hoes, large clubs studded with nails, *impiri* (heavy sticks). Many are still piled up on roadsides, churches, schools – everywhere there are Tutsi bodies. I doubt if his wife and children will survive; so many people have died.'

The sun slowly dimmed. I felt like my soul was leaving my body, like I was about to faint. I reached for the swing and carefully sat on it, allowing my weight to swing me to and fro as the unfolding story she told me devastated and numbed my feelings.

By the time my sister said goodbye, it seemed like I was watching or visualising a horror movie. I couldn't but wonder why that refugee I didn't even know escaped the carnage, while my brother couldn't. I thought of Jean Baptiste, his last hours before he was murdered in cold blood; the fear, walking home alone, knowing his family would die. That he too would die, alone, somewhere, from the blows of machetes, his hope that the UN would save him shattered. But in a way I was grateful that at least I had some news about him.

Jean Baptiste had been born with polio. His left leg was shorter than his right, so he wore a supportive shoe to give him balance. He could not run fast. I wondered if he had resigned himself to his fate because he could not run far before being caught. Or was it because he thought death was inevitable, and not worth trying to escape? Or because he had made his peace with God and was ready to die? Such thoughts, justifications, self-discussions and analyses ran through my head for days, never to be answered. But I desperately wanted to know how he died, his last moments.

I tried to picture Jean Baptiste asking the killers to spare his life, begging for mercy and pardon for something he had not done. I saw men hitting him as though he was a snake, six, eight, ten, twelve men, each hitting him until he was no longer moving and then continuing to the next victim. I heard him screaming – he must have, the pain would have been unbearable. Then I hoped the blow to the head killed him first, so he didn't feel any more pain, that his soul left him before the killers could cripple it. My grief was agonising, tearing at my soul and my heart. But I found that if I denied to myself that Jean Baptiste was dead, if I dissociated myself from his pain, I felt better. He did not die, so there was no pain. I held onto that image that my brother was still alive from then on.

With the border closed, I was forced to sit it out for a hundred days, anxiously wishing to enter the country but fearing the nightmare that was waiting for me. Part of me was extremely worried; thinking of a trip to Rwanda made my stomach churn with fear. On television, I saw corpses in lakes and rivers being washed ashore. Dead and dying Tutsis floated in the water like bloated logs, some heading north towards Lake Victoria, their rotten bodies easy meat for river hogs and dogs alike.

I heard stories from survivors who had escaped, the UN staff who had been repatriated to Addis Ababa; they made my emotions freeze. A stench of death filling the atmosphere, naked bodies crushed with clubs, arrows and machetes. Babies dead on the ground everywhere, tossed into rivers or drowned in bloody tubs, with their parents and relatives decaying elsewhere. I heard of pregnant women sliced open, their wombs expunging their unborn Tutsi children, and of burnt bodies filling churches.

I felt helpless and angry. I was at home alone with Richard junior, as my husband had started a new job and he was travelling in rural parts of Ethiopia. He would be gone for days or weeks. Unlike Nairobi, Addis Ababa had no shopping malls to keep me occupied. The biggest attraction was the British library, where I borrowed films and books to occupy my time. There was a large international community, yet no one had news of any possible intervention to protect Tutsis.

*

It must have been the end of June. It was a nasty day, damp and dull. When it rained in Addis it never stopped. The roads filled with dirty pools of water and the pavements were packed with people trying to escape the rain under the shop verandas. I was driving home after picking up my son from nursery. He was telling me about a new nursery rhyme his teacher had taught him. I was trying to keep my eyes on the road in case a cow crossed, as they often did. Richard was complaining, 'Mum, you're not singing along with me.' I was secretly extremely worried, but I tried to sing with him. Once at home I turned my attention to Richard, asking him to help me unload the groceries.

Inside the house the phone was ringing. I ignored it for a while, but it wouldn't stop. Eventually I picked it up. A friend whose husband worked for the UN was in shock. She told me that Rwandan radio was calling on all Hutus to unite and get rid of vermin, the *inyenzi* (cockroaches). 'The graves are half full,' it proclaimed.

With the foreigners gone, the only sources of information remaining were RTLM and the television station, Mille Collines. They broadcast hate, fomenting tension and calling on Hutus to hunt down and kill all Tutsis. The message was clear: no Tutsi should be spared, neither young nor old. As Lieutenant General Roméo Dallaire, leader of the UN mission in Rwanda, later wrote: 'We watched as the devil took control of paradise on earth and fed on the blood of the people we were supposed to protect.' There was no escape.

I tried to speak to the African Union, wondering if someone was following the news in Rwanda. After being shoved between different departments at the African Union offices, I was advised to speak to the Communication Department.

'Isn't there an obligation to protect Tutsis?' I asked the director of communication.

'Yes, but this requires a global response,' he replied. 'The USA is

86

reluctant to send its soldiers because of the recent Somali debacle. And the Belgians, after their soldiers were mutilated, have called for all foreigners to evacuate Rwanda,' he told me. 'The rest of the world in due time will recommend action.'

It became evident to me that the outside world had no grasp of how very little the Hutus valued humanity. Through its refusal to take action immediately, to stop the cold-blooded massacre of innocent people, the value of my brother had fallen, the value of our families. Although at the time I had no full understanding of how desperate the situation was, I still believed the world could and should have prevented the killing.

With every day that passed, the hope of finding anyone of my family still alive lessened. I had learnt from my mother, and my culture, not to speak about myself to anyone; that doing so was a sign of weakness, of not being able to cope. I did not voice my anxiety about Jean Baptiste's death to anyone, not even my husband. I only prayed for a miracle to find his family alive.

Weeks passed. It was now July and Richard senior's job was still taking him all over the place, so I was always alone with my son. Every night, after feeding Richard junior and reading him a bedtime story, I lay in bed awake.

I heard Richard turn in his cot, coughing and wheezing from his asthma allergies, trying to find a comfortable position before finally falling into a deep sleep. Then I turned my attention to the clock in the sitting room to distract myself from thinking about Rwanda and the madness that was slowly annihilating our families. I counted carefully, every tick. . . one thousand. . . three thousand ticks. . . Ticks turned into hours, and I still I couldn't sleep, my heart feeling heavy and my breathing getting faster and faster. This became my regular night-time experience.

EIGHT

A *thousand hills soaked in blood*

IT WAS NOT until August that I finally made it to Rwanda. The RPF secured the country that month, whereupon the international community – humanitarian workers, journalists, photographers, foreign nationals from all walks of life – lined up waiting for an opportunity to get back to Rwanda, a country they had abandoned for one hundred days.

I managed to get a lift on board a UN military Chinook helicopter that was flying multiple sorties, moving disaster relief and aid workers to Kigali. I was keeping myself busy with research on street children in Addis for a local charity, when I heard that there was a flight to Kigali every week from Kenya. The charity helped me get a place on the helicopter and arranged for me to stay with its staff in Kigali.

It was the first time that I had seen a Chinook. It was a camouflage green colour. Sitting on the runway at its base in Nairobi, it resembled a large deformed banana. Its engine was running with a lot of noise but little power. I began to wonder if it would fly at all. It had a large hump on its back with three rotor blades and a much smaller hump on top of the cockpit, also with three rotor blades. The interior looked like a warehouse, with seating cushions lining each side and belts everywhere. Towards the front, there was a large container full of aid supplies, well secured in place. There were ten of us on this helicopter. I was the only woman and, dare I say, the only black person on board.

My husband Richard remained in Addis with my son. It was early days after the genocide, and I didn't know what to expect, but I was relieved that at least I could find out if my family had survived and then return to Addis. Whatever the situation in Rwanda I was feeling lucky because I still had family to come back to.

'Is someone waiting for you in Kigali?' an aid worker sitting next to me asked.

'Yes,' I mumbled, cutting the conversation short, not wanting to give away my fear of the ride ahead. I was more worried about making it to Kigali, than what I would find there. I looked around. One person was reading a novel; three more were talking about the horrific events that had unfolded in Rwanda. I thought they must have come from the same agency. Others quietly held on to their seats. The Chinook was flying low, but I had no intention of looking through the windows at the horizon. The noise from the helicopter drowned out my thoughts of what was awaiting me. I could not anticipate or imagine what I was about to confront. I wondered if I would find my brother's body, whether his family had survived. I had no news at all of my family. I had spent months hoping to find them alive, yet aware that this may not happen.

As we descended through the clouds over Kigali the pilot warned us of turbulence. I wondered how there could possibly be more turbulence, as the ride was already so rough. I always feared flying, even in normal planes, but this time it was not just the fear of flying; I was full of emotions at facing the truth about the horror that had just happened.

We arrived at around two in the afternoon, in torrential rain. As we approached the runway, all I could see were the consequences of the recent fighting: homes that lay roofless, in ruins, with jagged black stones protruding; buildings with fallen beams and shattered glass, walls peppered with holes of every size. I saw a funeral procession: a row of cars and an ambulance with a siren in front, hazard lights flashing and horns honking.

The rain lasted for a short time. As arranged from Addis, a driver from the charity picked me up. On the way into Kigali from Kanombe airport, a twenty-minute ride, the clouds lifted and the sun started to peep through. Torrents of water were gushing down the hills, eroding trenches in the mud around houses and sweeping away everything in their path. The driver explained that the rains had been heavy the past three months and the drains were completely broken. The thought of bodies being swept away down the bloody streams and thrown against walls, disintegrating along the way, made me sick. Thank God Richard had introduced me to Dr Martens boots, a pair of which I was wearing. I would keep them on as long as I was in Rwanda.

I stayed first at a compound, hosted by an aid worker. The compound was gated and protected by a security company. Aside from the charity staff, no one was allowed in the compound without an appointment. My first impression was that it was not so much providing security as emphasising the different status of Rwandans and foreigners.

The compound contained many foreign nationals whom I came to know as journalists, researchers, and other people visiting Rwanda and searching for information. There was an abundance of food, the offices were well equipped with computers and the residence was comfortable, with maids and housekeepers. The compound was powered by a generator, possibly the only place in the neighbourhood with electricity. If it wasn't for another fortress opposite, with foreboding brick walls and filled with men and women dressed in pink, I would not have remembered I was in Rwanda because of the genocide.

This fortress was Kigali's central prison, housing genocide suspects, its gates guarded by armed men who ensured that the queue that snaked up to the main road was kept in order. Inside the prison I could hear people singing as though there was a big party going on. How lucky, I thought – the genocide suspects were happy because this was an official visiting day, and their families had brought supplies.

My host was kind and welcomed me, introducing me to everyone, so that I felt safe and included. He assured me that there was security and I could go anywhere because all genocide suspects were now in prison and would not harm me.

I was keen to find Jeanne d'Arc, who I had last seen eight years earlier, in 1986. So after a late lunch, I decided to place an announcement that afternoon with Radio Rwanda to say that I was looking for her. I hoped she listened to the radio, or someone who knew her would alert her to my message. I kept thinking that this was the same Radio Rwanda that had been preaching hate and destruction just a few weeks back, but I had no other way of finding her.

One of the Rwandan compound staff kindly offered to take me to the radio station, a short walk away. My guide was a very neat and smartly dressed man, in his mid-fifties, clean shaven and gently spoken. He was about 5 feet 8 inches tall and stockily built, a little overweight but really no different from an ordinary fifty-something man in Africa. I was not entirely comfortable with his offer. 'Is he a Tutsi?' I wondered. 'How did he survive? If a Hutu, did he kill? What is his story? How can I even risk being in his company?' Thoughts flooded my mind. I thought to keep him talking while I looked around for an escape route.

I turned my thoughts to the streets, lined with hibiscus, bougainvillea and avocado trees. There were a handful of people walking in different directions, seemingly in a state of shock, although that could have been my own anxiety playing up. Otherwise the place was empty and calm. It was as if everybody had simply disappeared.

The only vehicles around were large Land Rovers, driven by UN and aid workers,. They were draped in huge UN flags, which flapped aggressively in the wind as they drove past, often at high speed.

I plucked up the courage to ask a question of my escort to try work out whether I was safe with him. 'How did you manage to survive the carnage?'

Without much explanation, he replied, 'By the grace of God.'

I straightaway assumed he was a Tutsi survivor, because he seemed to suggest that his survival was a miracle, that God had protected him. Overwhelmed by my first encounter with a survivor, my fear and anxiety evaporated. I wanted to hear more. After all he was harmless. I felt at ease to ask more questions.

'How do you feel living with and seeing Hutus, knowing they were involved in killing your family?' I asked him.

'Well—' he began to speak, then paused. He looked back as if checking on passing traffic, avoiding meeting my curious eyes. He then cleared his throat and asked. 'Where are you coming from?'

I explain that I lived in the UK but part of my family lived in Rwanda.

He then said, 'I don't know how much you know of recent events.' He didn't call it a genocide, which worried me. 'Not all Hutus killed,' he told me.

I sensed a deep discomfort and awkwardness, and knew better than to ask any more questions. 'He is likely a Hutu,' I thought, fear gripping me again.

'How long is it before we get to the radio station?' I asked.

My guide pointed ahead to a gate. It was manned by young soldiers and there were others at the entrance to the radio station itself, about eight in total. I felt relief. I thanked him for his help as he hurried back.

As I crossed the road, I sensed that the soldiers were watching me. I looked up to catch one eyeing my Dr Martens boots and looking me up and down. I knew I seemed like a stranger, the way I walked, my shoes not feminine or flattering to say the least. I was different from the Rwandan women, who walked majestically, in a dignified and unhurried rhythm.

'How can we help?' a soldier at the gate asked politely. Very impressed by the manners of the young man, I felt relaxed with him. A thought crossed my mind: soldiers can be human after all. I explained I wanted to place an announcement on Radio Rwanda to find my sister, who was serving in the RPF.

'What is your sister's name?' he asked.

'Jeanne d'Arc,' I replied.

He turned to another soldier and said to him, 'This is Macho Ine's sister.' (*Macho ine* is a Swahili phrase meaning 'four eyes', usually used, as in English, for people who wear glasses.) I knew my sister wore glasses and I was surprised, but also relieved, that they all knew her. She worked in the president's office, just up the road. They directed me there. I thanked them, and bade them a good afternoon. I was visibly happy and excited.

I made my way hurriedly in the direction these young men suggested. By this time dark storm clouds were gathering in the heavens, threatening more torrential equatorial rain. It was soon pouring down, amid thunder and lightning. I had no umbrella, not that it would have helped anyway. In any case, I had to find my sister first, before it got dark. I continued into the stormy weather, to a place I did not know.

I arrived at the quarter guard (the description they gave me) at the Ministry of Defence. I was met there by a young army officer. He was excited, unable to contain his enthusiasm at meeting the elder sister of Afendi Jeanne. I came to learn later that 'Afendi' is a respectable way of addressing officers in the army, another Swahili word. The officer assured me that my sister worked there but had gone home for lunch. It was past four o'clock in the afternoon. Lunch? I wondered.

As it turned out, the young officer lived on the same street as Jeanne, Deputy Kayuku Avenue, which was a short walk away. He offered to take me there if I wasn't sure of finding the place, but said I would have to wait for another two hours before he could clock off. I couldn't wait that long, so I thanked him and set off looking for Deputy Kayuku Avenue. After searching a few streets, I found myself standing on the doorstep of my sister's house.

It was now getting dark. With no street lights, the only light came from a kerosene lamp, which was obscured by a net curtain. I knocked at the door.

'Come in,' a voice called from inside.

Pushing a curtain to one side, I entered the house. I could see three people sitting in the dim light.

'My goodness, Maria, is that you?' Jeanne d'Arc sprang to her feet and embraced me. I felt the strength in her arms. Her manner was brisk, her face had filled out and her soft feminine voice had gone. She wore the army uniform of camouflage trousers and shirt, with a pistol attached to her belt. She had become broader since we last met, which made her seem shorter. I put my arms around her.

'I'm so sorry, Jeanne, about Jean Baptiste's death,' I said.

'He's not the only one,' she replied. 'I never thought. . .' She spoke as if her voice was dragging her heart along behind it. 'I never thought, all these years I have been fighting for our rights, that Jean Baptiste would be a victim of his ethnicity. The worst part is, I can't do anything about it.' She looked at me. 'It should have been me. Jean Baptiste was a good brother; he was selfless.'

'He loved you like crazy and respected your courage. It was not your fault,' I replied. I wasn't sure this was the right thing to say given the circumstances, but I knew it was true. She looked down at the ground and nodded.

Jeanne introduced me to her friends, and signalled for me to sit next to her. I wasn't going to say anything else, not sure who her friends were, but then I did.

'Did anyone else survive?'

She reached over, still not looking up at me, and put her hand over mine, just for a second, like we were a team. She kept it there just long enough for us both to take a breath.

'Bitsibo is a graveyard,' she said. 'Everyone was killed in cold blood at the primary school. They lie in a shallow grave by the school.'

She let go of my hands as if to seal their fate and reached for a pack of cigarettes. Her friend also reached over and took one. Jeanne lit it for her, leant back in the chair and exhaled. 'Sorry, sis, I now smoke,' she apologised. She didn't offer me one – not that it mattered. I don't smoke.

'So how is everyone?' she asked, changing the topic.

'Everyone is fine,' I replied.

Then there was total silence, which made me want to scream. I had a sucking feeling, low in my belly. I took a deep breath and held in a bundle of grief that nearly sent me yelling. I filled my lungs as deeply as I could. I felt tears flooding my eyes, as if seeing Jeanne d'Arc was all I needed to have a cry without having to explain why.

She went outside, where a young boy was tending a pot on a charcoal stove. I followed her; there was an old white Toyota saloon parked in her driveway. 'Is this your car?' I asked, trying to make trivial conversation.

'No, I found it abandoned. I don't drive; a colleague called Jean Pierre drives me. I am only using it temporarily. If the owner claims it I will give it back.'

'It was probably abandoned by Hutus fleeing from RPF soldiers,' I thought.

95

The boy making dinner was not more than thirteen years old, but big for his age. Jeanne called him Kadogo ('the young one'). 'I found Kadogo alone and traumatised after his entire family was killed,' she said. 'He had gone to fetch water, only to return and find his father, mother and three siblings soaked in blood in the front room of his house.'

Jeanne took him to a safe zone – a refugee camp, hoping a relative would find him. After the genocide, when she returned to the camp, Kadogo was still there with no family. Jeanne brought him to Kigali.

'We are not paid a salary, we only receive RPF rations. I hope you don't mind the food, beans and maize flour,' she said apologetically.

'You know me, I'm not fussy, and as a matter of fact I'm starving,' I replied. I reached out and tasted the beans. 'Could do with a bit more salt,' I suggested.

Kadogo passed me a tin of salt, our eyes met and he smiled shyly. All this time I had been trying to catch Kadogo's attention, but he had been avoiding me.

'How did you get here?' Jeanne asked.

I explained about the lift in the UN helicopter. 'Are you going to adopt Kadogo?' I asked.

Jeanne told me she was hoping to send Kadogo home to find any surviving relatives when she got some money.

Everything I was hearing was overwhelming. I couldn't but wonder how Kadogo felt, the invisible wounds in his heart and soul that I could not see. Then I had a thought: this is my first call of duty. I am going to find the money and help Kadogo find his relatives. Just for a second I felt relieved; I was going to do something about the genocide.

During dinner, the young soldier I had met earlier joined us. His name was Célestin and he was one of the footsoldiers who marched into Kigali to stop the killing. He had a self-congratulatory air, a proud young man who was part of this gruesome history, but who was also one of the heroes who stopped a genocide. Célestin was keen to tell me of his experience and he proceeded to paint a picture of Rwanda during the hundred days of slaughter.

'There were miles of deserted villages,' he said, 'fields of crops unattended. The air was filled with the smell of rotting flesh. Corpses were lying in the fields, by the roadside, in churches, outside their homes. . . everywhere. The Hutus had fled when they heard the sound of our artillery.' He raised his voice as though he was irritated. 'I stumbled upon Tutsis still dying, warm pools of blood a sign of how if I had arrived a few hours earlier I could have saved them.'

Célestin saw men, women and children wandering on the road with gashed wounds rotting, maggots falling from their bodies, like living corpses. 'Please kill me,' they would beg. 'I have no reason to go on. I don't want to live alone.'

'What did you do with them?' I asked.

'Well, I was pursuing the killers,' Célestin replied. 'We simply left them behind and another group came after us and took them to the safe zone while we continued to chase the killers.'

When he joined the army his motive was to give Rwandans in exile a right to return home. As a soldier he had lost many comrades along the way, but nothing could have prepared him for what he confronted.

My sister was indifferent to our conversation. She suggested driving to town to see my uncle Eugène, who had survived.

Célestin gave us a lift. We drove in total darkness, and Kigali was silent and lifeless, except for occasional headlight beams cutting through the night. At almost every turn there was a roadblock. As we approached, Célestin slowed down and saluted, then some soldiers sprang up from nowhere and saluted my sister. '*Habari,*

Afendi.' (*Habari* means 'how are you', another Swahili word.) She straightened herself and saluted back. They waved us off.

I didn't know what to make of this. The discipline, order and good manners that the soldiers displayed begged belief. Were these the same soldiers that only three months ago had been fighting the murderers? I was angry and couldn't understand why they were so calm, as though nothing drastic had happened in their lives, as though they had just peacefully walked into Kigali and had not lost loved ones.

We arrived at my uncle's house a little after ten o'clock. Jeanne hadn't told me how he had survived. The knock on the door was answered with 'Come in if you want'.

My heart lightened. Uncle Eugène was the comedian in the family, he wrote a column in the local newspapers as a hobby about some of the funny things people do. It was difficult to take him seriously. I was expecting to see a vibrant 45-year-old, laughing and making jokes about everything. Instead, what I saw was a broken man, thin, old and haggard, his eyes sunken, wearing loose trousers and a shirt too big for him. When he got up to greet us he moved with a limp.

'Well, well. . . Where are these cockroaches springing from? We kill you and you bounce back,' he said, forcing a smile. He embraced me tightly and closely, a Rwandan greeting known as *uguhobera*, which means 'holding together'. I felt him shaking. He smelt of the cheep local booze.

The light from his kerosene lamp was faint, but I could see scars on his head and his arms.

'When did you arrive?' he asked me.

'Today,' I replied, shocked at his sorry state.

'Maria, you arrived late; everyone is gone. Only three months ago we were all here. What took you so long? Now all that remains is the shadow of the family we used to be.' This was the most serious statement I could remember Uncle making. He was a broken soul; he had lost his spark. I thought my presence must have shocked him and brought back rough memories of everything he had lost.

His house was modest in size and resembled my sister's. There was a small cupboard with basic cutlery and crockery, covered in dust as if it hadn't been used for months. In the middle was a table covered with a yellow crochet tablecloth, which matched the covers on chairs. The walls were covered with pictures cut out from magazines: Michael Jackson when he was still black, Mpongo Love, the African diva, and others I could not identify.

Uncle Eugène called out to a young man to go and buy us drinks, excusing himself. 'Sorry, this is a bachelor's house. There are no women to make African tea.' In the past that kind of statement would have enraged me, and I used to think he deliberately wanted war with me. But now, ironically, he was right. All the women were dead.

I gathered the courage to ask him what had happened to him.

'I have not spoken to anyone about my story,' he told me. 'What happened to me is unspeakable.'

Eugène's story took hours to tell, and his face was contorted in pain as he remembered it and struggled to get the words out. He spoke about death, despair and separation. He started by recalling previous conflicts such as the 1973 massacres of Tutsi students, which took place when he was in the seminary at Kabyayi parish church, thirty minutes' walk from my grandfather's village in Gitarama district. My grandfather was a respected Tutsi chief and so my family could find sanctuary in his village.

My uncle had qualified as a teacher, but he could not get a teaching job in Rwanda because he was a Tutsi. His passion was comedy, which was not terribly well paid or acknowledged as a viable career, being seen instead as a voluntary amusement. However, he managed to charm many people and was eventually invited to write a column for a newspaper in Kigali.

Once the RPF launched a guerrilla war against the Rwandan government, Eugène's relationship with the community became strained. The local mobs joined the army and harassed him. In our village and at work he was often referred to as an RPF accomplice, known locally as *ibyitso*. Although he would joke about it, he knew he was a prime suspect: an educated Tutsi with family in Uganda and a niece in the RPF. He told me he was always expecting to be arrested or killed.

On the evening of 5 April 1994, Eugène decided to go back to his home village. He couldn't remember what prompted him to go home. Maybe fate had something to do with it. After work he boarded a local bus which dropped him on the main road, where he hired a bicycle to take him on the next leg of his journey deep into the hills of Gitarama. He passed one of the local bars, where the usual crowd were drinking and eating *nyama choma*, roast goat. He knew everyone there. He had grown up with most of them; they had been to the local primary school and walked the beautiful folded hills of Gitarama together as children. He stopped to greet them and they invited him for a drink. Eugène liked his beer so there was no reason for him to refuse. The night was normal, no signs of aggression. He was making his jokes, which everyone laughed at.

Just before midnight, he left on foot to make the fifteen-minute journey to his house. The night was dark, but he knew his way around, for he had made the same journey for many years. After a few minutes on a straight stretch, he could hear people whispering, or so he thought. He was drunk and couldn't make out what was going on.

He started whistling and singing to stop himself from getting nervous. He sensed something weird but not very different from the usual night-time encounter. He wanted whoever it was to know he was there.

When Eugène got closer the voices became louder. Someone called out, 'What is this cockroach doing out late at night?' My uncle recognised that voice: it belonged to the head of the local defence force, who had been harassing him. Sensing danger, he ran down the hill, hoping to lose them. With his long legs, he made it to the bottom of the valley, but he was too drunk to keep going and the other people caught up with him.

More than ten enraged men, shouting abuse and insults, started hitting him. 'Your cockroach brothers tricked you; let's see if they will save your arse!' one shouted. 'The Tutsi betrayed us; you shall not live,' said another. He could hear them discussing who should cut his legs in two.

'The booze saved me,' Uncle Eugène said while telling this story. 'I would be dead if I had been sober that night. I was in pain but I kept telling myself, I'm not as badly hurt as I feel. I'm drunk; I will be alright once I sober up.'

The men beat him with machetes all over his head, and on his arms as he tried to protect his head. Eventually he passed out. 'The militia must have thought I was dead,' he told me, the pain etched on his face making him look older than his years.

Just before dawn he came to and remembered what had happened. He couldn't move his limbs. He was covered in blood, and wherever he felt himself there were gashes on his body as though part of him was disintegrating.

He knew he wasn't far from home and he inched his way back up the hill like a worm, until he reached the house of some Tutsi neighbours. He told them a drunken mob had descended on him because he had been drunk himself and had insulted them. 'I didn't want to tell them it was the local militia, because they would have panicked. The air in Rwanda was dense with rumours of revenge killings.' The neighbours cleaned and bandaged Eugène and took him back home. Everyone was horrified to see him in such a state and busied themselves looking for transport to take him to Kabyayi for treatment the next day.

But then there was a turn of events. In the early hours of Thursday 7 April, Eugène was listening to the radio and was just about to drop off to sleep when he heard a broadcaster announce that the RPF had shot down President Habyarimana's plane and that he and the president of Burundi were dead. He stayed glued to the radio all day and all night. 'I could smell what was coming; somehow I didn't think that anyone would be spared. In the past when we had problems, some Tutsis were killed but not on a big scale.' He recalled how, before my grandfather died, their neighbours protected my family, the same neighbours who the night before had nearly killed him.

The following morning, Uncle was taken to Kabyayi hospital. His wounds were so severe that he needed stitches, but meanwhile the doctors were trying to control infection and get his temperature down. The next day, many people were wheeled in with machete, spear and gun wounds.

The local parish church was beginning to fill with people fleeing from Kigali. They reported that the Interahamwe and local people were killing every Tutsi they came across. They talked of bodies littering Kigali's roads, houses, latrines, schools and churches. It was not until three days later that the gravity of the situation started to unfold. By this time the Interahamwe militia had elected roadblocks by the entrance of the church. Many more people, injured and frightened, were being brought in.

'I sensed I was going to be killed there and I wasn't about to wait until they found me,' Eugène said. 'Early on the morning of 11 April, I decided to take off my clothes and walk stark naked out of the main parish gate. I was laughing and telling jokes and turning around so that everyone could see me naked. The militia were laughing and cheering me.'

He pretended someone had brought him to the parish from Ndera mental hospital and he said he was going back as he missed all his mad friends.

'I was the only person walking back to Kigali, where everyone was fleeing. With my injuries, which I had exposed by removing the bandage, no one wanted to kill me. I was a walking corpse. I heard them say, "Don't waste your energy on the mad one, he is already dead."'

My uncle walked all day, stopping at the roadblocks to talk to the Interahamwe militia. They were variously embarrassed or amused to see the exhibition. Small boys and girls were particularly amused and they formed a curtain trail around him, following him and poking him. He would scream 'Help! The children want to kill me' then try and run, but his injuries were so bad he couldn't run away from them. But, even as the children chased after him, he managed to escape the Interahamwe. Some kids followed him for miles. As he continued, talking himself out of danger, he got further and further from the road blocks.

It took him four days to eventually make it to Ndera mental hospital. The Hutu attendants had no hesitation admitting him. He calmed himself down but sometimes he refused to sleep during the day, because he knew they would come and kill him in his sleep. He refused to wear any clothes. He would let the male nurses dress him, and then he would promise to keep his clothes on. When they turned away he took them off. Eventually they let him be.

The Interahamwe visited the mental hospital to see if any Tutsis were hiding there and Eugène would hear nurses saying, 'Everyone is bonkers here. They have been here for months.' He was the only newcomer to the hospital since the genocide started, but no one seemed to notice.

One day, while all the inmates were sunbathing, about thirty Interahamwe militia descended on the hospital. A truck stopped by the main gate and men with machetes jumped off and marched past the guards. 'We have information that RPF soldiers are hiding here,' they said. Wielding their machetes, they hurriedly turned everything upside down.

'One of them aggressively confronted me,' Eugène recalled. '"What is your name and where do you come from?" I kept my eyes fixed on the grenade that was attached to his belt and refused to answer. "Where is *inkotanyi* hiding?" he commanded. "Give me time to remember," I replied. The Interahamwe man was pissed and raised his machete to hit me, but his friends told him he must be mad himself if he was losing his cool with a Tutsi nutter. "Tutsi are snakes! He's not mad," he replied, spitting in my face. "*Genda sinkwica wambwa yu mu Tutsi we* [I will let you live, you Tutsi dog]."

'I was ready to die, but he let me live. I was so tired and emotionally exhausted I knew death would have been better.'

He reached out for his glass, his hand shaking. I put my hands on his arm to steady him. 'It's not just my hands; my whole body shakes every time I think of the anguish and fear I went through.'

He continued: 'I planned to tell the attendants the truth so that they could kill me. I awoke the next morning and the staff had abandoned us; the gates were open. I heard the sound of artillery nearby. In the late afternoon, some RPF soldiers rescued me.

'My regret is that I had to start wearing clothes again. You should all strip off one day, especially on hot days. It's nice and a wonderful feeling. I recommend it.'

By the end of my uncle's story, I had stopped laughing at his jokes. I was numb. It was as though I had just been reading a horror novel. I wished that his story was just that – a story, in a book that I could put on a shelf where it would gather dust over the years. But this book was my book, it was my uncle's story, my story, a story of death, grief, pain and helplessness.

We left his house in the early hours. I was worried about his drinking and his health. I was right to: he did not survive long.

Over the next two days, Jeanne d'Arc and I recalled the lives we led. She had learnt that a neighbour knew where Jean Baptiste's body was lying. He went to hide in a church, but the Interahamwe were by then attacking churches. With a sense of resignation he returned home to die there, only to be stopped a few yards from his house by a neighbour and a group of Interahamwe who beat him with nailed clubs known as *masus* and machetes. He was left for dead.

An old couple with whom Jean Baptiste used to pray witnessed the killing. They were hiding in their banana plantation, and watched him slowly die. When darkness fell, the couple stealthily buried him, with his Bible under his arm, in a shallow roadside grave, which they covered with banana leaves.

My sister sent for Valencia, Jean Baptiste's widow, and her children to come and stay with us. I had never met my sister-in-law nor her children, except through beautiful letters and photos that Jean Baptiste had sent to me, describing his family as a perfect gift from God.

I used to urge him to leave Rwanda, but after marrying Valencia he felt his life was there. I slowly gave up any hope that he would ever escape the ethnic strife. By this time my ageing grandparents, who had kept him in Rwanda because they had brought him up and he wanted to look after them, had long since died. But he loved the country so much he was reluctant to leave, even when times were hard.

One afternoon I was at home with Kadogo. I had just come back from my daily walk around Kigali, wandering the streets aimlessly until I was exhausted and then returning to have lunch and possibly a nap to ease my grief. Sleep always helped lower my anxiety; at least for a few hours, I would not feel anything. I was about to go to sleep, when Kadogo told me that some visitors were here to see me, and that they were my late brother's family. A young girl was walking up the driveway, carrying a small baby in her arms and with a little girl tugging on her skirt. She didn't look much older than fifteen. She was very short and walked with her neck at an angle, as if she couldn't straighten it. I thought, 'This can't be Valencia,' as we had a lot of visitors to the house.

But then Valencia introduced herself and her daughter Gigi, aged five, and nine-month-old Christopher. I didn't know whether to run, cry or scream. I hadn't felt so much love and happiness for days. I hugged the children and kept them on my lap as their mother told me the ordeal she had gone through. Gigi looked so much like Jean Baptiste; when she spoke she revealed a crooked tooth which was similar to his.

We spent an afternoon talking about my brother. The old couple who buried him had gone into hiding, Valencia told me, frightened that as they were Hutus, his family might take revenge on them or blame them for not protecting him.

I listened to Valencia, sitting staring at a wall, her eyes bloodshot, her face slick with tears as she recounted Jean Baptiste's death.

The morning after the president died, the family was awoken by the sound of gun shots. There was a commotion outside, people screaming, homes burning across the valley, cars racing past. Valencia went into the kitchen to make breakfast. Peering through the kitchen window she saw a notorious militiaman, a neighbour, sharpening his machete on a stone. She rushed to tell Jean Baptiste. Grabbing Christopher, then new born, and Gigi, they ran to hide at a neighbour's house. Another family joined them, telling them they had escaped through a roadblock manned by a gang armed with machetes and sticks. They didn't know where to go. They couldn't leave the house; there was nowhere to hide.

Valencia told me people were being smoked out of their houses all morning. A thick cloud covered the sky, obscuring the sun.

They saw groups of Interahamwe running across the hills, and heard shouts and the noise of guns and whistles nearby. The Interahamwe were running down the hillsides, chanting songs, wearing leaves on their heads and wielding machetes, killing everyone they came across.

In the chaos that reigned, Tutsis and their families tried to flee from the killers. Many were now gathering at the house. They decided to stick together and fight back. That was until a large group of refugees ran past asking everyone to try and make it to the church hall. Jean Baptiste and his family joined others and ran to the church at Masizi, believing the killers would not pursue them into a sacred place of God, a sanctuary.

Along the way many people fell. The Interahamwe cut their Achilles tendons with machetes to immobilise them. Once at the church, the Interahamwe retreated, sensing that the men would retaliate. All day long many people came to seek refuge at the church, which quickly filled with people crying, hungry, desperate and confused. Jean Baptiste and his family managed to stay together in the church.

For three days, from 7 April to 9 April, no one came to attack them in the church, but all around them the killings continued. On the fourth day, across the valley, they saw a Daihatsu pick-up drop off a gang of men who started to kill some people sheltering at a school in Kigali. Then the carnage began in earnest as grenades were thrown into the school. Men, women and children ran out screaming as the militia hunted them down one by one and killed them with machetes. Those at the church knew they had no chance of fending off the killers armed with just stones and sticks. The men decide to disperse, instead of waiting until they were encircled and easily killed. They all left except Jean Baptiste.

Valencia asked Jean Baptiste why he was staying. He would leave later, he told her. Jean Baptiste stayed for almost an hour and then, without a word to his wife, with his Bible in his hands, he walked out to the rear of the church. Valencia assumed he had gone to the toilet and would return. But he didn't. That was the last time she saw him alive.

The church echoed with crying, screaming and shouting. Women and children were packed in like sardines. They were hungry and exhausted. Many were wounded and some had broken limbs. Blood mixed with sweat on that hot sunny day. Jean Baptiste had only been gone for a while and Valencia was still hoping he would return.

The Daihatsu drove up the valley and stopped in front of the church. The gang asked where all the men had gone.

'We don't know,' the women replied.

Then a voice called out, 'If you're Hutu and you are here by mistake, get out now.' At that, an old woman picked Gigi up and safely walked out with her. She was a Hutu. Valencia didn't know this woman, but she was relieved. Other Hutus were allowed to go, leaving only the Tutsis to face their fate.

Meanwhile, reinforcements arrived, Interahamwe in their thousands, wielding machetes, spears, sticks and hoes. Then the massacres begin in earnest. Hours of chopping, beating, stabbing, slashing. Chaos reigned. People were screaming, children holding onto their mothers, bodies piling on top of each other.

Miraculously, Valencia, bleeding from wounds at the back of her neck, managed to hold onto Christopher. The baby was unhurt, but he was very hungry and dehydrated. Valencia crawled under a pile of bodies as the Interahamwe continued to kill. Eventually they left, hoping everyone was dead. When darkness fell, those who were still alive and able to move crawled out from under the dead and walked all night. They met other people along the way. They kept walking, hiding in the bushes during the day and walking to different hiding places at night. During her escape,

Valencia met a man from the neighbourhood who told her that Jean Baptiste never made it home. He had witnessed his death.

That night, after Valencia told her story, was filled with emptiness, the loss of innocent blood. I comforted Valencia although I felt I didn't know how to. I knew whatever I did would not heal her broken soul, that she could still see my brother walk out of that church for what she now knew was the last time.

We went to visit what was left of Jean Baptiste's house the next day. I wanted to see if I could relive my brother's last days. Or even to feel the happiness and comfort he had created in his home. A modest two-bedroom house lay in ruins, the roof gone, beams sticking out. It was an open shell, just like my father's houses years back. And just like my father, Jean Baptiste had built a thick wall that even the Interahamwe would not bring down.

My niece was happy to show me where her room had been and took me around. She showed me a mango tree in the front garden where her father used to sit in the afternoon to shelter himself from the burning sun, while he kept a watchful eye on the children playing. I could visualise and feel his presence looking down at us. I knew he lay not far from the grounds I was standing on.

We then went to the neighbour's house past the banana plantation. I looked around, wondering where my brother was lying. Any piece of ground here could be his resting place, but with the old couple in hiding we had no way of finding Jean Baptiste. Still I felt relieved that with time the couple would return and show us where they buried my brother.

I think I had become so numb that I don't remember being sad about Jean Baptiste's death at this point. All I could think about was rebuilding his home and resettling his family. Valencia, though, could not return to this home, as it brought harsh memories, a reminder of the Hutu neighbours that had killed her husband. She said she wanted to live somewhere removed, detached, where neighbours wouldn't stare at her or, worse yet, assault her with insincere kindness.

She was suffering from depression and still in shock. The machete wounds at the back of her neck and back healed without being treated, and left her neck facing sideways. On her legs and body there were scars, a reminder of the many blows she survived. Thankfully, her children were unharmed. She had managed to find Gigi, and Christopher was safe. I had so much to be thankful for about my brother's family. I could feel a renewal of life through their eyes.

I arranged to visit my home village to witness where the rest of my family fell and where they were dumped. Jeanne d'Arc refused to come with me: 'I will not be responsible for what I may do if I see our neighbours.' With a pistol permanently glued to her belt, and a shotgun that she kept at home, not to mention her bodyguard and colleagues, each one of them armed to the teeth, I was relieved she didn't want to come. I don't think I would have trusted myself either if I had had access to any form of ammunition.

I wanted to meet survivors of the Bitsibo massacres, and Jeanne d'Arc organised for me to meet Adella, a relative of ours who was a guardian of the memories of Bitsibo. I needed to confront the gravesite. Then I wanted to visit a cousin, Oliva, who had survived the massacres at the site and was living with her aunt in Kigali.

I spent the night remembering the faces and names of my relatives that fell, some of whom I hadn't seen for a long time, and others whom I had never met.

NINE

My first visit to my motherland

MY PREVIOUS VISIT to my home village was the first time I had set foot in Rwanda. It involved a different kind of anxiety and expectation. I had just turned thirteen and I was meeting my paternal family for the first time; I was also meeting Jean Baptiste and Jeanne d'Arc, from whom I had been separated since they were toddlers. I was travelling in a country where my safety was compromised but nonetheless I was determined to meet my relatives. It was an emotional adventure, and I was frightened and racked with doubts, but I kept my composure.

I remember my mother giving me snatches of her life in Rwanda when I was a girl. In a black book containing her life's journey, she made me record the fallen: her grandparents, her parents and her favourite cousin Bwanakweli, founder of the Rwanda National Union Party – all of whom died during the 1959 revolution – and my father, who died from natural causes. She made me record the names of her stepsiblings who survived the revolution and fled to Tanzania, Congo and Burundi. Most of the relatives in this book were either dead or separated from us. Mother seemed like a stump that would not fall despite life's trials.

She had no immediate family and focused on us to replace her lost relatives. Each of us children was named after a relative that had died. I was named after my mother's grandmother, who was known to be a tough negotiator; even as a woman in those days, she would have a say in any decisions such as going to war. My mother must have noticed that I was old enough to understand my history. In this black book, her life story slowly became mine, her grief, her loss, her laughter and her anguishes mine.

My mother had aristocratic connections and was among the first educated women in Rwanda. She trained as a midwife at Astrida, later renamed Butare University, and later went for further education abroad, across the border into Burundi, which was then a Belgian colony.

Instead of carrying a passport, my mother had *indangamuntu* – a Tutsi identity card, which she was proud of. The Belgians had introduced these cards and described Tutsi as closer to Europeans. Mother was not affected by her given status until 1959, when Rwandans' identity cards were used to mark divisions among them, bringing about the beginning of resentment and the disintegration of indigenous social and political structures. Mother had been brought up in these structures, and acknowledged that the identity cards changed the relationship between Hutu and Tutsi, who initially lived in a reciprocal relationship that allowed Rwandans to move ranks and get rewarded and promoted to better status in the community. She described the relationship as a class society that shared the same language, name, culture and religion.

Over a period of months, mother would remember events and names and make me record them. I began getting interested in Rwandan history and found her background fascinating. I treasured this black book for years, but at some point, probably during one of our frequent moves, I lost it. All my history went with that book, but fortunately my mother's story remained in my memory, safe and secure. Apart from the book my mother never spoke much about her feelings to me.

My knowledge of Rwanda was also enriched by the many Tutsi students from Rwanda whom mother welcomed into our home whenever they came to study English in Uganda. Among them was Jabu. He was much older than me, perhaps around twenty, very handsome, polite and extremely respectful. He reminded me of a Catholic priest; he had a strange feel of purity and righteousness about him.

After his studies, Jabu went back to Rwanda and traced my grandfather and my siblings. Mother was excited at this news; she had not seen Jean Baptiste and Jeanne d'Arc since my father died and my grandfather took them back with him to Rwanda. She suggested I should go and bring the children home and Jabu would help me find them; she always had confidence in me. I had never contemplated going to Rwanda before and I am not sure how I felt about the trip, but in any case I didn't have a choice. There were never many discussions about children's feelings; it was a task and someone had to do it. And so at the age of thirteen years I made a solo journey to find my siblings, cast into the world in ways that I was not ready for.

Jabu had told us how Tutsis were treated as second-class citizens. He spoke of discrimination, in education and employment, and killing. I don't think I understood the reality of living in Rwanda for the Tutsis. 'Everyone in Rwanda has an identity card,' Jabu had told me. He held a Tutsi card. He was now back in Rwanda, so I couldn't ask him how safe it was to go to my grandfather's village without an identity card. I would pretend I couldn't speak Kinyarwanda and show my Ugandan travel document.

Preparations for the trip began. For days, Mother repeated instructions, names and places, and made me memorise them. I repeated them constantly. 'There are no phones or any form of communication,' she told me. 'When you leave home, you're on your own. You have to remember all the tiny details.'

She instructed me not to speak to strangers about my business, and to be careful and respectful of myself. At thirteen, I didn't understand what she meant by that. I had spent years being told to respect adults, and others, but never myself. I was puzzled but didn't ask any questions. Mother always knew what was right.

One hot afternoon, my mother and I had been at the immigration office getting my travel documents. We stopped at a café nearby to grab a drink. A businessman whom I had seen a few times before was there; he was planning a visit to Rwanda soon. Mother asked him if he could give me a lift on his next trip.

He said he had no date for his next visit, so I would have to be on standby, but as it was the school holidays, that didn't matter. I waited day in, day out. I was literally not allowed to leave home. Others went to church, or to fetch water, but I anxiously stayed at home, jumping every time a car raced past our house or stopped at the market.

The businessman, Mustafa, agreed to take me to Jabu's cousin in Kigali, who would connect me with Jabu, and he would escort me to my grandfather's village. I had to keep to the schedule, to return with the same lift in ten days' time. Everything was well planned. I had nothing to worry about, although I was anxious about missing my lift back home.

A few days later, two men walked into our front room. Mustafa, who I recognised, was tall, thin and light skinned. He introduced his business partner, Haji, who was overweight and had a dark mocha complexion. He had a black patch on his forehead, a result of touching his forehead on the floor five times daily during Muslim prayers. Both men were Muslims and chewed green leaves, which they told me was good for the immune system.

Mustafa was in a hurry. 'We need to get going,' he instructed.

I collected my suitcase and said goodbye to my family. We set off in a dark blue car which seemed to have passed its sell-by date. As we drove off I looked back to wave to my mother, and she waved back. Fear made my stomach turn. I wanted to call out to my mother, to tell her I was frightened and felt sick, but the car accelerated away and soon I couldn't see her any more. Thoughts dashed through my head. Would this trip reunite my family? What if my siblings didn't agree to come back with me? How would mother cope? What did my siblings look like?

The two men were now laughing, and my thoughts returned to the car. The radio was tuned into Muzungu Kanga on Radio Rwanda. Muzungu Kanga was our favourite presenter. Every afternoon, after school, we put the radio on full blast so each one of us could hear the music whichever part of the house we were in. Mother was usually in her clinic, someone would be peeling bananas for dinner in the kitchen, and someone else would be taking down the washing from the line. For the rest of the journey, I listened to Muzungu Kanga. Every record made me want to dance, like I did at home, and soon my worries were washed away. I nodded my head and wiggled my waist a little bit, as much as I could in the back seat. For nearly four hours I forgot the purpose of my going to Rwanda and I just enjoyed the ride.

It was six-thirty when we arrived in Nyamirambo. Even before the car had a chance to stop, there were cheers from the crowd standing in front of a busy shop. 'As-Salam Alaykum [peace be upon you],' they called out.

'Alaykum As-Salam [upon you be peace],' Mustafa and Haji responded.

When we finally stopped, fifteen or more people surrounded the car. They opened the doors and everyone was embracing, hugging and laughing.

Welcome home! A man I didn't know kissed me on both cheeks three times. It was the first time I had been greeted like this. I felt uncomfortable. There was no time to reason, as everyone took a turn to kiss me on both cheeks. They seemed genuinely warm and friendly, and they didn't even know me.

Mustafa introduced me as Mariam's niece; I was led to her house to meet her. Mariam was a beautiful, slender woman with sunny eyes and a ready smile. Her nails were manicured and her hair long and curled. She was no older than thirty. She was clearly happy to see me and had been expecting me. In fact, she was almost hysterical, telling everyone her niece had arrived from Uganda. But she wasn't my aunt; I had never even met this woman before. I couldn't understand the fuss. Everything seemed larger than life here, doors of each house wide open, people walking in and out, a maid constantly refilling pots of tea and coffee. I became overwhelmed by the attention.

Mariam prepared a warm bath and gave me her kaftan to wear for the evening. I was honestly treated like royalty, and, though I was uncomfortable, I was enjoying the rich tidings.

Mariam's husband returned from work – a sporty figure, six feet tall, with a black moustache and dark, almost black eyes. He was very trendy and smelt of expensive cologne. He smiled and spoke warmly to everyone at home. Meanwhile, the atmosphere changed, everyone rushing and signalling to prepare dinner, movement everywhere, people, tables, chairs, salt, pepper, jugs, rugs, everyone frantically moving in and out of the kitchen, the sitting room, nearly walking into each other.

At a lavish dinner, I expected people to sit at an already set dining table, but instead everyone was sitting on the floor, which was covered with multi-coloured rugs and small cushions. A huge dish with a variety of foods – lamb stew, aubergines, fried rice, roast chicken, chapattis, spicy lentils – and jugs full of ginger drink were placed on the floor. Many people were there to celebrate after Friday evening prayers.

They ate with their right hand, cleaning their fingers by licking them. The food kept coming: as soon as a dish was empty, another one was placed in the same spot. Then one by one the diners drifted away, but not before they had stuffed themselves with dates, figs, nuts, olives and dried fruits. Mariam told me her husband was rich and liked to give something back to the poor.

I was trying to keep up with the conversation and look interested when I heard a commotion outside. No one seemed to take any notice, though, so I ignored it. Then I heard a voice: 'I'm sorry, I have an important person that I need to see. Please give a moment.' I thought the voice sounded familiar, and my mind raced to try and place it, but I couldn't. It was disturbing, though, to hear this familiar voice when I was in Rwanda and had no sense of bearing. I was becoming overwhelmed by events and the voice was part of the confusion.

A split second later, a tall elegant man entered through the front door; he looked mature but also slightly cheeky. I could smell his strong spicy perfume. Everyone clapped and stood up, but I remained seated. I was totally off balance and I didn't know why; something wasn't right but I was a guest and couldn't confide in anyone.

The man, whose face was unfamiliar, walked up to me and put his right hand out towards mine. 'I've looked forward to this moment all day. How delightful to meet a beautiful young woman! You must be Maria.'

I extended my hand to touch his, and he gently raised me up while everyone was cheering. 'My lovely young lady!'

I blushed. I knew now who it was, and I felt a burning sensation and excitement. I screamed, 'No! Muzungu Kanga!' I was shaking with excitement and passed out. I came round in a quiet room, a few people standing by and watching me. Muzungu Kanga was sitting next to me squeezing my hand, and someone, perhaps a nurse, was applying cold and hot towels to my forehead. Or maybe it was my body temperature dropping. I felt so ashamed of myself. I had let everyone down.

That afternoon, Muzungu Kanga had been reading all the postcards that had been sent to him with requests and special messages. We had sent many postcards to my siblings with messages of love, asking if they could get back to us. We never heard from them. Sometimes we thought they didn't have a radio, or the money to buy a postcard and send it to Radio Rwanda. Nonetheless, we religiously listened to the programme hoping to hear from them, besides enjoying the wonderful music Muzungu Kanga played.

I apologised for the trouble, but no one seemed to mind. They told me I was tired and needed to sleep. But I knew I was not; I was just shocked to see my hero, the one person that we had listened to every day for years. I was also overwhelmed by the warm, rowdy and friendly people and I suppose anxious about my visit. And I had just eaten a hot and spicy dinner, and washed it down with a ginger drink, which Mariam had convinced me helped with digestion. A combination of all this disoriented me.

I never did discuss this incident with anyone; it was my shameful experience that I didn't want anyone to know about. Mustafa knew I was a fan of Muzungu Kanga, and, to my sweet surprise, he told him about me, and he made an appearance specifically to meet me and to applaud my act of bravery, at thirteen years, venturing to find siblings after many years of separation.

Mariam told me her family was poor, but her husband provided for them. She was a second wife and her husband was Hutu, but he loved and protected her. Being a second-generation Tutsi, growing up outside Rwanda, I didn't know much about Rwandan history and the life they led. I listened to her intently, not sure whether she expected my approval. I couldn't tell a Hutu from a Tutsi, so in a way I didn't comprehend her explanation. She then told me she felt closer to me than anyone else around, because my mother treated her cousin Jabu as her own son, so the warmth was reciprocated.

'Tutsis have suffered,' she said. 'No one understands us. We always stick together. We have each other.'

In Uganda, the only country I knew and identified with, I was struggling to be accepted as a Ugandan citizen. I didn't feel Rwandan or Tutsi. My mother always said that changes in regimes decided Tutsis' destiny and she was always optimistic that one day Rwanda would be for all Rwandans. She didn't dislike Hutus or Twas, and never aligned our thinking to either Tutsi or Hutu. She always warned us to be careful, however, as Hutus harboured a deep-rooted resentment and hatred for Tutsis. At the time, I couldn't understand this.

A couple of days later the moment of truth arrived. Mariam drove me in her posh car to the taxi rank, and told the taxi driver to show me where to disembark. I had memorised the name of the village, the names of Jabu's family. Besides, I still had my note with instructions, which I read through before tucking it away carefully in a bag of clothes that Mariam gave me. 'It's easier to carry than a suitcase,' she said. Then, as the sun began to peep through the clouds, Mariam drove off and I took a local taxi to Gitarama province, deep in rural western Rwanda, to find my siblings. This was the test of nerves; the past three days had been an escape.

I pushed my fear into the background and focused on seeing Jabu again. It was nearly a year since he had stayed with us in Uganda. Soon we would be on the way to see my family. I had seven days left, which made it easier for me – before long this ordeal would be over and I would be back home, with or without my siblings.

The ride only took twenty minutes. The taxi driver dropped me off, picked up more passengers and drove away. I was left standing by the roadside.

I looked for a trustworthy face. An older woman sat nearby, selling soft drinks, cigarettes, chewing gum, sweets, matches, safety pins and other stuff, set out on a flattened cardboard box. I bought some chewing gum and asked her if she knew Jabu's family. (Mariam had told me everyone at the trading centre knew Jabu's family, because his mother and father were teachers at a local school.) Yes, she did know the family and she had seen one of Jabu's brothers around.

She called across the road, 'Has anyone seen Calixte? He can't have gone far.' She summoned a boy of about seven who was hanging around, shaven headed and with a snotty nose, to help me find him. I thanked the woman and followed the boy along a winding dusty road. He walked on the sharp stones and the hot earth without shoes. He told me he would show me the house, as his home was on the way to Jabu's. I felt relieved.

A few metres away, I heard the woman calling me. 'You, girl, stop, stop. Stop that girl, *yewe. . . yewe. . .* hello. . . hello. . . stop her.' I looked back and everyone was staring at me.

'Calixte, that girl from Uganda is asking after your brother Jabu.'

I wondered how the woman knew I was from Uganda. Calixte told me my accent was a giveaway, and everyone knew Jabu had been studying in Uganda. He assured me there was no problem. Like Jabu, Calixte was tall – about 6 feet 4 inches – lanky and very handsome. He was fifteen years old.

Jabu and Calixte's family welcomed me; everyone was elegant and gentle. They spoke in turn, and in tune, patiently waiting for each other to finish their sentences – a big contrast from Nyamirambo's rowdy audience. Jabu was at work when I arrived but returned home in the evening. He had taken leave to escort me to my grandfather's house the next day.

In the morning, after a breakfast of boiled eggs, bananas, bread and sweet tea, we boarded a pick-up that took us to a trading centre. The driver went very fast and the passengers sat with nothing to hold onto as they snaked their way up and down the steep hills of Rwanda.

I have a fear of heights. The ride up the hills was just manageable, but as the pick-up started to descend it went even faster. My hands were tired and hurting from gripping onto the side of the body. I squeezed my eyes shut to try and distract myself, but it didn't work, and I was finally overcome with fear and dizziness. When we arrived at the centre, I ran to a bush by the side of the road and threw up. I could smell the eggs and taste a mix of my earlier breakfast.

The walk to my grandfather's house took us through some beautiful scenery: terraced hillsides, greenery everywhere, patches of banana and eucalyptus trees. We crossed over streams that run between the green hills. There were few pedestrians; most people were riding bicycles. There was even a bicycle that operated as a taxi. But you had to get off and walk up the hills! Every time I thought we were getting close, yet another hill appeared, and the walk took just under two hours. When we arrived it was nearly nightfall, and I could see homesteads scattered across the hill that Jabu said was our destination. As we were descending through a banana plantation and fields of sweet potatoes Jabu pointed out my grandfather's house, which I could not see clearly. I was feeling anxious and uncertain of how my family would react to me, but Jabu was excited to be a witness at a family reunion, having worked so hard for nearly a year to trace my family.

We entered through a gate in a tall cactus fence and made our way into the dusty front courtyard. A small corrugated iron hut nestled among some huge trees to the south of the house and there were three huge stones which seemed to have been deliberately positioned to terrace the slope to the north. Jabu called out, 'Anyone home?'

'Yes!' a voice replied, swearing. '*Yampayinka!* ['Someone gave me a cow!' – an expression of surprise in Kinyarwanda]. That's my grandchild.'

A tall, grey-haired old man appeared from the back of the house and lifted me into his arms, embracing me and shaking with excitement, even crying for a moment. This was an unusual display of emotion and I felt embarrassed to see an old man shed a tear. I grew up knowing that men do not cry. A proverb in Kinyarwanda says 'The tears of a man flow to his stomach'. The moment was overwhelming for my grandfather, but I didn't appreciate it in the same way.

Jabu had sent a message ahead, and grandfather had been expecting me for some time. He took us round to the back of the house and sat on a stool, studying me with great deliberation in deep silence. My grandmother was sitting on a mat a distance away under a mango tree, cleaning milk jugs. I could see two girls sitting by an earth stove, their faces illuminated by the fire, tending a pot of food in a small hut.

My grandmother, quick on her feet, ran and grabbed me, squeezing me so hard and pinching me. It spooked me. Why was she hurting me? The girls heard the commotion and came out too, my sister jumping towards me, her face luminous with happiness, the other girl standing and watching in disbelief. With Grandmother still shaking me, and my sister joining in, we lost balance and all three of us came down, now laughing. Grandfather helped us up and again he held me so close I could hardly breathe. Everyone was speechless. They hugged me and looked at me. There were no words to describe what they were feeling; as for me, the explosion of excitement was too much to comprehend, although I was pleased to feel warmth from people I hardly knew.

Grandmother then took me to meet my great-grandmother, who they called Mucyecuru, meaning 'old woman', unsurprisingly, as she was 112 years old. She barely looked up when I went to her and showed no emotion. Grandmother repeated to her several times, 'This is your second great-granddaughter.'

Mucyecuru was making strange, scary noises – short high-pitched squeaks and quiet chattering sounds. Grandmother assured me she could still understand what was going on around her at least half the time. She told me she could hardly speak properly any more; she squeaked if she wanted attention or when irritated and chattered when she was content, but most of the time she used signs. If she wanted to eat she brought a plate or a cup, or else she pulled you and made gestures until she got what she wanted.

Having grown up without any grandparents, it was strange to meet one of the oldest women alive and to find she was related to me. Mucyecuru was so small you could have scooped her up easily. Grandmother told me to hold her hand. Her skin was dry. I could feel the bones in her fingers sticking out like branches of a tree. There was also a strong smell in her hut, a mixture of urine and a powerful soap or detergent. I couldn't wait to get some fresh air. Grandmother said that Mucyecuru would now die contented. Before she stopped talking, she had said she would not die before her grandchildren came home.

Meanwhile, Jean Baptiste was fetched from where he was tending cattle. He was the coolest person I had ever seen. He was slightly taller than me, of medium build, and looked older than his twelve years. He was very gentle and unhurried, with a penetrating gaze. There were no introductions, not that there had to be. He stood silently for a while, looking at me, then calmly embraced me, as though we had seen each other before. After this greeting, he continued to stand and watch every movement I made. I was aware he was looking at me but carried on talking to the others. I think he was in shock.

I kept wondering if I hadn't turned out to be what he had expected of his sister. I wished he would talk to me or ask me questions like the others did. I retained eye contact with him, but I could not think what to talk to him about, although I felt close to him. This was his moment, but I guess he was not the kind to get excited or overwhelmed easily.

Darkness fell and we gathered around a big fire and ate roast beef. Grandfather had ordered one of his cows to be slaughtered for the occasion. This had to be a special event as Tutsis did not kill or sell their cows for money. We also had maize, bananas and sweet potatoes, all baked in the ashes of the fire, which I enjoyed. We washed the food down with sour milk that was passed around in traditional wooden jugs. I don't like milk, but I politely held onto one of the jugs and pretended to drink. But the jugs came around so fast I couldn't keep up. Everyone who had one kept passing them in my direction.

Word of my arrival spread rapidly, and soon a crowd of neighbours had arrived in the courtyard. They didn't seem to have any work to do, and for the next few days they stayed in the compound, only leaving to go to sleep after midnight. The conversation that night was easy, Jabu occasionally interrupting to stop the many questions I got from everyone.

Mucyecuru made her way through the crowd and sat next to me. When she walked, her back was so bent she was nearly crawling on her knees, even with the help of a walking stick that was nearly as tall as she was. She put her hands on my lap. I could see her white knotted hair and sunken eyes in the firelight. She didn't look up at me, but I held her hands and she kept wiggling them. Everyone said she loved attention and wouldn't stay in her hut alone.

We had been sitting together for a few minutes when I felt something trickle from beneath her clothes. She had wet herself. My sister and I joined Grandmother to wash her and change her clothes. All the while she didn't let go of my hand. It was bedtime and she pulled me towards her. Everyone laughed. 'Mucyecuru wants to sleep with you. Someone always sleeps with her,' Grandmother told me.

I didn't know if this was love or what it was, but it was certainly the most awful night of my life. Her bed wet, her hut stinking, she pissed herself all night. She put her arm around my waist and it felt like a scary snake crawling up my skin. I tried to push her away, but she wiggled back. During the night I wondered if she would die in her sleep, now that she had seen her great-grandchild. I was scared and didn't sleep all night. I longed to be back home. I couldn't possibly survive another night with her.

Grandmother had warned me this would happen, but she didn't want to deny the old lady her wish. She told me to try and cope for one night, giving me a long dress to sleep in. 'Her urine is like a dye, you never get it off. You don't want to sleep in your own clothes,' Grandmother said.

The next day Jabu left, as he had to go back to work. I had four days to spend with my family. On one of them Grandfather took me on a tour of his land and showed me a plot that he had given my father before the 1959 revolution. My father had used his salary as a teacher to build a house with walls 2 feet thick. Over the years, whenever there was trouble it would be set on fire or smashed with heavy implements but the walls remained standing; it would not come down completely.

'This is your land when you return to Rwanda one day,' Grandfather told me. He then took me to the stones and showed me the graves of my fallen relatives, naming each one of them. There were thirteen or so, nieces, cousins, aunts, grandparents. Grandfather then said, 'I have never fled from Rwanda. When I die this is where I will be buried, and you can come and visit my tomb. This is where I will be laid to rest.' This was a scary conversation. But death, like life, was something Grandfather celebrated. I wasn't old enough to understand why he was talking of dying when I had only just met him, as if I would never see him again.

Every day, more and more relatives came to join the family reunion – aunties and uncles with their children, and distant cousins – together with friends and nearly the whole neighbourhood. They drank the local beer out of jerry cans, and there were always pots of potatoes mixed with beans, a favourite dish, on the go, with sour milk and all. Everyone was keen to get close to me and ask questions. It was lots of fun, but tiring. At night I would be exhausted, but instead of allowing me to rest, Grandmother, Jean Baptiste and Jeanne d'Arc each took turns to sleep with me, asking me yet more questions until the early hours.

I suppose I would have asked them questions too, only Mother had caned me several times because my mouth had got the better of me. Every time I offered an opinion or asked questions I got into trouble. My mother was so strict that even miles away I couldn't forget her voice. 'You should not answer back to adults,' she would say.

In Rwandan culture, children are supposed to be seen and not heard. I could not bring myself to ask anything, overwhelmed by so many people. The only thing I must have asked is whether my siblings could be given permission to come back with me. Even that was my mother's request. Grandfather agreed that I would return to Uganda with Jean Baptiste, and Jeanne d'Arc would follow. Jean Baptiste was excited and so was I. At least Mother would be pleased to see one of her children.

Early on Saturday morning, the sun still cool, we trekked through the hills and boarded a pick-up to Jabu's home. We spent the night there and he escorted us back to Kigali, where Mariam was waiting for me. Mustafa had visited to remind her when we were to return to Uganda.

At around midday we set off for Uganda. Mariam asked me if I had heard any messages from Muzungu Kanga. I hadn't. Apparently he had sent out messages on each show to me and my siblings. Mariam said she would send another message to say I was on my way home. She asked me if I had anything to say.

'Yes,' I replied. 'I would like to send my love to my family, all my sisters and brothers, in Uganda. I wish everyone in the car with me, including Mustafa and Haji, a safe journey.'

Muzungu Kanga read out this message too. Afterwards, as the next record started to play, Jean Baptiste turned to me. 'You didn't mention me.' I still remember his expression; he was so disappointed in me.

Now here I was, nearly twenty-one years later, back in Rwanda. Not to enjoy another reunion but to bury my relatives, almost my entire family; to see where they were massacred in cold blood, all those whose faces I remembered even if their names were a struggle. Tomorrow I would take the same journey, visiting the same village, to see where the people I got to know and love fell, where they lay. I cannot describe the grief that weighed on my shoulders; the thought that I was to bear witness to hundreds of people who shared a mass grave with my family left a taste of despair in my mouth. I wanted to blame someone; I wanted a reason that would justify the extermination of my family. I hardly slept, torn by the pain of losing so many and the thought that I could never get over the loss.

TEN

Fifty members of my family murdered in a primary school

I BEGAN THE dreaded journey to my home village to confront the death of my relatives in the genocide. Accompanied by an old friend that I met back in Uganda, we set off from Kigali early in the morning. It was warm and sunny, no different from any other morning. We drove through the muddy congested slums and as we came out of the city there were brick houses scattered over the hills. Many beautiful birds were hovering over the eucalyptus trees that lined the main road from Kigali to Gitarama. We passed well-tended terraced fields of potatoes, maize, beans and bananas. Rwanda appeared unchanged from my last visit.

On the way, I recognised the route I had taken when I came to find Jean Baptiste and Jeanne d'Arc. This time there was hardly anyone left alive, yet on our journey there was little evidence of genocide except for some collapsed and burnt-out houses.

We stopped at Kamonyi, twenty minutes from Kigali, where I was meeting Adella, a relative who had survived. She was going to take me to the gravesite. Jeanne d'Arc had given me instructions to stop at the trading centre and ask for Adella. Everyone knew her; there were not many survivors left in this district.

We arrived at the trading centre. I was feeling anxious and frightened, and I was convinced there were still killers at large, especially in the countryside. As the car stopped, everyone watched, motionless, as if they had to register every movement, every gesture. It was obvious we were not from here. I asked a woman if she knew Adella. It didn't take us long to be shown her house, in the distance on the opposite side of the road. It was a small mud-brick house surrounded by bushes, and it looked like no one had lived there for years. The only sign that there had once been life was a local cactus-fenced compound.

As we approached the house, I could see a woman sweeping the compound, spirals of dust whirling in the air and settling on her shoulders. The noise of her brushing was so loud that she didn't hear us approach. I called out, '*Muraho*? [Are you well?]', a Kinyarwanda greeting.

This was Adella. She had never met me but knew Jeanne d'Arc and Jean Baptiste. I introduced myself and my friend as she led us into a small room with wooden stools and a side table, and African mats on the floor. It was decent and clean but it had no window. The only light came through the main door. She gestured to us to sit on the stools, while she took her place on one of the mats in the corner of the room. 'This used to be my kitchen. My house was torched during the genocide. I lost everything,' she said apologetically.

She was wearing a blue headscarf, a white top and a black skirt. I thought she was a nun, but she explained that she had machete wounds on her head, and when she walked in the sun, her brain melted. She lifted her scarf to reveal a deep hole in the left side of her head and another wound at the back of her neck.

She told me that almost every day since the genocide she had made a journey to the school in Gitarama where my relatives were slaughtered in order to visit the families she left behind. She had no job or any source of income, but she grew food on her patch of land and survived somehow.

Adella never married; she used to look after her elderly mother. She had two sisters and three brothers, all of whom lived in Gitarama. She used to babysit her many nieces and nephews and would spoil them, she told me with a smile on her face. Now in her late forties, she had no hope of rebuilding her life. Her mother had been killed, and only she and her two sisters survived out of the entire family – all the children died. She told me she had dedicated her life to safeguarding the memory of families that had fallen.

Adella believed she had survived so she could protect those who had died. She swept the ground and pruned the flowers at the site. During termtime she sat by the gravesite to stop the schoolchildren from playing football on it. Sometimes, of course, the ball would drift across onto the site, and when it did she picked it up, carefully avoiding stepping on where the bodies lay. I found this interesting. How did she avoid the bodies? Did she know who was lying where?

We went to the school together. On the way she recounted what happened.

The genocide began on the night of Wednesday 6 April 1994. Adella had no radio, so it wasn't until the following morning that she was told that President Habyarimana had been killed. She had left that morning as usual to dig her vegetable plot. An old man came by around noon and told her that he had heard Tutsis were being slaughtered in Kigali. He said she should go home and await her fate.

'My brother was tending our cows. I went to warn him,' Adella continued. 'He went to the trading centre to find out what was happening. There were rumours of roadblocks at every road junction in Kigali, where people carrying Tutsi identity cards or who had no identity card were being killed. We believed we might be in danger but we didn't think the situation would escalate as it did.

'A week into the killings, we sensed an impending disaster. We were now aware that elsewhere in the country massacres of Tutsis had begun immediately after Habyarimana had been assassinated.

'The horrors slowly unfolded. My siblings and their families boarded a minibus and came home. They were in a state of shock, having just about managed to get through the harsh roadblocks. They told us that Tutsis were being hunted across the country. The following day, the Interahamwe started to burn Tutsi homes. Fires were started in the neighbourhood, and the army came and killed some Tutsis in the local marketplace.

'Meanwhile, the stories we were hearing from refugees fleeing from neighbouring communes, some of whom were injured and distressed, were alarming. They told of mass killings, but we did not think it would spread to our home village. Their accounts confirmed that well-organised gangs of armed men were looking for Tutsis to kill, and that roadblocks were being erected everywhere to stop Tutsis from escaping the slaughter.

'Then it was our turn. A group of local mobs known to us torched our house. We scrambled out and managed to get away safely, but we lost all our belongings. We decided to make our way to the village, believing we were being targeted because we lived near the main road. With unruly mobs at the trading centre and no roof over our heads, we were not safe.'

On the way to my home village they walked along small footpaths to avoid the roadblocks which were now erected along the main road from Butare to Kigali. 'There were trails of people going back and forward. It was difficult to know where to escape to, but we made it to the village safely. It was calm, and the neighbours even stopped us to ask what was happening. There were no roadblocks and life seemed more normal. We found many of our family members, from Butare, across Gitarama and from

Kigali, already well settled in. Your uncle Joseph, well known in the village, went to ask the mayor to protect us and our families. By this time we were more than seventy people, Tutsi friends and family, all sticking together.

'In the meantime the stories we were hearing were terrifying: massacres intensifying everywhere else in the country, mass slaughter. The scale of the carnage started to become a reality. The men were planning and organising to fight back and protect the women and children, but they were armed with just a few spears and knew they would be outnumbered. In the village the killing hadn't begun yet.

'One day, I can't remember which, everybody in the family and all the Tutsis were rounded up to assemble at the school. All day the militia were going from house to house calmly telling everyone to make their way to the school. Some left with no belongings or even food. Once at the school everyone felt relieved and settled down. The adults had nothing to eat, as the refugees divided what little food they had come with among the children.

'The heat was soaring; people were sweating and some fell asleep from heat exhaustion and fatigue. Still, everyone appeared calm and hopeful; some were even telling jokes and singing hymns to keep up morale. They believed they were secure, that the classroom was their sanctuary. But as time went on they began to get desperate, confused and frightened; nonetheless there was no sense of what was to come.

'In the late afternoon, some trucks pulled up at the school. The men in the trucks surrounded the classroom, armed with machetes, clubs, *masus* and spears. There was no hope of survival.

'I was exhausted. When they cut my Achilles tendons, I must have fainted. I only remember the blow to my head and then there was no more pain. I don't remember anything else. When I gained consciousness I was in a hospital, being looked after by

RPF soldiers. I don't know how I was pulled out of the burial pit, except from stories that I was told later – Tutsis who managed to get away found some people still alive. Apparently they pulled us out and dragged us to a nearby swamp, where we hid until the RPF rescued us.'

Adella led me to a shallow gravesite. At the time of the massacres it was raining heavily. The topsoil was washed away, exposing hundreds of lifeless limbs. There were 200 people buried in this grave. Not everyone in the grave had been identified, so it was impossible to reinter all the victims. Instead, the site was covered with earth and flowers were planted to stop the soil from eroding.

Seeing the gravesite where my family lay provoked the unbearable image of skeletons that were once people whose faces I knew, my blood relations – men and women who had trustingly given up without a fight, fathers unable to defend their children, men and women too tired and hungry to run or fight back, their sanctuary turned into a death trap.

I stood silently, taking in everything: the beautiful flowers, blossoming red, green and purple, the only sign of life on the gravesite; the gentle breeze fluttering in the surrounding trees; the breathtaking hills of Gitarama that were now killing fields. The horrors kept replaying in my head like a stuck record. A people betrayed, who had gathered together, as they had many times before at my grandfather's home, where they had found sanctuary during the Tutsis' troubled times. They trusted their neighbours, hoping and believing that this time was no different. But for one after another, the school was the end of their journey.

My sadness turned into a sort of a relief because I didn't have to worry about where they had fallen. It would only be a matter of time and I could give them a decent burial and erect a memorial in their names; they still had a place in the village, a home in the community that had stood by while they were slaughtered. That would be my revenge on the killers. I would ensure their victims were never forgotten, that their lives were not in vain. That's all I could think of. They would be here for many years to come. I blocked any sense of emotion; it was too much to take in.

I put flowers on the gravesite and, without a word, left and returned to Kigali. I could fully appreciate why Jeanne d'Arc did not want to come to the grave. Grief turned into anger. I wished I could win a lottery and buy mercenaries to kill all Hutus. It was the first time that I understood what my mother had gone through in 1959. Generations later, Hutus were still annihilating Tutsis. I couldn't begin to understand why Hutus had turned into animals. All these years Tutsis had never killed any Hutus, yet many Tutsis had met their death at the hands of the people they lived alongside and even intermarried with.

I counted myself lucky to have been out of the country, otherwise I would be lying in the same grave. I would have been hunted like an animal. The world would have abandoned me to the mercy of Hutu killers, because my life was worthless. How could I possibly have survived, where no one would?

I got back to Kigali around three o'clock. Jeanne d'Arc was still on duty. Kadogo told me someone was waiting for me in the house. A young girl in her early teens, who I had never met before, was humbly and patiently sitting in my room. I was feeling tired; I wanted to close my eyes and sleep to drown my anger and mental exhaustion. But I didn't have a chance.

Jeanne d'Arc had called for this girl to come and tell me how she had survived the massacres. Her name was Oliva and she was a thirteen-year-old cousin of mine. She went through her ordeal, matching Adella's recollection almost word for word. It was as if I was hearing the same story again, but Oliva's account was even more moving and cut deep into my heart.

134

Oliva was living in Kigali with her family when the genocide began. On 7 April she awoke to the news that the president had died. Her father gathered the family in the sitting room and told them that Tutsis were not safe.

'Our friends and neighbours started to phone us,' she told me. 'They told us our house was surrounded by the Interahamwe. They also told us which of our close friends had already died. I was so frightened. My father tried to comfort us, and then we heard of the death of the ten Belgians and the Prime Minister. I could see my father getting desperate but he told us there had been previous unrest which was usually contained and that the United Nations would protect us, especially now that some of their soldiers had been killed. He believed that the UN would intervene to stop the unrest.

'On 8 April the phone lines were cut. The first attack was launched against us at three o'clock on 9 April. A group of Interahamwe that had surrounded our house came looking for my father. He gave them money and they left, but at night they came back and asked him to get dressed and to man the roadblock. When he said goodbye, he looked very frightened.

'I will never forget the look in his eyes. That was the last time we saw him,' she told me, lowering her voice and suppressing her tears. 'We later heard that he was taken to the roadblock and macheted to death by a mob of Interahamwe militia. My mother suggested we take refuge with her sister, who was married to a Hutu.

'We got up at dawn on 10 April, around 5 a.m. My aunt's Hutu husband organised a military pick-up and drove us to our grandfather's village. Everyone was happy to see us. We felt relieved to get there and thought we'd been saved. Every day, more relatives and friends arrived for safety, telling of the horrific killings they had escaped. The neighbours did not bother us. But everything changed when the mayor told us to go to the school, where he would protect us.'

Oliva explained that this was four weeks into the massacres. Many people were telling of horrific deaths in the capital. 'We heard that foreign nationals were being airlifted from Rwanda. At this time the killings were selective, targeting mainly men. People didn't think they would spill over into the general population, believing that only those involved in politics and business were being sought. No one anticipated the massacres that followed.

'It was literally unimaginable then to believe the scale and scope of the killings. Every day, the Tutsis in the neighbourhood came to check what was going on. I remember hearing that men were gathering weapons to protect women and children. Some people, such as the old woman who lived near the school, came to stay with us, because her children were in Kigali and she lived alone with her two grandchildren. Over fifty family members had gathered in my home village – a place of sanctuary, so they thought. Not this time.

'The district mayor came and told my family, and other Tutsi villagers, to congregate at the local school, where their security would be discussed by the local leader. But they were soon herded into a classroom where they were locked up until the Interahamwe could be trucked in, all armed with machetes. From morning to late afternoon, women, children and men stayed in that room with no food or drink, waiting to be addressed. Everyone was hungry and exhausted.

'At around three o'clock, the Interahamwe surrounded the school and it was then that they started chopping people up inside the classroom. All hell broke loose. The carnage began as men and women tried to jump through the windows, only to be butchered. The stampede was unbearable, people crushing babies as they tried to escape, crying, screaming, and falling over each other as they tried to run for their lives.

'But outside men with sharpened machetes and clubs were waiting for us. They severed people's Achilles tendons, which prevented them from fleeing as they were bludgeoned to death. Our neighbours were catching anyone who tried to escape as the Interahamwe hacked them to death, one by one.'

Oliva paused and held her head in the palm of her hands. She stayed fixed in that position for a while.

Listening to Oliva, I couldn't rid myself of my anger and resentment. I felt like I was carrying a deep wound in my heart which was constantly bleeding. I felt desperate and incredibly lonely, sinking into a well of emotions that I could not stop. Yet I was hungry to hear more, to piece together the last hours, the last words, the last time my family was alive.

Later, when Oliva was able to compose herself again, she continued. 'They dumped us in a pit, many people still alive.'

Oliva recalled the carnage. After she had been macheted, she could see many victims on the ground. No one was running and the Interahamwe came to finish them off, while others dragged them to a pit near the school and pushed them in the grave still alive. Neighbours she recognised were throwing stones into the grave to suffocate and kill off those who were still breathing. Oliva survived through being hidden by bodies which had fallen on top of her in a pit that she shared with 200 others, murdered in cold blood.

As I listened to Oliva, I remember this feeling of numbness. She recounted almost without emotion the tragedy of my family. In the pit there was my uncle Joseph and his wife and children, and my aunts and their children: over fifty relatives. I fixed my eyes on Oliva, my heart bleeding with grief and sadness. I felt as if a rock had lodged itself in my throat, but I didn't feel I had the right to cry. A million people had died, and although my family members were among them, I still had my brothers and sisters who were outside Rwanda during the genocide. In fact, only Jean Baptiste was in the country at the time.

Oliva went on. 'Our uncle Joseph was injured badly, but still alive. After the Interahamwe left, he started calling out names to check if there were other people that had survived. I awoke from a dream, lying close to Uncle Joseph in the pit, listening to all the names he was calling out, some answering that they were injured and couldn't move, others crying. The crying turned into groaning, pain and agony. Slowly the voices disappeared, as one by one people began to die – women and men, children and old people alike. No one was spared.'

Oliva told me how Uncle Joseph kept calling out people's names, asking if anyone would go for help from the neighbours. He was complaining that his legs had been macheted and he couldn't climb out of the pit. Oliva came to her senses and shouted that she was still alive. Somehow my uncle helped her out of the pit and she staggered up the hill to find help from a good neighbour called Daudi.

The machete that had slashed the back of her neck and her legs had missed her Achilles tendon. Her wounds hurting dreadfully, she staggered to Daudi's house to ask for help. His wife was at home, and she cleaned Oliva's wounds and gave her food. Meanwhile Daudi's two sons came home with goods they had stolen from the Tutsis. They said they would help and left, but when they returned later that evening they claimed everyone was dead when they arrived.

That night, the older son raped Oliva and told her, 'You are now the family spoil. You have no choice. You will be my wife.' Oliva knew she didn't have much choice. There were no Tutsis left in the village and she had nowhere else to go.

She gazed outside, avoiding looking at me. 'The pain was unbearable, the machete wounds on my neck and legs, but still he raped me all night and every day for months. When he was not at home, his brother raped me too. Their mother was aware of what was going on but she didn't stop them. I became numb – nothing mattered any more.'

Both of the brothers would leave early in the morning to go to work, so they said, and would return with stolen goods such as clothes, household items, food, goats and cows. They would discuss how many Tutsis they had killed, comparing notes as though killing Tutsis was an honour.

'I spent most of the time at home with Daudi's wife, my mother-in-law as she claimed. She seemed to guard me so that I would not escape. She fed me and nursed my wounds. I helped with her chores at home, but I couldn't get out of her sight,' she told me.

Then one evening Oliva was outside minding a pan of potatoes. She loved the night-time because she could gaze silently at the stars. She believed everyone had gone to heaven and this was the only time she could get to communicate quietly with them. The brothers were having an argument, which they did often, fighting over money or goods they had stolen from the Tutsis they had killed.

'I overheard my captor saying, "Oliva is *my* spoil, *I* am the one who finished off her uncle." I don't think they knew I was listening. What a shock!

'I felt hate and betrayal. I escaped through the back of the house. They heard me running and followed me. I stumbled and fell into a thick bush and held my breath. I heard them run past me. I hid in this bush until I was sure they were gone and then crept to a nearby swamp, where I found some other people hiding. There were many Tutsis here. I survived in the swamp until the Rwanda Patriotic Army rescued us.'

Oliva believed that everyone in the pit died, that Daudi's sons did not attempt to save Uncle Joseph or the rest of our family;

they went to the gravesite and finished off anyone who was still breathing. When she emerged from the swamp, she discovered by the mercy of God a total of seven people who had escaped from this grave, all of them with visible wounds to the head, neck, legs, arms and body.

I spent three months with Oliva. She would recount her story every day, remembering the names of people in the classroom and the men who killed them. It was not until ten years later that most of the victims were eventually identified, named and buried with dignity in a permanent gravesite.

Ironically, the neighbours who finished off my family helped to bury our relatives, those very people that had stood by and done nothing when the killing began. Whether it was out of guilt I don't know, but they spent all day helping with the digging, exhuming bodies, identifying the remains and placing them in coffins. Daudi and his wife were there too, but I could not bring myself to speak to them. Their sons left for Congo after the genocide and have never been seen back in the village.

Over the following days, I watched as Jeanne d'Arc and her colleague Jean Pierre left for work. I would then get ready and venture wherever I could. The whole country was eerily quiet and smelt of death. There were bodies everywhere, and I knew any of them could be someone close to me. But I couldn't cry. I was just numb. It was an unthinkable horror, a story of shame and incomprehensible grief. It was very difficult to find words to describe or make sense of what was going on in my mind.

For days I walked the streets of Kigali trying to figure out what was unfolding in front of my eyes. I visited churches and schools that had become houses of butchery. The scale was enormous; occasionally I stepped over fragments of skulls and femurs, ribs and fingers in silent houses. I watched dogs wandering aimlessly on the streets, possibly looking for Tutsi remains for dinner. I wondered how many people they had fed on. I tried desperately to understand the scale of the murder and killings, but it was beyond imagination.

Around this time, the UN had begun to dig up the bodies that had been thrown into the mass graves. Bodies literally piled up as they were exhumed. The sirens of ambulances carrying the dead could be heard from all corners of the city. Only God, and the survivors, knew how horrendous it must have been in Rwanda over those hundred days of genocide.

I could not come to terms with the loss of humankind as I stood watching people at work exhuming men, women and children from mass graves. Sometimes I felt like I knew each victim. Then I wondered about those I didn't get to see, washed down rivers and streams, burnt in pyres, eaten by dogs, rotting in pit latrines. I felt sad for the survivors who were not with their families when they died, who were living in hope that they would find them alive, looking for their remains with increasing urgency.

I became preoccupied by the dead. Who were these remains, who would claim them? What if an entire family died? What would happen then?

The horror of finding my family was my introduction to what was to follow. In all, fifty members of my family had been slaughtered; in fact everyone in my immediate and extended family in Rwanda, except for Valencia, Gigi, Christopher and Oliva.

And that seemed OK. Everything had to go on as normal. I wondered if I was going mad, or whether survivors would soon be tearing their hair out and their clothes off, running insanely on the street, overcome with trauma and grief.

I sometimes took stock of my grief. I am lucky, I would think. At least I had managed to locate my family and temporarily bury them. Those not so lucky, who have been unable to locate their missing relatives – how anxious are they, I wondered. Would they ever gain closure, having been left to wonder forever what became of their loved ones?

One afternoon Jeanne d'Arc returned home early. She was frantic, agitated; she had come to let me know she would be home late, because Jean Pierre's sister had been exhumed from a mass grave in Kigali with her seven children. They were looking for coffins and transport to take the remains to a designated gravesite. How could I help? I didn't know anyone. What little money I had on me I gave to my sister, although I knew it was nothing compared to Jean Pierre's grief. I had met Jean Pierre, a handsome and extremely polite young man; he always wore a smile and always had time to speak to me.

I forgot my own dead, and wanted to protect all the other dead; I wanted to give them dignity. Then I found the answer: I will not only bury my dead, but I will raise money and bury all the victims and give them a peaceful resting place. But now, Jean Pierre needed all his friends to help him do the decent thing: give his sister and her children the respect taken from them by the Hutu murderers.

I visited the gravesite, where thousands were being unearthed every day, and stood communing with the corpses. Identifying the dead was the most distressing moment. A sickening sight met my eyes: the bodies lay quietly, the countenances of many distorted in agony, bloodstains that had soaked into their clothes still visible to the eye. I didn't have to be related to the corpses to feel the connection.

I met a young woman in her early twenties called Solange. She had come to identify her husband, Pierre, who had been killed the morning after the president was pronounced dead. She had just got married when the genocide occurred. Pierre, a teacher, left for work saying only politicians had anything to fear. He was killed before arriving at his school. Someone told Solange that he had been dumped with many others in a mass grave somewhere around Kigali, and she was visiting all the sites to try and find him.

I stayed with Solange as she went through the remains. She carried a photo of Pierre, which had been taken at a friend's wedding. Pierre was laughing, a missing tooth visible. He looked much older than Solange, and she was quick to point out that she was still in love with him. 'I often reconstruct him in my mind to keep him alive. If I see his remains I will recognise him from his missing tooth,' she told me. 'He also has very long hands and feet.'

Solange spoke about Pierre as if he were alive, even though she was here to identify his remains. During this time, the stench that hovered in the air didn't seem to matter. The bodies of the dead seemed to talk to me, asking me to dress them and cover their nudity, their hollow eyes expressing calm beneath the storm. Having failed to identify her husband, Solange left without him and went to the next gravesite.

After this horrific experience, there was no going back. I regained my anger, and my frustration drove me closer to the survivors. I saw Hutus gathering around exhumed bodies, a community that had stood by looking with no emotion, as if they were there to confirm that the dead would not be resurrected, watching families tear their hair out, seeing survivors die for the second time as they relived the death they had escaped. I promised myself that I would not let them triumph over our dead. I would build memorials so that their names live on.

Then I had my very first encounter with the scale of the massacres at Ntarama church in eastern Rwanda, where 5,000 men, women and children were slaughtered. I stopped to speak to a young boy, eleven years old, who told me he had escaped the massacre, but his brother and his parents had not been so lucky. They were lying in this church.

He took me into the church and pointed out the remains of a woman still fully dressed in a brown and red patterned African dress. '*Uriya mugore uryamye munsi yintebe ni mama.*' ('That woman lying under the bench is my mother.'). Alongside was the body of his younger brother, Philis, lying close to his mother's. Victims could easily be seen on the benches, against the walls, across the floor, with clothing and personal belongings scattered everywhere. Some had machetes stuck in their skulls. The scale of human destruction was beyond imagination.

The boy's father had been burnt to death nearby, and he pointed to a corrugated iron house within which a pile of black and brown ash could be found. The only signs that these were human remains were the skulls, bones and fingers sticking out of the pile.

He showed me a deep scar running all across his back and neck, and told me that he had been hiding in the church when the Interahamwe attacked and started hacking people to death. Bodies fell on him but he remained alive. Eventually, after the killers had gone, he crawled out. He told me that every day he visited the site to see his mother and brother. He is a keeper of his family's memory. His immediate family gone, he lived with his surviving grandmother, who was all he had.

I held the boy's hand firmly and stood communing with the dead. Decomposing cadavers covered the floor, still clothed, skulls with visible machete wounds emerging, decaying bodies with signs of struggle, ribs poking through rotting cloth, skin still attached to bones, body parts, hair, personal belonging, bibles, identity cards, household items, shoes and clothes scattered around. The dead were displayed on benches, robbed of their dignity. The loneliness and the rude nudity of the corpses on public display, lying face up, open mouthed, were a screaming reminder of the pain and horror the victims faced in the hundred days. The horror that this little boy had gone through bore no comparison with my own loss. I had no words to comfort him.

I was incredibly saddened by the boy's story. I thought about how badly the world of adults had let him down. Yet somehow his resilience offered some hope. He was alive, and I had to help him rebuild his life. I felt I had a role as a mother, to give this boy a chance. But there were many more like him. I was determined to try to help every survivor. I knew it was an impossible task, but nothing would stop me trying.

I spent the next weeks speaking to survivors and confirming accounts that I'd heard before I arrived in Rwanda. I started slowly piecing together the last journeys of the victims: the thousands of Tutsis that perished in the massacres in churches, schools and community centres, a reminder of my family in Gitarama; the hundreds more like my brother murdered individually in the genocidal frenzy, hunted down in their homes, chased from swamps and forests, and stopped, raped and slaughtered at roadblocks. Many victims now in mass graves were being exhumed, while countless thousands more unnamed skeletons lay in unmarked graves. The scale of the dead was beyond grief.

The stories from survivors only helped my resolve to defeat the killers, to find a way of showing them that Tutsis will not perish. I was determined to prove them wrong: they would not annihilate a race, they would not annihilate my race, even if I were the only Tutsi standing. I made that promise to myself and to the victims who fell because they were Tutsis.

I remember one of the first stories that raised my resolve to hold my head up and be counted. I will not be a killer, but I can have my revenge. By helping survivors rebuild their lives, they would live and face their killers every day, a reminder of the shameful animals the Hutu killers had become.

Sheema was only fifteen when the Interahamwe came to her house early one morning in 1994. 'My parents were terrified, and looked desperate and helpless. Even they could not protect us. I escaped and climbed up a tree. As I sat trembling, struggling to stay still, my mother was brought out of the house alive, begging for mercy. She was chopped to death. To this day this is the only memory I have of my mother. The Interahamwe left, taking with them our belongings. I gathered my mother's remains, warmed by the hot sun, and put her back in the house. My father and four brothers were dead. I walked aimlessly all night, in deep shock. Many people were walking in different directions. Eventually I was stopped at a roadblock. The Interahamwe pulled off my clothes and gang-raped me. I was kept there for weeks.'

I will never forget the look on Sheema's face when she told me her story. I decided I would raise the voices of those who had survived, so that they would bear witness to the failure of humanity to intervene and save those who had perished. By some miracle the survivors had defeated the power of evil. How many people would we have saved if even on the eightieth day we had come to their rescue? I found myself wondering how I could put that right. This became my preoccupation; I didn't yet know how to do it, but I needed to try.

ELEVEN

Resilience and survival

BEING IN RWANDA, where my life had begun, where my history had been wiped out in a mere hundred days, where entire families had just been annihilated, meeting survivors and speaking to the dead, I had to dig deep to find ways of coping. It was always comforting to know I was not part of the genocide, I was not a victim. Like my mother before me, I could not let the world beat me down. I would focus on the task ahead. My personal experience as a refugee helped me face the world to some extent, but genocide was beyond human understanding. Nothing could prepare me to accept the death of an entire family, killed simply because they had a different ethnic background.

I revisited my life, which began in exile in Burundi. One event had stuck in my mind: my mother on a motorbike, wearing a skirt that seemed too short even to a five-year-old. The skirt was grey and pencil shaped, and it tightly caressed my mother's curvaceous African hips, making it hard to get on and off without much drama. I asked her not to wear it again on the motorbike, and I don't believe she did.

I should mention another event that has remained fresh in my memory. Our house was full of people crying. My parents were not at home and people I didn't know were coming in and out and speaking in whispers so that I couldn't make out what they were saying.

My father had left the night before, after tucking us into his bed, to bring Mother home from hospital with our new baby. We loved sleeping in my parents' bed, which seemed so big. Riisa and I topped and tailed with Jean Baptiste and Jeanne d'Arc. We hardly touched, but in any case Riisa and I each moved our legs to the edge of the bed to avoid kicking the others.

Eventually Aunt Ancilla, my mother's stepsister, told us in a low voice that my father had died and wouldn't be coming home. I was too young to understand death. 'Why won't Father come back?' I asked my mother when she came home.

'Your father had dinner in a hurry, and then he had a cold shower. He developed sharp stomach pains and was rushed to the hospital, but he died,' she told me sadly. He had had an intestinal abstraction, a condition that only affects one in a million, I came to learn later. But why did it happen to my father? My mother's explanation was simple and made sense to me. As long as I didn't make the mistake my father had made, I would never have to die. There was no fear of death provided I didn't eat and have a cold shower immediately afterwards. In my mind, I justified my father's death: it was his fault, and that was all I suppose I needed to understand.

My father's death left my mother in a foreign country with five children to care for. Her only relatives were Ancilla's family; she had neither parents nor an extended family network of her own to call on for support. My paternal grandfather came to Burundi for my father's funeral. On his return, to ease the financial pressure on my mother, he took Jean Baptiste and Jeanne d'Arc with him. We were to remain separated for years.

I was so young that I can barely remember the separation, and cannot recall my mother speaking about it much. I can only imagine now that this must have been her way of dealing with tragic situations, a way of coping that I was to see again and again in life – silence, and acting as though this was how life was meant to be. She refused to wallow in misery or self-pity; she coped by focusing on tasks.

When I returned to Rwanda in 1994, someone passed my family a photo of my parents' wedding, which had taken place in 1957. My mother never spoke about the wedding, which looked civilised for the time. She wore a full white wedding gown and a white veil, and my father was in a black suit, with a white shirt, black bow tie, and smart and stylish shoes. The photo seems to imply that my parents were well off. In those days many people wed in traditional dress, partly for cultural reasons, but also because they couldn't afford the Western wedding attire.

In the photo my mother is smiling shyly, like a little girl, behind the veil, her hair cut short to fit the headdress. I imagined her being fitted for the wedding dress. She must have been genuinely happy then; perhaps those days leading up to her wedding were the happiest time of her life.

The mother I came to know as I was growing up was a fighter. She would not let life beat her down. I suppose she numbed her emotions and focused on making us self-reliant and resilient. This was to become my trait too; I turned my personal tragedy into a collective tragedy. It was easy to focus on the survivors, and to think less of my personal loss in the genocide.

After my father died my mother married a previous fiancé. I have a clearer memory of living with my stepfather, who was a doctor. He was tall and broad shouldered, quite light skinned, and his bushy eyebrows and narrow nose gave him a severely thoughtful look. He was not much of a talker, and I don't remember his smile. He was always serious, but he never raised his voice – he didn't have to. He gave you a look so long and silent that it spoke a thousand words.

Once we had settled in Uganda, we seemed relatively privileged. We didn't have a lot of money, but we were not poor either compared to other local people. My mother and stepfather both had a job and as for us children, we were always presented as a shining example of a respectable family. Unlike other children we didn't visit our friends or hang around playing with local children. The only playtime we enjoyed was at school. We had no friends visit us either. We were expected to behave properly, infallibly polite and respectful towards our mother and stepfather. If we disrespected them, or argued, or did anything silly, as most children do, there was always a punishment waiting for us. I was always in trouble for meddling in people's business and controlling the flow of information and gossip both at school and at home.

My mother had nicknamed me 'United Nations'; there was nothing that ever happened without me having an opinion on it. I always defended anyone who was being punished, even when I was not directly involved in the incident in question. Most of the time I would be correct. I was sharp, argumentative and witty. I easily picked up loopholes and inconsistencies, and I was good at stating the facts correctly. Sometimes, I didn't know when to step back, though, and my parents would punish me for speaking out of turn.

I remember very well Reverend Mugisha, a local priest, furiously asking my mother about a missing letter. '*Musawo* [Nurse], someone travelling on the local bus gave one of your girls a letter to deliver to me.'

'Maria! Come here,' Mother called. 'What did you do with the letter addressed to Reverend Mugisha?' she asked me.

Reverend Mugisha's son was working in Kampala. He had sent some money to his father in a letter, but the letter never arrived. There were no post delivery services those days; mail was given to individuals travelling on buses. Our house was in front of the bus stop, so people were always dropping off letters for us to pass on. My mother automatically assumed I had received the letter, since I was the one who always knew what was going on, the one most likely to have been standing and watching who was getting on or off the bus and who was travelling with whom. I was made a culprit.

'Mother, I swear to God, it wasn't me,' I cried in terror.

She couldn't believe that I hadn't received or even seen the envelope. To extort the truth from me, she made me kneel in a corner.

'Think back quietly; maybe you will remember what you did with the letter,' Mother ordered firmly. She knew I wasn't a liar, but she was also aware that I was capable of covering up to protect anyone from being punished.

I knelt for a long time. I couldn't think of anything to say to get me off the punishment. This was a serious case, involving a furious and deeply disappointed local pastor. This man put the fear of God in my heart. He was our school reverend, and he taught us about the Ten Commandments. '"Thou shalt not steal", nor tell lies, because God knows when we lie,' he would preach at the school assembly.

I knew I was innocent, but had no way of proving it. Feeling nervous, I started giggling. For this giggling, I received an extra punishment: I had to raise my arms up into the air and hold them there until I had permission to put them down. That really hurt. My giggles turned into cries for pardon. Eventually Mother let me go. The next day she told the reverend that she did not believe I had taken the envelope.

I couldn't face school or the reverend. I had no idea who knew about the incident, and worried about being mocked by my peers. A few weeks later, it turned out that someone had indeed delivered the letter to the reverend's house. His daughter Florence, who was found with a stash of sweets under her bed, had opened the envelope and kept the money. She confessed to her parents and admitted hiding the money to buy sweets. No one apologised to me. I was glad not to be the suspect, but I wanted Reverend Mugisha to acknowledge my innocence. He never did.

For months I hated Florence, until one day I had my sweet revenge. Every Friday evening, I stayed at school, waiting to help Mother carry her clinical equipment from her outreach clinic in the village. One Friday I got bored of waiting and started walking from one classroom to another. Everyone had left. To my delight I found some pink chalk on the floor. I was fascinated with the colour pink and chalk was very scarce. If we ever found a piece, or a pencil, we handed it to the teachers.

Without a thought, I picked up the chalk, pulled up a chair and stood on it so I could comfortably reach the top of the blackboard. I composed a love letter to my imaginary boyfriend. I loved the way Florence crafted the letters 'g' and 'q' and had been copying her handwriting for months. This was a unique opportunity to perfect my writing, carefully twisting the letters, almost in italic script.

Dear Kato,
I love you, like the chicken loves millet
If you hold up six roses in front of a mirror,
You will see seven of the most wonderful things God created.
The seventh is you.
Yours in love. . .

These were phrases that we all used at school, and no one was sure where they had read or heard them. So any one of us in school could have written these words.

I surrounded the letter with heart-shaped roses and carefully filled the petals with pink. I made sure I covered the whole blackboard. The chalk slowly wore down until there was none left. I sat back and read the letter over and over, happy with my creation. It was a bit of fun, and I meant to erase the letter and clean the board before leaving to meet my mother.

'Hello, anyone here?' a voice from the back of the classroom called out.

I quietly dropped behind the teacher's desk, held my breath and prayed that no one found me. There was movement, and I heard footsteps, which slowly retreated. When I was sure there was no one around, I ran out of the classroom and made my way to the crossroads, where Mother was waiting for me.

Relieved to be out of the school, I totally forgot about the letter until Monday morning, when the teachers discovered it. Interrogations went on for days, as there were many potential suspects. For instance, a girl named Erena had an admirer at school called Kato, but she had an alibi: she had left school with friends and lived far away, so she could not have come back. I was known to stay behind every Friday, but I managed to deny ever entering the classrooms. Then there was Florence, with her distinctive handwriting. She lived a stone's throw away and could access the school anytime during the weekend. In the end Florence was punished. The fact that she had recently lied about her father's letter and the money didn't help her case. Her punishment was lighter than the hours I spent kneeling and agonising over the letter: She was made to dig the school flower beds for a whole morning, and to write and repeat 'I will respect my school' one hundred times. I didn't see a need to own up, nor did I feel guilty then. I thought Florence deserved the punishment for stealing her father's cash and for making my mother give me a harsh punishment for something I had not done.

Months passed. One day I went to confession. Being a Catholic, eventually the guilt began eating away at me. I spent the whole of Mass telling God, 'Florence deserved it. It wasn't my fault. I was having some fun.'

In the end, when I knelt to make my confession, I found myself giving a long-winded explanation of my sin to the priest, who impatiently said, 'My child, God reminds us not to lie and to treat others as we would wish to be treated.' I got away with the Lord's prayer and a few Hail Marys.

My mother and stepfather ploughed great energy into bringing us up right, forever reminding us that we were in a foreign land and had to work hard to prove ourselves, but also ensuring we knew how special we were. We had no land or property to inherit from our parents; our heads and our pens were the only way to success, we were always told. Education became our driving force. We were told that there was nothing we could not achieve.

Because of my parents' professions, there were always people who were reliant on them, young people who came to stay at our house so that they could have access to schools, and I think this taught me the great value of education and giving support to others.

My siblings and I were student role models and always came top of our classes. The school had a requirement for parents to send in contributions or buy presents to give to different categories of pupils who had reached some kind of achievement. On one occasion my mother bought two rather expensive diamond-cut drinking glasses.

'How much did the glasses cost?' my stepfather asked.

'The cost is irrelevant. I know my girls will bring these glasses home.'

My mother was right. My sister Riisa won both glasses, having come top of the class with the highest scores across all subjects, and being voted the most polite and respectful girl in school. I managed to bring home a plate for coming third overall in my class and a book for achieving the best English language score in the whole school.

I was so lucky to grow up with such special and strong parents. They instilled in me a confidence that no one can ever take away from me. This confidence made me different from my contemporaries. I wasn't especially clever, and I always left my reading to the last minute, but I had the capacity to learn quicker than my peers and get good grades, and this always surprised people.

The only subject I couldn't cope with was maths. I hated it. Sometimes my stepfather tried to help me with my coursework. When it came to maths I had a very short attention span and that frustrated him. In the end he got an elderly man to tutor me, but after a few months he declared: 'Riisa is smart and I am happy to tutor her; Maria is unteachable: she is incapable of managing sums. She doesn't get it.' He stopped teaching me, and I never recovered from the fear of maths. I couldn't wait later to drop the subject in high school.

Besides academic discipline, we routinely helped Mother at home with the housework. She also taught us how to knit and create all sorts of decorations using beads, and soon we started making decorations and selling them for wedding gifts. Mother created a unique market that brought in some extra income, a small family business which kept us all busy and us children out of trouble.

Settling into a new culture was not always easy. Some of the children in my class sometimes threatened that they would take our home if we were deported back to Rwanda. One day at school during morning playtime, a popular boy who played football for the school told us that the radio had announced plans to return all Rwandan refugees and their children back to Rwanda. A group of girls came to ask me if I had heard the news.

There were no more than twenty Rwandan refugees in the whole school. Our schoolmates gathered around us, some curious to hear what we had to say, others laughing at us. '*Empungi* [Refugees]! You're going to be returned to Rwanda,' I remember them saying. 'Your parents are taking our jobs.'

'What is your family going to do?' one friend asked, concerned.

Before I could answer, a girl who was a bully said, 'Hey, Maria, I want the dress you were wearing on Sunday. I will take all your clothes and shoes when you leave and send a team of looters to grab your family belongings.'

I was terrified. I tried to picture my family being forced to leave their jobs and my siblings and me stripped of our familiar life. Although this seemed a light-hearted joke to the others, it left me with a feeling of alienation that remained with me into adult life. None of the other children from Rwanda seemed to worry about returning to Rwanda, let alone understand the implications. If they did we never discussed this matter between us.

One girl whose name I can't remember, but whose face I will never forget, used to terrorise me on the way home. She wasn't particularly clever, so she made me do her homework. She would say, '*Empungi*, you think you're clever and a teachers' pet. Why should I waste my time if you can do my work for me?' For peace and quiet and to buy her favour, I would give her my book to copy my homework.

She looked like a terrier: muscular, short and rough. She ran like a cheetah and used to drag both boys and girls to the ground and wrestle them. She tormented me mentally for years at this school; I worried and lived with the thought that she would take my books and dresses off me if we were forced to return to Rwanda. She didn't beat me or my siblings up, she just hurled insults and verbal abuse at us. We didn't report her to my parents or teachers, as those pupils who did endured months of torture: she made them carry her books and ate their school lunch.

I sometimes worried that on returning home from school we would find that our parents had been repatriated without us. The radio ran campaigns from time to time, threatening to get rid of refugees that were now gaining some capital and buying land or taking on local jobs. This fear lasted throughout the course of my primary education. I don't remember ever telling anyone about my anxiety, but in those days children were seen and not heard. If we told Mother and Stepfather, they would tell us not to let anyone dictate what to think. They stressed that we were as good as others, and not to let anyone say otherwise, reminding us always to honour our principles and forever be true to ourselves. 'The truth always wins', as my mother said. That seemed sufficient.

My parents were frequently transferred from one health centre to another, so we changed schools sometimes three times a year. Once we had learnt the local language, my siblings and I adapted well to our new schools. No one could pronounce our long Rwandan names, and the other children made jokes about us. But being called names didn't really bother me. I heard it so often I almost got brainwashed into believing and accepting it. We even joked at home and called each other by these ridiculous names.

Even the teachers mispronounced our names in ways we had never heard before. At a Protestant school my original birth name, Emeriana, would be registered as Mary, as the teacher said it was the equivalent name; when we moved to a Catholic school, I would be registered as Maria. I was always either Mary or Maria, never Emeriana. Our parents also decided we should change our names to fit into the Ugandan community. I dropped my surname, Nyinawamariza, and changed it to Kayitesi.

One school made a particular impact on my life, a Roman Catholic primary school. It taught me Catholic values, selflessness, self-respect, dignity and empathy, not so different from the ones my parents had instilled in me, which I believe shaped my life today.

I admired my teacher, a nun, Sister Modeste. She was very young and beautiful and looked immaculate in her uniform, always spotless and neat. I wanted to be like her, a nun. I took to the Catholic teaching and I started believing in Heaven and Hell. I was terrified of burning in Hell, as I was always in trouble for interrupting conversations or stating my opinion on any topic when I wasn't asked. I believed this was a sin that would land me in Purgatory. I often went to confession, but still I couldn't stop interfering.

In later years, frequently changing schools started affecting our school performance. Adjusting from one place to another was becoming difficult. Mother decided to apply for a licence to operate as a private midwife. She would be gone for days, I think to do interviews. Riisa and I took on my mother's role, making warm water for the bath in the morning and getting breakfast ready for my stepfather before going to school. Mother hired a housekeeper, who made meals for us.

My mother gave up her job with the local hospital. She registered as a private midwife and established a new clinic in a rented house about 50 miles from where we lived. This was a remarkable achievement: even midwives trained in Uganda found it hard to get registered. Although mother struggled with learning English, having trained in Rwanda, her privileged upbringing and education gave her a headstart compared to other midwives of her generation. She was extremely good at her job and local people sought her services.

I know now that my stepfather objected to Mother taking this job. She was a wife and mother, and those roles came first. When they both worked at the same clinic, he always collected the pay cheque and determined where the money would be spent. I suspect my mother's independence and potential opportunity to earn more money than my stepfather posed a threat and represented insecurity for my stepfather. But she went ahead despite his objections.

Mother moved out, only visiting at the weekend. I was excited about her new home; I couldn't wait for the holidays to visit her there. Initially everything seemed relatively normal. My stepfather spent most of his evenings as he had before Mother left, drinking with his friends at a local pub, and would join us for dinner and sometimes help us with our homework. I noticed that he seemed less strict and authoritarian with us.

There had been a change at home, though. My stepfather's mother and sister moved in when Mother left. His nephew Gite also came to stay with us and enrolled in the school we attended. Gite was four years older than me and would beat me up for no reason. He was annoying, but I wouldn't let him have his way with us. My step-grandmother said I provoked him, and that no one should have as sharp a tongue as I did.

With Mother away and my stepfather spending most of his time with his friends, I endured months of battering. If I told my stepfather he would call Gite and tell him to apologise, and my step-grandmother would intervene in his defence. Then Gite would laugh and mock me – he always acted like an innocent lamb to my stepfather, who couldn't see through him.

Months had passed since Mother left, and she now visited irregularly. But one weekend, everything changed. We woke up to find our clothes packed. 'I was instructed to pack your belongings. You're taking a local bus this evening,' the housekeeper told me. 'Riisa, Louis and you are going to live with your mother, but Francis and Lois are staying with your stepfather,' he said. Francis and Lois, then aged four and three, were my stepfather's children with my mother.

I remember feeling excited – I had longed to visit my mother. I hadn't listened properly to what the housekeeper had said and I thought I would be coming back home on Monday ready for school.

The last time I saw my mother, she'd asked Riisa and me to see her off at the bus stop. She sat us down on grass by the roadside and gave us sweets. This was a rare treat, which I was grateful for. Mother was more relaxed and friendlier than normal. 'Girls, I am working hard to make a home for us. Please be responsible and look after your siblings,' she said. I slipped into a dreamland, thinking of the day Mother would take us to her new home. I vaguely recall mention of my stepfather's name, but don't remember the actual conversation.

The bus arrived, and before Mother boarded, she gave my sister and me a long hug. I remember a strange feeling, as though she didn't want to leave us behind.

'I will visit soon.' She hopped onto the bus.

Now, the moment I had waited for had arrived. I was bursting with energy, hopping and jumping everywhere I went. Later in the day I got anxious because my stepfather hadn't come home and we had no money for transport. The housekeeper had told us that my mother was expecting us and would pay our fare when we arrived. But Riisa wasn't convinced. So she and I ran to the local pub, arriving breathless; it was getting late and we would miss the bus. There was only one bus to my mother's place. My stepfather was drinking with his friends. He didn't seem surprised to see us. We were sent back without a penny, my stepfather saying my mother would pay for the fare, but nothing about being expected.

When the bus arrived, to our delight, Mother was on board. It was packed with passengers and stopped frequently so that people could get on and off. It took four hours to reach my mother's house. By this time it was dark and cold.

Mother seemed calm; I suspect she knew we were being sent away; maybe that's why she was on the bus. She told us not to unpack our suitcases; she was taking us all the way back the next day to live with her cousin Buse until the end of the school year. Buse lived 3 miles from our stepfather's house. I was torn: I wanted to live with my mother, but that would mean leaving my school at Cyabirukwa, ruining my hopes of becoming a nun, like my teacher Modeste. But it made sense to go and live with Buse. We would only be with him for four months.

It was only now that it hit me: our stepfather had sent us away. I loved him, and couldn't understand why he was throwing us out of his life. There were no signs of anger, no changes in behaviour that could have prepared me for the separation. I thought about Francis and Lois, whom I would miss. Everything was happening suddenly, out of my control. But I don't remember having any resentment towards my stepfather and his decision to push us away with no explanation. I think I was too focused on making Mother proud of me to be angry with anyone. We had been given so much love and confidence and coping came naturally.

Before meeting my mother, my stepfather had spent seven years in a Rwandan political prison. He had been arrested during the 1959 revolution, like many other educated Tutsi men, and charged with treason. My mother had witnessed death and destruction first hand. Neither had any help or support, except from each other, to deal with their past experiences and the pressure of living in a foreign land. I suspect this took its toll, and played its part in their separation. But today I am left wondering how this happened. It still amazes me that despite everything they had been through, they never shouted or argued, and at least in front of me, never allowed their despair to show or hate to rear its ugly head.

Looking at my own ways of coping with the genocide, I suspect their denial, helplessness, guilt and despair were forced into the shadows in order to focus on the immediate needs of providing food and shelter for the family. They literally had no time to think of their loss and grief.

The next day we took another bus back to Uncle Buse, whose five children attended the same school as me. He was a tailor and didn't have much money, but he had cows and grew his own food, so we never went hungry.

My uncle's wife looked after us very well. She was a beautiful, calm woman who never raised her voice. I remember her with fondness but also with sadness. She suffered from chronic headaches, and doctors had tried to diagnose her illness and never succeeded. When they eventually did, she was dying of a tumour that had slowly engulfed her brain.

The return to school was normal, except that Mother and Uncle Buse came to school with us and spoke to our teachers. My stepfather used to give us money to buy lunch, while Uncle Buse's children brought packed lunches, often leftovers from the previous night's meal. Many children who could not afford school lunches brought a packed lunch. They ate in a separate dining room. It was easy to adapt to packed lunches; besides I loved my aunt's food, especially cassava mixed with beans, with a touch of ghee.

It was not in our culture to discuss our personal lives with anyone, but it became difficult to explain to the other pupils why we were living only 3 miles from my stepfather's house. 'We met your stepfather yesterday with your brother and sister,' a boy who lived next door to us said one day. I spent the whole day in tears, missing them. I couldn't tell anyone; there was no one to tell how I felt. I didn't understand why I could not walk home and see them. I didn't ask either, because I was used to being told what to do, and I believed my mother and stepfather knew best.

Life was always full of changes for us, and this was just one we grew accustomed to. We let people come to their own conclusions and got on with the task of getting our grades. I found the change particularly difficult, because I was very fond of my stepfather. I used to walk to the local shops with him to pick up groceries in the evening, and I would have thousands of questions to ask him.

I learnt the names of trees and birds, and enjoyed the short stories he made up. I would hold his hand and run to keep up with him.

But what I looked forward to most was constructing sentences in English. My stepfather had been educated in a French system and spoke French. He had to teach himself English, so he practised with me. We had ten sentences that we repeated all the time. One I remember well is, 'I congratulate you for coming top of your class.' Every time a teacher at school asked if we could make a sentence using a particular word, seven times out of ten one of the sentences my father had taught me would fit.

Soon I was the master of English at school. During playtime I would teach English to my friends using the same ten phrases. I don't suppose I was always correct, but none of the other children spoke English, so it didn't matter. I confidently led the assembly, and read bible verses in English. I even learnt to memorise English songs, whose lyrics I wrote down as sentences and taught to my peers. Everyone wondered where I got my vocabulary from, but I wouldn't tell them. Bob Marley's lyrics were popular in the school then. Not many children were familiar with the songs, and I would sing them with my father and make sentences. 'Stand up for your rights' was especially popular; the teachers even gave me an award for providing an outstanding role model of morality. Little did they know that it was Bob Marley playing in my head. Later I became carried away, getting into trouble for writing 'I shot the sheriff, but I swear it was in self-defence'. My English teacher was mortified.

Following the separation, my stepfather remarried and later got a job in Tanzania, where he worked for a charity. There was less contact between us, so that I can't remember exactly when and where he lived and worked. I never had the opportunity to see him again before his death from a snake bite.

TWELVE

Growing up fast

AFTER MY STEPFATHER left, when I was eleven years old, Riisa took over the role of being my mother's confidante. She was always at home, looking after my siblings, while I would be sent to fetch water or buy groceries. Mother would tell us that Riisa was in charge when she was away. Riisa would make sure we were fed and did most of the chores at home. She had little free time to play with us.

I think my mother always protected me from her pain, because she never discussed her anxieties with me. Riisa wasn't so lucky. Being the first born she was the keeper of my mother's secrets. Knowing my mother's troubled past – the events in Rwanda that saw her privileged upbringing shattered, and the escape to Burundi; the loss of her family members, during the 1959 revolution; the sudden death of my father; the grief of enforced separation from her children, who didn't seem to be hers to claim; and finally a divorce – I can't but feel overwhelmed by my sister's responsibility. I don't think I appreciated her pain then, as my sister did. We were not a family that hugged each other but we greeted each other every morning with '*Mwaramutse* [Have you woken up safely]?' And we always went to bed saying '*Muraramukyeho* [Wake up safely]'.

As I said earlier, Riisa liked my mother liked to sing, and they would sing together. As a child, Riisa never smiled much, and was always sensible. I have no doubt Mother confided in her because she saw special qualities in her. She was a year older than me, calm, quiet, shy and reserved, unlike me.

Mother built us our first home with her own money. It was a one-bedroom house, with a sitting room and another room that Mother used as her clinic during the day and an extra bedroom if we had people staying. Otherwise, in the small bedroom, mother had a double bed which she had carried with her from Rwanda years back. It was quite big and three of my siblings shared it with her. At the bottom of the bed sat a metal trunk filled with all our clothes, bedding and valuables. There was also a dark brown wooden suitcase where my mother kept all her useful documents. It was not very large; it had room for a pair of shoes and a few personal belongings. I suspect it was my mother's wedding present from a rich family. Wooden suitcases were not common in those days and we treasured it.

The sitting room, the same size as the bedroom, had a round table, a few chairs, and some African stools. If many people were staying we borrowed a bench from the clinic or spread a colourful mat on the floor, where we sat with our legs folded sideways. At bedtime, if we were alone, we moved the table and chairs to the clinic and arranged a mattress and cushions on the floor. We nearly always seemed to have people staying, though – mainly students from Rwanda studying in Uganda. We slept on mats without protest when visitors came, giving up our mattresses and sometimes sleeping next to the many relatives who also frequently stayed with us. It was a comfortable feeling sleeping close to each other, telling stories and giggling before we fell asleep.

Mother enrolled my sister and me at a school 12 miles away which was attended by Rwandan refugees. It was at the refugee camp in southern Uganda, built by the United Nations High

Commission for Refugees (UNHCR). I believe Mother wanted us to learn Rwandan culture and to face the new challenges of growing up. Until now we had been protected by two loving parents but we needed to be toughened up. Mother also wanted us to receive the best education. Rwandan refugees were high performers.

I can't say I was excited, but in those days you didn't ask questions. I was still getting used to being separated from my stepfather and, having then lived with Uncle Buse for four months, I was keen to stay close to my mother. But she always made the decisions, and she knew best.

The new school was difficult to adjust to. It had a strict regime and lots of homework, and it was very competitive. Everyone spoke Kinyarwanda, and although we spoke Kinyarwanda at home, we found learning in the language particularly difficult, let alone catching up with the syllabus. However, the teachers and students alike were kinder to us than at my previous school. They didn't mispronounce our names or call us things. They almost gave us an honoured position in school because we were outsiders. Everyone knew about us; the community was small and tightly knitted, and everyone knew each other.

In this school I met many refugees that lived in the camp. The adults had a collective responsibility for the children, and it was a safe environment to grow up in. There was a high level of discipline and respect – even, you might say, blind obedience. The camp had elements of a Big Brother/Big Sister community, which, I came to learn, was part and parcel of Kinyarwanda culture.

Rwandan culture, as Mother told us, is like an onion: you peel off the top layer and there is another underneath. Although she gave us a full Rwandan cultural education she wanted us to keep our identity and to take only what we felt comfortable with from our culture. She told us as a young adult how she had rebelled against some aspects of the culture, and she made us promise, for example, that we would never allow a bride price to be paid when we got married, that cows were a sign of enslavement for a woman.

She taught me not to take everything at face value, to question anything I wasn't comfortable with, never to take anything or anyone for granted. This always made me and my family stand out in our culture, because we did not accept or obey the cultural rules. In Rwanda there is still a lot of cultural policing. Many of my friends, I know, will not speak out or question anything. They are paranoid and would rather live under total cultural control, and in an environment which is sometimes claustrophobic. Everyone knows and minds everyone else's business. As an adult I can see what Mother meant: that a regime that could make its citizens blindly kill each other, kill families they intermarried with, friends, godchildren, neighbours, can only be explained by years of total compliancy and obedience.

My mother had arranged for us to stay with a family at the refugee camp. The family comprised the mother, the father and nine children and they lived on a homestead that they shared with a hundred or more cows. Riisa and I were the youngest. African round grass huts kept us away from the scorching sun. There were five such huts, small and packed with belongings. There was the main hut, slightly bigger than the others, where the parents slept and where all their important possessions were kept. Then there was a boys' and a girls' hut and the kitchen, which was used to store utensils and where women sat in the afternoon to churn milk into butter. The calves had a hut too.

The roofs were full of holes. At night, rain fell on our mats, compelling us to move from one spot to another. In the day, shafts of sunlight pierced the holes. We had no mattresses; we spread straw on the floor and covered it with a mat, rugs and shared blankets. The tricky bit was getting up in the night to visit the lavatory in the backyard. It was pitch black, except for a glimmer of light from the fire burning in the middle of the kraal, cows sleeping around it. The night would be filled with a horrible smell from the cow dung which fuelled the fire. It burnt slowly, releasing a dark smoke that penetrated your clothes and clogged your nose with a nasty stench. No matter how much you washed, the smell lingered on. I can still smell it.

Some nights were filled with drama, people scratching themselves and turning until we were all awake, tearing at our skin, fleas leaping away or attached to our flesh. The next day we mixed cow dung with water and made a paste which we sealed the floor with, to trap the fleas. We burnt the straw and hung the rugs and blankets outside in the hot sun to burn off the fleas. On the way home from school, we would cut fresh straw in the forest. With cattle sleeping so close to humans, we often shared our beds with fleas.

Our host family was kind to us. We joined in their domestic chores, clearing the heaps of cow dung every morning and sweeping the compound before going to school, while the boys milked the cows. Life revolved around the cattle. The family had no regular income; they sometimes sold milk and butter to earn a bit of cash. Once in a while, if more money was needed, they would sell a cow at a local market. Cows are sacred to Rwandans; therefore selling even one is very painful to the owner. Cows represent wealth and prestige, and are supposed to be nurtured, not sold for meat.

The camp was in the middle of a drought region where no food would grow. At the weekends, refugee children would walk to my home village and work all day for food. Sometimes Mother cooked them lunch so that they had the energy to carry the food back after a day's work. Life was difficult at the camp. The staple food was dry maize known as *impunguri*, which had to be soaked for days to make it soft enough for cooking. There was also sorghum bread, called *rukacarara*, which had a rubbery texture and tasted like mud. It sat in your stomach for days. It was common to be constipated for weeks and months. The maize and the sorghum bread would be washed down with sour milk. Some days there was no food at all, and everyone just drank the milk.

Initially Riisa and I stayed at the camp from Monday to Friday and spent the weekends at home with Mother. On Monday, we would wake up at dawn and walk to school. On Friday, we would excuse ourselves from afternoon games, run to the main road and catch the bus home.

I don't know if it was selfishness, but I found the food in the camp difficult to adapt to, especially as I don't particularly like milk. I particularly hate sour milk and yogurt. So I started walking home every day to escape the camp conditions. Apart from the food, I missed my mother, and I think she was happy to have me back every day.

I looked forward to Fridays, because my sister would come home with me. Mother couldn't always afford the bus fare, so sometimes on Fridays we hurried home on foot before it got dark. We would run from school, jumping on stones placed along the path, chasing the sun, while the cloud shadows played hide and seek. It would take us three hours to walk home, getting there when the sun was setting. I didn't want to burden my mother, so I asked her to buy me bags of sweets which my sister and I sold at school during break time. If we made a profit, we took the bus home.

We stayed in the refugee camp school for a year and then moved to a new school in the village, and settled down again with our mother. For years we had lived with the shadow of separation hanging over us. Christmas, Easter, New Year, birthdays passed, and we hardly spoke of our siblings in Rwanda, or the ones my stepfather took with him. During our time with my mother, we slowly rebuilt our lives. We didn't have much money, as my mother had only her private clinic as a source of income and although sometimes there were patients, at other times there were none. The local dispensary was miles away and many villagers couldn't afford the cost of private healthcare, so they trekked for hours to get free treatment.

During such periods we often had no money for food. I remember Mother sitting in the front yard on an African stool waiting for days for a patient to come through the gates. She would wait until late if we didn't have food, and then ask a neighbour to help and loan us bananas or anything else. We never went to bed on a completely empty stomach, though; mother would make us sweet tea and a loaf of bread which she sliced thinly so that we all had a second helping.

Mother always said to us that whatever happened we must never beg or let people know that we were hungry. On bad days, when we had no money, she covered us with Vaseline to disguise our pale and hungry faces. We would sit in the kitchen surrounded by the sounds of laughter, Mother laughing along gamely even though half the time she didn't even know what was going on. We were almost at our best when we didn't have food; Mother would lift our spirits until she worked something out.

To subsidise the family income, mother rented a hectare of land, hired a tractor and planted beans and maize. The harvest gave us food, and Mother sold any surplus locally. A small piece of the land was put aside for the family to plant aubergines, cabbages and carrots, which Mother would share with the villagers. If patients came for treatment and she had some money, Mother would buy sacks of rice, maize and beans. We would sell some of the food on, to make the money stretch further and to try to keep food on the table.

When I turned thirteen, I helped subsidise Mother's income by making doughnuts to sell at the local market. Market day came once a month, on a Saturday. The traders would set their stalls up at dawn, each one trying to get the best location. They laid their goods out on pieces of fabric spread on the ground.

We would be awoken early in the morning by the sounds of peasants' calls coming from the streets, goats and sheep bleating and cows mooing, the animals examined one by one in a shed and released for slaughter. The air would also be filled with the sounds of birdsong and the beep of car horns cutting through everything.

There would be chickens and ducks too, clucking and occasionally breaking out of their pens and escaping into the crowd. A chase would ensue, under the stalls, behind the traders' screens, the birds flying over the butcher's knife and under the women's long skirts, causing a commotion, dust particles swirling in the air and everyone joining the chase, 'Catch it. . . hey there, get it!', people laughing and knocking over goods and the elderly alike.

Soon the streets would be transformed. Women with their multi-coloured dresses on a hot sunny day, and kerchiefs tightly knotted on their heads, would stand or squat on the pavement in front of their array of wares. Stalls of new and secondhand clothes, shoes and watches would be set up. Farmers spread out their wares on the floor: sweet potatoes, maize flour, bananas, cassava and so on.

My mother's house was at the heart of the market. I would jump out of bed and start baking at dawn. My brothers moved around with baskets full of warm doughnuts, which they sold to market vendors. They would run back to get more, while my sister and I sat behind the stove, either kneading more dough or frying more doughnuts. There were lots of people around, friends staying and sometimes patients who were unable to make it back home on the same day. It was very exciting. We always made a bit of money and mother would be guaranteed patients and some income.

On weekdays, we made a large pot of porridge every morning. I would fetch water from the well, running barefoot down steep hills covered in stones and bushes that tore the soles of my feet. I would invariably hurt one foot and limp back home with a large pot of water balanced on my tortoise neck. Mother would clean the wound and put antiseptic on it, to stop tetanus as she always said.

Mother got up early as well, getting her clinic ready, sterilising her equipment while humming a song. She always hummed songs and often looked across the road to greet a neighbour. 'Good morning, and how is your daughter? Has the diarrhoea now cleared? Give her plenty of water; it will do her good.' There was always easy harmony, order and responsibility.

Although we were happier at the village school than at the one in the refugee camp, we weren't doing well academically. I think it was because we didn't have enough time to study, or sometimes we couldn't afford books or tuition. Mother was only just keeping her head above water. We were always late for school because we would be so busy in the morning, though we tried to make it before the assembly bell rang. Sometimes the bell went as we were going down the hill to school. We would run barefoot, the soles of our feet bleeding from the sharp stones, taking a short cut to reach assembly before the teacher's third whistle signalled everyone to stop wherever they were. For arriving late there was a price to pay: six of the best on the back and sometimes up to twelve if you were mischievous or hadn't done your homework.

Adults seemed to enjoy caning children for all sorts of reasons. They hit us on our backs, bottoms, legs and especially hands. They hit us when we didn't give the right answer in class, when we spoke out of turn or when we didn't speak because we didn't know the answer. The teachers walked around with canes; I don't remember seeing any teacher with a pen or ruler. Sometimes they caned us when we brushed past them in the corridor, or when we passed them while they were caning someone else. 'Maria, I forgot to cane you yesterday for giggling at assembly. Put your hands out.' Two hard slashes but no tears. We were likely to see someone being caned every time we looked through the window of our classroom.

School had its fun times too, though. I enjoyed eating sugar cane which we bought from other students at lunch time, gnawing off the hard green peel and chewing the juicy, white pulp. There were always lots of fresh fruit; friends who had farms brought us mangoes, oranges and sometimes the rare jackfruit. I received kindness from people outside my family, and always felt accepted.

During my childhood Mother would leave us for days, weeks, sometimes months at a time. When she reappeared she would bring us new dresses and food or announce that we were moving again. It wasn't easy for my mother to put food on our table, so she often had to relocate her practice to somewhere she hoped would be more lucrative, and it would take her months to save enough money in order to arrange accommodation and schools. She always left us with a relative or a maid.

When Riisa and I went to secondary school, there was less upheaval, and my mother's work became more stable. She would visit me often, I think to find company, since my sister and I had left home the same year. My school was nearby, so she could visit, bringing me bananas and sugar.

I salute my mother for her outstanding representation of the human race. She taught me human values, above all resilience, which came to influence my decision to devote my life to rebuilding the lives of the survivors of the genocide. I could not bring back my brother but it was my duty to help my people, my race.

THIRTEEN

Making sense of the genocide

I HAD SO much negative energy, I needed to use it to find a productive way of supporting the survivors. My anger that the genocide had been allowed to happen, that the survivors were not being helped, made me decide to remain in Rwanda to provide more support.

I took voluntary work with the Ministry of Rehabilitation. It was the only functional ministry in Rwanda, and it became a one-stop service for most people looking for their families. It contained a Department for Reunification, where the names of survivors and those they were searching for were recorded and sometimes matched. The Ministry of Rehabilitation was also charged with registering all foreigners coming to Rwanda. There was a lack of skills in the country, and I was asked to help the NGO (non-governmental organisation) coordination unit, charged with setting up guidelines and registering any humanitarian agencies coming to Rwanda. This was to become my task for nine months.

The ministry was housed in an empty building: no electricity or running water, no chairs, no tables, no computers, no stationery. The minister and his staff had no vehicles or even any budget to run the ministry. One had to literally resource all the materials needed to do any job at all. I had no idea what was required of me, so I flew to Ethiopia, Kenya and Uganda, paying out of my own pocket, and learnt how they managed and registered humanitarian agencies in those countries.

The United Nations Development Programme (UNDP) lent the Ministry of Rehabilitation a small office, which I shared with two translators. I had a secondhand computer, also borrowed from the UNDP. The office was covered in dust and cobwebs; it hadn't been occupied for months, since the war and genocide began. A half-broken chair and a child-sized table, which seemed to have been looted from a school, stood in one corner of the room. A small window was the only source of natural light. I had hardly any light where I was sitting. I spent months working in this office. I studied the guidelines from all three countries I had visited and wrote a guideline document for Rwanda, which the government adapted and used for the next five years after the genocide.

The suffering in Rwanda provoked enormous public generosity from the West. Many humanitarian agencies working in Rwanda before the genocide had left the country, but after the RPF secured Rwanda and stopped the genocide, over 200 agencies went back into the country, as a first step. The new government in Kigali was unfamiliar with humanitarian agencies and their methods of working. The government operated an open-door policy, even allowing agencies that were operating in the refugee camps in Zaire and Tanzania to operate across the border, partly as a demonstration of the government's goodwill and partly to encourage innocent refugees to return to Rwanda from the camps.

I started organising and facilitating debriefing meetings between the ministry and the agencies' representatives. The government was quick to recognise their support and contribution and welcomed all the agencies to operate in Rwanda. It was open about its financial bankruptcy and lack of human capacity. It was obvious to see, just visiting ministries, that the infrastructure of government had been almost completely destroyed; the interim government had also emptied the bank vaults as it fled. Rwanda had lost half of its human resources either through death or as a result of people fleeing the country.

The process of registering the humanitarian agencies had its own challenges. The agencies were of all kinds: the traditional big ones; smaller ones who flew in young volunteers starting their careers and making their presence felt in Rwanda, a country they could not easily point out on the map; new agencies formed on the back of the genocide, competing for donor funds, many not even registered in their home countries. The agency staff came from all over the world. Some spoke English, others French, even Chinese and Japanese. It was difficult to interpret what everyone was doing in a country that was just setting up a new government. Different agencies had different values and principles, and they were in competition for resources and disapproved of each other's professionalism and approaches to emergency work.

At first, the agencies were required by the government to register with the UNREO (United Nations Rwandan Emergencies Office), which was an intermediary between agencies and government. It was set up to help, guide and facilitate the work of the agencies, and covered areas such as registration and issuing certificates of operation, facilitating duty-free imports, issuing work permits to qualified staff, evaluating the relevance and impact of agencies' programmes, liaising with donors and assisting coordination to stop duplication and overlaps, and maintaining communication with other ministries on the agencies' behalf. Some of the agencies did register with UNREO, but it had no powers to enforce them to respect the arrangement. Others, usually those with no knowledge of the country and no experience of emergencies, simply went through Kigali into the countryside without registration, erected tents, camps and offices, and put their flags up everywhere along the main roads and in the towns. The failure to record, let alone regulate, the humanitarian influx at this stage would have serious repercussions on the capacity to coordinate the response.

The government announced its intention to draft working guidelines for humanitarian agencies. This was the first hint of restrictions on the hitherto total freedom enjoyed by agencies and it met with mistrust and finally coordinated resistance. I found myself drawn into an all-out war of words with the agencies, who felt that they had the money Rwanda needed and that they should call the shots. I would spend hours writing a guideline which no one wanted; nonetheless, I was in Rwanda to support the government, so I persevered.

The most resisted condition was declaring income brought into the country and for what purpose or programme. Many agencies were operating in camps and did not want the government to know how much money they were spending there. Agencies were also requested to provide names and qualifications of expatriate staff, information on where they were operating, and the number of assets such as vehicles they had brought into the country.

The government was determined to reinforce order and coordination. At a meeting on 15 November 1994 held at UNREO's offices, a government representative reiterated that all agencies wishing to operate in Rwanda were required to register with the new office. The humanitarian agencies responded with threats, saying they were prepared to abandon Rwanda if such registration was enforced.

One of the obstacles to cooperation was the agencies' political analysis. Many agency representatives appeared to believe that the new government was merely a temporary interlude before the exiled extremist government returned to power. The agents that operated in the camps were particularly prone to this view. More generally the attitude of agencies towards the government was one of arrogance. They assumed that the government needed them because of the resources they were providing; they also enjoyed diplomatic protection with their embassies and at one point they even got the European Commission Humanitarian Office (ECHO) to pressure the government into scrapping the registration process. The agencies knew they had a privileged position with the international media.

The agencies demanded to see the minister or the President, wasting valuable time that Rwandans needed to deal with the genocide. Still, on 10 January 1995, I organised a government meeting, attended by all the foreign representatives – diplomats, donors and humanitarian agencies – at which a government representative openly declared registration a government directive that would not be compromised. The agencies then called a meeting which I attended in a non-official capacity and declared they would boycott the registration. I was supposed to register over 200 agencies in two weeks' time. I had spent over eight months caught up in this controversy, and it was a test of nerves. Would anyone come through the registration doors or not?

Meanwhile, the Rwandans I spoke to felt that the foreign presence in Kigali was excessive or even offensive. In a shattered country in a state of mourning, the expatriates were holding parties and filling the few clubs that were open. One of them, Kigali Nights, was home to many young volunteers. It was common to see a half-mile-long trail of new vehicles, Land Rovers, Pajeros, Corollas, outside an agency office, where more than a hundred foreigners, agents, journalists and UN soldiers would be attending a lavish party with loud music, staggering home rowdy and drunk in the early hours.

Mille Collines, a hotel which was famous for having sheltered refugees, became a meeting place for all the expats, whether they were interviewing Rwandans, attending government meetings or just going for a coffee or a meal. There would be men and women, half naked, sunbathing by the pool and downing fine wines, taking photos of themselves as memorabilia. I would be spending days with survivors who had hardly any food, while the aid workers enjoyed the beauty of Rwanda, its weather and its fabulous cuisine. How offensive and insensitive could this be in a country just emerging from genocide?

Come registration day, I was surprised to find around a dozen major reputable agencies hurrying to be the first to register. Then things fell quiet for about four hours, until at 2.30 in the afternoon all the other agencies swarmed into the office, as though they had been released from prison. We were not able to register everyone by the end of day, and as we closed the office people were harassing me, asking to be given guarantees that they could register the next day.

I later learnt from unofficial sources that the twelve major agencies were planning to hold a media conference to explain why they had opted for registration. When word of this got around, it acted as the trigger for the others to race to register before the conference. In two days we registered well over 200 international non-governmental organisations (INGOs).

It was only now that the government could establish when the various agencies had arrived in the country, many having set themselves up in strategic sites, mostly in Kigali. The majority of these INGOs spent their money supporting refugees in other countries, committing few or no resources to assess the needs of the survivors living in Rwanda. Worse still, some agencies were raising money on the back of sympathy for victims of the genocide which they then channelled to refugee camps – especially the one at Goma, in Zaire – to support the people and structures that had caused the genocide. Aiding the killers who had executed, and were planning to resume, the genocide was not intentional – but the diversion of aid away from Rwanda was. You cannot imagine the frustration I lived with.

Through the registration period, it became obvious that virtually no funds were being committed to the survivors. Many more gravesites were being identified and excavated and the bodies transferred to new, properly consecrated, mass graves. In order to support those searching for the remains of their dead relatives, I used my free time after work to meet survivors and track back and forth to all the UN institutions and charities, begging for funds to help buy coffins, and identifying and relocating both survivors and victims.

This was the most trying time of all. Humanity was brought to shame as the survivors, who had been abandoned once, were left to emerge from their nightmare with no support whatsoever. The situation was desperate because the agencies I was registering, the very people who had come to Rwanda in response to the failure of the international community to stop genocide, told me that they were not mandated to help with these burials, that because of security reasons they could not lend me vehicles to help transport the dead.

I could not get them to support the survivors' needs, although they were happy to be seen to support refugees. One charity worker told me, 'Agencies need a high profile to be able to raise funds back home. The media is not focusing on survivors but on refugees. They are the priority and that is where charities are visible.' The competition between agencies for a media spot overtook the need to consider who it was they had come to support.

I needed space to work and my sister's house was now overcrowded, so I moved out and lived with the charity that had helped me come to Rwanda. I had the chance to meet other Rwandan charities and lobbied them to support the Ministry of Rehabilitation. After a few meetings, and a little persuasion, they all pooled their resources together and provided the ministry with office furniture, equipment and vehicles. I also managed to secure support from the Ministry of Social Affairs. The minister was a survivor, and he knew prominent businessmen and other individuals who were able to contribute. With their help some

My parents on their wedding day in 1957.

At primary school. I am second from the right in the front row.

At Maryhill High School (*centre*), enjoying a visit from two of my cousins.

Graduation party at Makerere University.

With Shirley in the flat in Barnes.

Typical machete wounds inflicted by the Interahamwe during
the genocide.

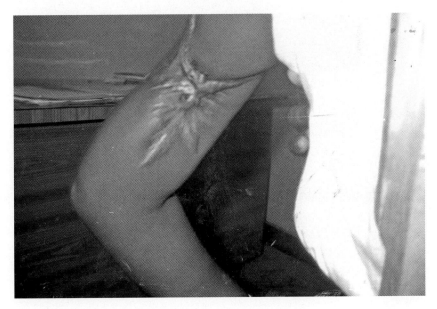

Skulls and other remains from the genocide on display at
Ntarama church, where 5,000 were slaughtered.

Coffins awaiting burial laid out inside the Kamonyi Never Again
memorial site.

Above a makeshift home typical of where many survivors lived immediately after the genocide. SURF was able to construct replacements like the house *below*, built for orphans in Kigali. (Bottom picture: Andrew Sutton)

The Kamonyi Never Again memorial site for 11,000 genocide victims, partly funded by SURF. (Andrew Sutton)

The Shorongi memorial site in Gitarama for 3,600 victims, partly funded by SURF. In the background are the remains of the church where the massacre took place.

The memorial site at Bitsibo, my home village.

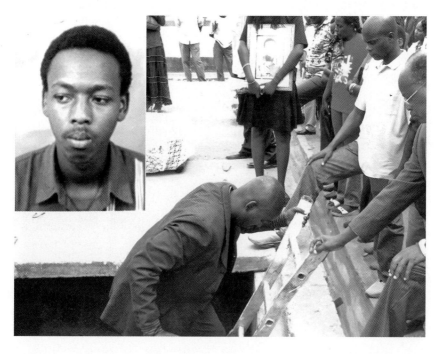

My brother Francis steps down into the grave to receive the coffin
of Jean-Baptiste (*inset*) at his reinterment.

At a Downing Street reception hosted by Cherie Blair, with the newsreader Moira Stuart, a SURF supporter.

Receiving the Window to the World award at the 2004 Women of the Year lunch from Lorraine Clinton, Women of the Year council member.

Collecting my OBE, accompanied by Christine, Richard senior and Richard junior.

lucky survivors found their loved ones and we could help buy coffins and bury them, but many others were still searching, not knowing where their family members had fallen.

I remember Chantal, a beautiful, tall girl, whose father had been exhumed from a pit latrine in Kigali. She had come to the ministry to ask for help. She was the sole survivor of her family, and was hoping to bury her father at her home village of Nyamata. Chantal's father was a security guard. He was on duty the night the president died. In the early hours of 7 April, he was preparing to go home when a group of Interahamwe beat him to death and threw him into the latrine.

I managed to get an old Land Rover, which we used to transport the body. There were seven people sitting in the back, and we had to tilt the coffin at an angle so that we all fitted. We had asked a priest to come with us to pray for Chantal's father, and he sat in front with a plain-clothes army escort and the driver. Apart from Chantal, none of us knew the dead man.

On the way, we broke into church songs. My colleagues were Tutsis from Burundi, and I was from the UK, and we didn't know all the verses. So everyone was asked to improvise to keep the song going. Chantal's improvisation cracked us all up: '*Mana turagushimye kuduha iyi modoka, utubabarire gucurika papa, ntitwakwirwaga mumodoka*' ('Dear Lord, we thank you for the transportation, forgive us for tilting my father in his coffin, we couldn't fit in the Land Rover otherwise'). Soon we were laughing and falling over the coffin. The laughter didn't stop as the only man in the back composed another verse: '*Ndagushimira mana kuba arige mugabo urikumwe nababategarugore beza*' ('I thank you, Lord, I am the luckiest man living, stuck with these beautiful women').

'You're damn right, the other one is dead,' someone responded. I just couldn't believe I was laughing all the way.

The journey took less than an hour. Friends who had survived at Nyamata had already prepared the grave, and soon we were all standing by the graveside and the priest was giving the eulogy. The mood changed, the reality of this girl's life hitting us all as we listened to the priest's words.

Then the next of kin was asked to say the last word. Bravely Chantal looked up and said, 'Father, I wish I could trade places with you.'

Suddenly a voice from the crowd of about twenty people called out, 'Tell me if there are any more dead volunteers wishing to swop places.' Someone laughed, and soon everyone was laughing. I couldn't understand it, but I was to witness more jokes and black humour (or 'grey humour' to be politically correct) about the genocide.

This kind of humour gave me hope. The laughter, although to my mind inappropriate, reflected the beautiful lives the survivors had once lived. The quickness to respond to strangers cemented trust between people who didn't know each other, brought together by a tragedy that we all shared.

On the way back Chantal asked if we could stop at the church in Nyamata. It was a genocide site where her mother and two siblings had been killed, and she wanted to say a prayer for them. The door to the church was shattered, a sign of forced entry or a grenade attack. We went in. Chantal told us the church had been cleaned and the people that had perished here lay in a mass grave. She made the sign of the cross and closed her eyes to pray.

We observed a minute's silence to honour the victims, the 20,000 people who had died in the church and its compound. My eyes wandered to the altar, spattered with bullet holes and blood stains, the roof riddled with holes and debris from what seemed to be grenade attacks. There were traces of blood everywhere, even on the roof, lumps of body tissue still lodged up high; it was not difficult to imagine the agony and horror the victims had gone through in this church. Chantal led us behind the church, where a mound lying between some eucalyptus trees marked the resting place for her mother and siblings.

Chantal told me how for eight days the authorities played cat and mouse, pretending to care about the refugees who had gathered at the church but occasionally killing some. On the eighth day the Interahamwe threw grenades into the church and started macheteing everyone. Those who fled outside met a mob that finished them off. Chantal was in the church. She was hit on the head and fell, bodies piling on top of her. She could hear the Interahamwe chopping people up, then when the struggle stopped, she heard them say they should strip everyone of their clothes and money. The Interahamwe started pushing the bodies around as they robbed them. Chantal stayed still and waited her turn. Eventually the Interahamwe left, saying they would come back the next morning as it was getting dark. Later Chantal heard movement, people crying. She turned and asked for help, and a man pulled her out from the underneath the bodies. She saw her mother and brother lying among the dead, naked. She pulled them together, put her African wrap over them and joined other survivors making their way to Nyamata's clinic. On the way she was rescued by the RPF.

Sitting in the back of the Land Rover, this time with our legs stretched out, Chantal told us the horrors that she and her family had gone through. She had a handful of distant relatives who had survived, the only family left. I invited Chantal to the widows' evening meetings which had been set up. I got to know her better after a while; sometimes she smiled and gave me hope, but most of the time she would sit quietly, gazing into space.

I remember once speaking to a group of widows, where I was the only outsider. I mentioned something about my husband, and someone said, 'Some people are lucky they have husbands.' I was terrified of saying anything after that, because although this person meant it as a joke, I felt lucky that I had not been in Rwanda because I would be dead or no doubt a widow. I had a family to go back to, but who was there for the survivors?

After tending to the dead, I turned my attention to those who had survived. They described how once the killing had started, it spread through the country like evil wildfire. Within three months, a million people had been killed. The statistics were cold; behind them lay death upon death, of a wife, a mother, a father, a husband, a sister, a brother, a daughter, a son, an aunt, an uncle, a grandmother, a grandfather, a friend, a neighbour, old and young, boys and girls, women and men alike.

Many survivors thought it a miracle that they had escaped with their lives. When I spoke with them, the full impact and implications of the genocide slowly started to sink in. Every story I heard added a new chapter to my understanding of what had happened to my own family, as I began to absorb the pain of the survivors and better understand all they had endured. I could feel the loneliness the survivors felt, the anguish about their relatives, the hope that they would find anyone alive. I felt a duty to listen to them, because that's all I could do. I had no way of taking the grief away. I couldn't imagine the hundred days of hell they had emerged from.

Many trusted me with the only possession they had after losing their entire families: their memories. It was like opening Pandora's box. In their thousands, they told me their experiences. Every day after work I would sit through testimonies of despair. I soon begin to experience a physical, as well as mental, numbness from sharing their pain. I would literally block my mind and focus on how to help those who were pouring out their feelings and stories to me, while at the same time seemingly listening. I had the urge to give the survivors their hope and dignity back, and to defeat the Hutu murderers.

Sometimes the stories replayed in my mind for days. I particularly remember Espérance's story. On this day I had been at work from 7.30 a.m., writing up the INGO guidelines for registration. Most evenings I would look forward to meeting survivors and hearing their stories. But this evening, I felt tired and grumpy. I didn't think I would be good company, so I stayed at work until late.

I had just left the office and was about to cross the road, lost in the day's events, feeling thirsty and hungry. As I was checking the traffic, someone tapped on my shoulder. I jumped with fright and pulled back to the pavement. A woman who I recognised from a meeting the evening before was standing there with a bewildered expression. Is she stalking me, I wondered.

Gasping for breath and composing myself, I said, 'How are you today?'

'I'm fine. But I came to the meeting today and you weren't there,' she replied.

I explained I had a lot of work and couldn't make it today. 'What are you doing here? Do you live around here?' I asked.

'No,' she said. 'I came to see you!'

'How did you know where to find me?'

'I went to see you at the Ministry of Rehabilitation, and someone told me where to find you.'

Across the road was St Famille, a church where many survivors had hidden during the genocide. I suggested that we go to their canteen for a bite to eat, and we could speak there.

The woman hesitated. 'Sorry, I haven't been to St Famille since the genocide.'

'Alright. I am heading into town; we can find a good spot there,' I said.

I hailed a taxi. It smelt of cigarette smoke and burnt rubber. It was packed, with six people sitting on seats designed for four, plus three children sitting on their parents' laps. Normally I avoided taxis, preferring to walk, to stretch my legs and get some exercise after sitting in a gloomy office for a straight eight hours every day, but also to avoid the sweat, dirt and smell of passengers perspiring under the hot sun.

We sat quietly together in the taxi and went round the city until we found a restaurant. It was basic, its tables covered with fading multi-coloured plastic sheets and plastic chairs, once white, placed untidily around them. The tiled floor was stained, but clean. There was a delightful plastic flower placed in the middle of each table.

I ask the woman where she preferred to sit. She pointed to the far corner of the restaurant, where she could sit facing the wall, her back towards the entrance so that no one could see her face.

I pulled up a chair and sat next to her. 'What is your name?' I asked.

'I am called Espérance. I saw you at the last meeting at Kabuga, speaking to widows.'

'I have been coming to support the widows every day,' I said.

'I know all the women are surprised you have time for widows.'

'I lost my brother in the genocide,' I replied. 'This is the least I can do to understand what he went through.'

'I'm sorry. I lost my family too. I didn't really want to survive. I am condemned to live. Even death didn't want me!'

I thought how stupid I was to speak about my loss, my brother. This was not about me. Espérance was here to speak about herself.

'I have been trying to kill myself, but have failed,' she blurted out, turning her head so that I couldn't see her eyes. Over her left shoulder, I could see two men drinking beer, and then a party of six, four men and two middle-aged women, chatting and laughing, no doubt celebrating some deal. Jackets on the back of their chairs, collars unbuttoned, ties in their pockets. The girls were neatly dressed like professionals. The bottle of Moët & Chandon in their ice bucket was emptying quickly.

I asked Espérance if she would like something to drink, buying time to find an response to her comment.

'I would like lemon soda.'

I called the waiter and I also ordered myself a pot of tea.

It was getting dark. The night was cool and filled with the fragrance of flowers in window boxes. A waiter turned on the lights and closed the curtains. I could see Espérance more clearly now, under the light. She was pretty. She also had something more substantial about her, what you might call an unpredictable fatalism, and a shabby panache. Her hair was thick and tangled, and her clothes were rather too big, as if she had lost a large amount of weight from her emotional shock. She wore light sandals, revealing machete scars on her Achilles tendons. I could also see scabs, scars and marks on her arms. I had noticed that she limped when she walked.

'I have been trying to throw myself into the river Nyabarongo, but the water throws me back.'

Two thoughts cut through my tired brain. First: the woman was beyond help; let the river take her. Second: she had a glow to her, an aura that I could not explain.

'Do you think I am mad?' she asked.

How could I answer such a question? I knew, no matter what or how I answered, it would be wrong. I hesitated, not sure if I would be the last person to see her alive. Then I asked, 'If you had to choose one, which would you choose? Life or death?'

I didn't know anything about her life. I could only guess she was unable to cope with her experiences, like many I had spoken to before. I could fully imagine the grief that made her want to end her life. I pretended to pick something out of my handbag, which was on the floor, as if I would find the answer in some book or magic box inside it.

Espérance turned and faced me. She pulled her chair closer, but not uncomfortably close. She was tall, and her stature revealed the beautiful and elegant woman she had once been.

'I have thought about it myself, and have heard so many testimonies,' I continued. 'Death is the more difficult.' She waited for my explanation, her face lightening a little. A good sign, I thought, or was I imagining her face responding to my answer because I wanted desperately to help her or at least say what she was expecting, although I had no idea what that might be? I questioned why this woman had sought me out. Why was I spending days listening to survivors? I didn't have the answer; all I felt was a duty to absorb some of their pain and relieve them of their loneliness.

'To choose death', I said, playing along, 'is to choose a journey that requires a strong will and a lot of energy. It requires one not to attempt to be rescued. It's quick and sharp, end of story. No conversation or reasoning, just personal willpower. I don't have that.'

'Go on, what is there for me to live for?' she asked. Her face was now looking vulnerable, nervous and anxious.

'If you choose life, though there will be twists and turns, along the way you may find something to smile about, an answer to why your life should bear such a terrible circumstance.'

'I have nothing to expect from life any more,' Espérance replied.

I wondered then if she would ever have an opportunity to restore her sense of humanity, to give her a 'why' to live for. I felt like giving her a hug and telling her I would be her friend, that she wasn't alone. I found myself telling her, 'I have all the time in the world to listen to your story. If there is no "why", I will bear witness to your death, if you choose death.'

It was a daring statement. I have no idea where it came from, but I guess I thought that, whatever I said, she would kill herself anyway. I had no time to think through what the implications were.

She looked less pleased.

How could I stop her committing suicide? What if I was the last person to see her alive? Did I really want to be her last witness? I was now praying for a miracle from God.

Luckily, over the next four hours she told me her story. 'You see, when the war began, the militia started looting and destroying houses, taking away all our belongings and raping women. My four daughters, and then later I too, went to St Famille Church to escape the rapists, leaving my husband and three sons at home. The militia came every day to the church and took men or women away to rape and kill. My daughters and I were taken out of the church, marched to the river Nyabarongo with many other people and thrown in.'

Espérance stopped, sipped slowly at her soda and took a deep breath. She continued, 'When the militia realised that the flow of the water would wash me ashore, they followed me downstream. They slashed me with a machete and I passed out. They also beat me. Fortunately they hit me on the shoulder and not the head. I believe they thought they had killed me. I was lucky that the waves threw me onto land again and by morning I had started to regain consciousness.'

I noticed Espérance's choice of words, 'fortunately' and 'lucky', which meant she wanted to live. Her ordeal had been unbearable but she had been given a second chance to live.

'My body was hurting badly; I could hear the voices of my

children as they plunged downstream. There was no sign of them on the shore; I knew they had died as none of them could swim.'

She pulled at a cotton wrap tightly tied around her waist and wiped her sweating face with it. I could see her stomach was hollow. She probably hasn't eaten for days, I thought. I wondered if she was starving herself or whether she just didn't have any food.

'The pain was too much. I decided to throw myself back into the river so that I could drown. But the river coughed me up onto land again. Another group of militiamen found me and beat me up with *masus* and threw me back into the river. God protected me once more because the waters brought me to land again, this time in a different area, I made yet another attempt to drown myself, but every time the river brought me back to land,' she told me disappointedly.

'By this time I was very weak and I passed out by the river. I don't know how long I was lying there, but when I awoke I decided to walk back home to see if anyone had survived. I wasn't frightened of death then. I wanted someone to kill me, so I walked past roadblocks covered in blood. The Interahamwe laughed at me, saying they wouldn't touch me so that I would die from my wounds.' She took another sip and turned to look straight into my eyes.

'When I arrived home, the bodies of my husband and my other three children were lying in our compound. I had expected that but couldn't imagine what pain they'd endured. They looked peaceful. I longed to die and join them.'

Espérance could not contain her pain. She shook as she sobbed silently. 'I am so sorry,' she apologised. 'I should be strong for them.'

At this point, I thought, I had the 'why'. Espérance should stay alive to be a witness for her family. She might have one ray of hope. She longed to die and join her family, but not even death would have her. I didn't want to interrupt her, so I sat close to her. As I reached out to hold her hand, she tried to pull away. But I held her firmly. I thought that no one had touched her for a while, and a human hand, one little gesture, might warm her grieving heart.

It was getting late. She needed to get back home, and Kigali was not safe for her to travel alone. I suggested continuing the story the next day.

Espérance smiled sneakily. 'You haven't been listening. Not even death wants me. I am not afraid of death. I wish they could kill me, and then I would rest in peace!'

'I didn't realise you had chosen death over life already.' Thinking I wasn't comfortable walking home late, I didn't want to choose death myself.

Her body rocked back and forward, but she regained her composure and went on. 'My journey continued to Taba, where my sister lived. At night the militia men attacked us. My sister, her husband and other people who were hiding in the house did not survive. Everyone was killed apart from me. I don't know why no one wanted to kill me, as I had nothing to live for.'

As she told her story, I felt that she trusted me, that she would agree to meet up again if she wanted to speak some more. I still wasn't sure, though, how I could make it better for her.

'I sought refuge with my sister's neighbour, a Tutsi married to a Hutu man. I stayed for three months and by then, the RPF had reached the area. I tried to return home. Because my house had been destroyed, my neighbour, who was a Hutu, sheltered me, but even then his relatives intimidated me and threatened to kill me if I talked about the atrocities that had been carried out.'

She pulled her wrap even tighter around her and adjusted her position, her back still turned against the entrance. I guessed she didn't want anyone to see her vulnerability, especially those who might mock her if they saw her cry.

'I am not frightened of death or intimidation,' she told me. 'In a way I wished they had killed me as I failed to kill myself. I live a miserable life because I have nobody to help me with the day-to-day work at home. I am handicapped, have no family, and survive by the grace of God and well-wishers.'

I had been listening quietly to Espérance's horrific experience; I knew that she wanted help to begin her life again. I promised I would ask around and find some help for her. She didn't want to kill herself, but if she didn't get help, the only option available to her was death. I had no idea where I was going to get help from, but somehow I gave her my word. 'I will try my best to help, please give me time.' I had been told of a voluntary organisation in Kigali that comprised widows of the genocide. I thought that would be the first port of call to help Espérance.

Espérance bade me goodbye. She stood up, straightened her clothes and told me she was walking home. I gave her a little money for a taxi and promised to see her at the meeting the next evening. To my relief, she replied, 'OK. I'll see you tomorrow and thank you. God be with you.'

I was relieved to know she hadn't chosen death over life, for now at least.

As she walked away, I went over to the window and opened the curtains so that I could see her leave. I felt so sad for her. I couldn't imagine how she managed to live with such memories. On the way home, I cried for a long time. I cried and cried, incapable of stopping the tears, yet not quite knowing why. Maybe for Espérance, maybe for myself, and maybe for all those bodies floating down the river Nyabarongo, maybe for the months that I had spent listening to survivors' stories.

On this particular night I lay on my bed, staring up at the ceiling, when I was seized by a tremendous sensation. I felt voices, people, or a sort of movement in my room. I turned nervously when I heard a cracking sound at the window. I lay immobile, completely stock still. There was a peculiar silence, filled with the creaking of the wooden floor, and the hollow barking of dogs outside.

Suddenly the room started to spin. I leant against the wall to prevent myself from falling out of bed. When I woke, I could see that day had already broken. I felt lost and disoriented. A distant voice was howling.

Every morning I was awakened by the distant call to prayers from the Nyamirambo mosque across the valley. I liked to watch the sun rise in the cool, misty morning. It often helped to set me up for the day ahead. But this morning, with sleep still in my eyes and the bright sunlight stabbing at them, I felt like I had slept through many days and nights. I wanted to carry on sleeping. It was like being dead, or rather part of the living dead.

I remembered I was due to facilitate a meeting between an NGO steering committee and the Ministry to discuss registration. The thought drained me of energy. I sat up, but my head felt heavy. I closed my eyes, squeezing them tight in an effort to try to refocus. It didn't work. My heart beat so painfully loud, I was afraid I was having a heart attack. I was mentally exhausted and I could feel the extent to which Espérance's story had affected me.

There were many aid workers and visitors, mainly British media, staying at the charity compound. On my way home the previous night, I had stumbled over a body lying in a sleeping bag on the sitting room floor. I could see in the light from the window other sleeping bags dotted around, two or maybe three. As I regained my composure, I heard voices coming from the sitting room and the toilet flushing constantly. The smell of Rwandan coffee, bacon and eggs filled the room and made me hungry. I heard car engines, warming up for a trip to Zaire, I thought. Many aid workers spent their days in the refugee camps helping families that had just committed genocide. In the evening they would return to safety in

Kigali. I had tried telling them about the survivors I met every day, but there was little interest.

A BBC journalist once told me, 'The refugees are the victims, they have been kicked out of Rwanda by the Tutsi minority. We can't have a situation where the minority rule. The voices of the masses must be heard.' During the genocide the media had portrayed the killings as just another outburst of 'tribal' violence on the African continent, suggesting that nothing could be done to stop 'savages' from killing each other in their 'barbaric' outbursts of violence.

I was so frustrated that I couldn't forgive the journalist's ignorance, but it wasn't only the media that got it wrong; some of the established INGOs working in Rwanda then considered themselves more legitimate than the newly established Rwandan government. The government was highly criticised and much maligned by these INGOs, a matter that did little to enhance stability in the country, or the perceptions of stability so critical for prospective donors. The government was often depicted as an illegitimate Tutsi minority government.

I told the journalist that the majority-led elected government, which she had recognised pre-genocide, had endorsed, supported and armed the very people that had killed over one million people in just one hundred days. The reports and debates at the compound were so hurtful, insensitive and ignorant of the situation that sometimes I had to turn a blind eye and mind my own business.

Today, I thought, I will get up like other days, introduce myself, half smile and avoid their questions. There was no time to feel sorry for myself. The survivors had no one, and I felt a call to be with them, to defend them against any further hurt, whether deliberate or due to ignorance. Many survivors travelled to meet me each evening, to tell me that they felt safe and were able to speak to me precisely because I listened to them. But they had no idea. I was in my own fantasy world, thinking of how to fix. . . fix. . . fix *something*. How to turn the clocks back, so that I could tell them it was all a dream. But it wasn't a dream. These were real people. This was real life. It was fact.

So there I was. I listened and each night as I fell into bed, I cried myself to sleep. I cried for my family. I cried for the survivors, for the pain their families went through before they died. I cried for all the dead who wouldn't see another day to tell their stories. I cried for myself, and the trust placed in me to help all those who had witnessed the worst nightmare of their lives. But every night, I emptied my mind to make space for more stories the next day.

For months, the stories came in their thousands. Every day a new person and a new story, the content similar but expressions, recollection and emphasis differing in each case. They entrusted me with stories that will live with me forever.

FOURTEEN

Meeting the genocide widows

THE FIRST GENOCIDE widows I met were two beautiful women, Angélique and Jacqueline. They were both volunteering for AVEGA.

Angélique was in her early twenties. She had a light complexion, and was gentle in manner but authoritative with a serious expression. She was a very dynamic woman and a good communicator, a born-to-lead kind. She had no fear of expressing the anxieties of the survivors she represented. Jacqueline, also in her twenties, was slightly shorter than Angélique, and looked older than her age. Dark skinned, she was an agreeable person who smiled with ease. Warm and attentive, she was less assertive than Angélique and a good listener, always receiving and speaking to survivors at the AVEGA premises.

I meet both ladies at their office, in a back street in Kigali. It had two counselling rooms and a reception area. The latter was packed with women and children, each waiting their turn to be seen, or trying to catch someone's attention as they passed. All the benches were full and many women were sitting on the floor, with their backs supported by the wall.

Angélique explained that a few widowed survivors, struggling to recover from the social upheaval of the genocide, formed an association called AVEGA–AGAHOZO. AVEGA is an acronym derived from the phrase *Association des Veuves du Génocide*

(French for 'Association of Genocide Widows') and *agahozo* is a Kinyarwanda word, which means 'dry one's tears'. They met to support each other emotionally and to talk about their experiences. From the first meeting they invited more widows to join.

Unlike the normal situation where widows are mainly elderly, thousands of the women widowed in 1994 were young, many still in their twenties. Beyond their own struggle to stay alive, most of them had to assume responsibility for looking after relatives, orphans and child survivors – often single handed, with very limited hope of assistance. They had no choice but to pick up the pieces of their and other people's shattered lives. Furthermore, a lot of them were homeless. Under existing Rwandan law, widows had no right to their husband's land or property. In many cases that meant the male members of their husband's families had claimed priority over any property. Some of the widows also had to cope with children born of rape and a lack of means to bury their dead.

The association operated on a voluntary basis with no budget or assistance whatsoever. Members who had jobs contributed to keep work progressing. The most important contribution was the office, which provided a confidential space for widows to speak. It had been rented with the help of a grant from the Ministry of Social Affairs.

While we were speaking a woman burst into the office in tears. She had a little girl with her aged about six. Jacqueline asked Angélique and me if we would step outside. She took the little girl's hand and sat close to her, while holding her hand. As we made our way out, the mother began to calm down.

Angélique took me to meet the widows; she asked some at random if they were happy to share their stories with a stranger. I looked around, and their piercing eyes and the questioning expressions on their faces made me feel uncomfortable. 'I am your friend,' I said.

'You don't have to speak to me, but I came to meet you because I felt a close connection.' I couldn't explain what connection I felt, but part of me felt as though I had a duty to be part of them.

Then a young woman said she was prepared to tell me about her experience. 'My name is Claudine, and I am twenty-two years old,' she started. 'I was a mother of two and lived in Muhazi in Rwamagana province when the genocide happened.

'In April 1994, our world collapsed. The horror, the death of our loved ones, the cruel rapes, the machetes, that noise, the smell, the complete destruction of our properties and belongings, the end. But it didn't end. The world didn't stop. We didn't die even if we wanted to.

'I survived, more or less; survived with some visible wounds, scars, but mostly I survived with invisible wounds, inside the heart, the head.'

With a desperate look on her face, Claudine told me how she had been raped and deliberately infected with HIV during the genocide. She had been forced to watch her son being killed with a single machete blow. Her life was spared, but her rapists told her, 'You alone may live, only so that you will die of sadness.'

This beautiful young woman guiltily told me the story of how her two young sisters were killed during the genocide. When the killings started Claudine had a week-old baby, and her two sisters had come to help nurse her. On the morning of 7 April, one of her sisters had gone to look for milk for the baby when the Interahamwe militia raped her and shot her in the stomach. She died a week later from her horrific injuries.

Unable to focus and to articulate details, Claudine went on, 'We arrived a little late to save my sister.'

I could see it was too painful for her to speak about her ordeal. I patiently sat and waited for her to regain her composure.

After a while she continued. 'There was no escape after that incident. The killing was spreading everywhere. People were afraid to leave their homes for fear of being assaulted. We had no idea of the scale of killings that awaited us.' Tears streamed from her eyes. 'We held a small funeral for my sister in a cemetery not far from our home. During the service a group of Interahamwe militia approached, singing and shouting at the top of their voices, "Is the grave large enough for all of you?"'

The mourners scattered in fear and ran off. But Claudine's other sister was too shocked to run. Claudine pulled at her but she kept slipping from her hands. 'I believe I could have saved her, but I was so frightened, I left my sister behind and ran while holding onto my baby,' she told me.

The killers chased her husband and other male relatives and friends. All five men and her younger sister were killed near the grave, then thrown into it. Meanwhile, they also caught Claudine, dragged her into a neighbour's house and gang-raped her.

'The only thing that kept me alive was hearing my baby crying as they raped me one after the other. I don't know why I am still alive. They told me they would not kill me, but that I was as good as dead, because they were HIV positive and had infected me.'

When the ordeal was over Claudine left the house, covered in blood and holding her baby, ashamed of herself. She then walked to her home, which she shared with her husband and parents-in-law. At this time she was unaware of what had happened to everyone who had been at the funeral. To her horror, a friend who had witnessed the killings and hidden her five-year-old son told her that her husband, sister and in-laws were all dead. She took Claudine to her house to comfort her.

Everywhere around them, friends, relatives and neighbours were being killed like flies. There was no time to mourn or find out what was happening. Claudine decided to go to her parents' house in a neighbouring commune, to tell them the bad news.

While her two sisters had died, Claudine and her two children were still alive. 'I was so ridden with guilt,' she told me. 'How was I to tell my parents that two of their daughters had come to visit me and had died, that I could not save any of them?'

Though they were her sisters and she could feel the pain of losing them she kept thinking that her parents, whom she assumed were still alive, would ask why two of their daughters had been killed but not Claudine and her children.

Claudine arrived at her parents' house after negotiating several roadblocks. To her horror they were dead, their bodies still lying in the house. She dug a grave that night and buried them.

Not long before, a Hutu man that she knew had come and raped her. He told her she was now his wife and he would be coming back to take her to his house. She didn't want to wait until this man returned, so she went to seek refuge with a Hutu friend of her mother's. At first this friend was kind, giving Claudine food and hiding her and the children. She kept them for three days, then she brought bad news. 'I cannot bring myself to kill you and your children myself,' she said. 'You have to leave and hopefully someone else will kill you along the way.'

Shocked, Claudine left with her children and just walked around randomly. The children were hungry and weak, but she couldn't carry them because she was feeling ill. She headed to Lake Muhazi, where other Tutsis were hiding in the papyrus swamp. The children were cold and started crying, whereupon she was told to quieten them or leave because the killers would hear them and find everyone.

Claudine survived in the swamp for a week, but then her children became dangerously weak. 'I knew they would die of hunger, so I left the swamp desperately to find food for them,' she told me.

She meet a group of Interahamwe, who stripped her naked in front of her children and raped her. 'My five-year-old was crying, and he came to me asking them to leave me alone. One of the Interahamwe struck him with a machete and he died immediately. Meanwhile others were raping me, one after another. I passed out.' She pulled up the wrap knotted around her waist and buried her head in it, sobbing.

I sat watching her and imagining the pain she was carrying, unable to find words to console her. What do you tell a mother who has been stripped of her human value?

In time, she carried on. 'When I came round I had a machete wound across the back of my neck. I searched for my children. My five-year-old was still there, his face soaked in blood, and the baby was lying apparently lifeless not far from me. I went to pick him up, thinking he too was dead, but he was still warm. I panicked, pulled him to me and tried to breastfeed him.

'I must have been lying there for hours. In the evening I heard some people say, "This woman is not dead." It was two Tutsi women. They pulled me and the baby off the road, and covered my dead son with grass. They were kind to me; they helped me with my baby and took me back to the swamp. They had some carrots and cabbage, which they gave me. I gave my son swamp water to rehydrate him. That night the refugees sneaked into someone's garden, brought back whatever they could find and fed me.

'One day a large group of men came chanting and singing to where we were hiding. I heard them mocking someone and beating him with clubs and sticks; he was crying in agony. I couldn't take it any more. I got up to give myself up and die with him. But they refused to kill me; instead one of the men dragged me behind a bush and raped me. I felt numb. I asked him to kill me and my son, but he wouldn't.

'There were many men, all happily congratulating themselves for getting rid of the "cockroaches". When the killers left, I stumbled back to the swamp, but the other women had gone. That night it rained a lot and I collected some water on a leaf and gave it to my son. I got some energy back, and I left the swamp to find food for the baby.

'A Hutu woman felt sorry for me and hid me in her kitchen. During the night, two men came and knocked on the door, claiming they were looking for cockroaches. They broke the door down, seized me and raped me. My baby saved me for the second time; I focused on listening to him crying as I was being raped, to take away the pain. Thereafter men came and raped me every day and every night. The woman knew I was being raped, but I guess she couldn't stop them. She gave me food and some African medicine to dress the wounds on my neck and arm, but my arm was beginning to rot.

'Sometime in May, I can't remember the date, the woman told me she was leaving for Tanzania and she was taking me with her, because the cockroaches were approaching and would kill people. I didn't understand a thing she was saying and I couldn't make sense of anything around me. I thought I was already dead. But I was rescued by RPF soldiers, who took me to a refugee zone, gave me food and treated my wounds.'

Claudine survived with her son; she had no home, no family to take care of her. She had come to AVEGA to find help.

By the time Claudine finished her story, I couldn't but see the scale of devastation the survivors were going through. I could visualise Claudine's son being struck on the head with a sharp machete as he tried to protect his mother. I didn't want to believe any human being could do that to a child and then rape its mother. I wondered how children who survived such ordeals coped. I had sat through stories of children who had survived denying their parents so that they had a better chance of survival, or mothers who had denied their children.

I thanked Claudine for trusting me with her memory.

I joined Angélique and Jacqueline, still concerned with the woman with the little girl I had met earlier. Jacqueline told me that the girl had been raped by a neighbour, a forty-something man, and they were trying to find money to take the girl to a doctor, as she had a high fever and infection. The mother had only just found out her daughter had been raped a few days previously. The girl had not told her mother of the incident at the time.

The woman had been raped herself during the genocide but had managed to protect her daughter then. She was distraught that her daughter could be raped after the genocide by a Hutu neighbour; she felt responsible for neglecting the girl. She had left her daughter in the small shack they called home to find some food and work. A Hutu neighbour took advantage of her absence and raped her daughter. She felt helpless that she wasn't able to parent her only surviving child.

I offered to pay for the little girl's treatment. I was so furious I swore I would have the rapist castrated. The police had already arrested him.

The scale of these women's responsibilities daunted me. I started paying them regular visits and working with AVEGA to find ways of making sense of its role. Until then it was a social support organisation. Many women travelled from all corners of Rwanda to seek help. The organisation had nearly a thousand members, of whom maybe thirty were especially active.

I met with many women, every day after work, to chat about the day's events. The scale of rape by and infection from the Hutu killers was increasingly shocking. Claudine was not alone, as thousands of women endured the same dehumanising and degrading experience, often in front of their own families, who ended up dead. Many women were infected deliberately and told they were being spared so that they could die a slow death from HIV/AIDS. This widespread use of rape as a weapon was a deliberate strategy to destroy the fundamental fabric of interpersonal relations in the community and to shatter the victims' sense of security and identity. More than three-quarters of the women I spoke to told me how they had been raped and feared they had been infected. The attackers also sexually assaulted women with objects such as sharpened sticks or gun barrels, and subjected them to sexual mutilation. Pregnant women and those who had recently given birth were not exempt from rape: the attackers were indiscriminate.

Others died from botched abortions when they learnt they had been made pregnant by their killers. Those who had children by their abusers called them 'children of fate' or 'children of bad memories'. They abandoned them at roadsides or delivered them to orphanages, because they reminded them of their ordeal.

One widow told me, 'I was forced to lie on the ground while still carrying my baby on my back and raped. My other child sat beside me.'

Her husband had been dragged out of their home and killed on the road. She fled with her children and made her way to a school where other refugees had gone to seek sanctuary. Soon the Interahamwe arrived and took her and other women behind the school to rape them.

'I put up a struggle, but the rapist hit me with the back of his machete and pushed me, so that I fell to the ground. He said he wasn't worried about the child I was carrying. He made me lie on my back, on my child, and he raped me. My child was crying, and I tried to hold my weight off the ground so that I did not suffocate him. I twisted sideways, relieving my baby's head so he could breathe. The other men seized hold of the other women and raped them one after another.

'Eventually the Interahamwe left us and with the other women we left the school, but we soon met another group of Interahamwe who were carrying machetes and clubs. They too raped us, while they laid their weapons on the ground next to them.'

Another woman told me how the killers took her dignity away when they undressed her and raped her in front of her children. The Interahamwe attacked her family's home and killed her husband straightaway. She was told to choose between being raped or having her children killed with machetes. They gang raped her and left her almost unable to walk, but she managed to stagger to a neighbour's house for refuge, only to find another horde of killers waving machetes. An Interahamwe man forced her to march towards a mass grave, saying that he was going to kill her and her children to save them from the misery of being a Tutsi.

To the woman's relief, they were intercepted by a soldier who insisted that she was his wife. He took her to his house, which he shared with his mother and two brothers, who were Interahamwe. 'As soon as he got to his house, he took me to his room and raped me. He locked me up in the room so that I would not escape, and left the key with his mother. Every day he went out to murder Tutsis.

'One of his younger brothers came with his bandit comrades. They climbed on top of me and raped me. They did so in front of my children, the eldest of whom was six years old. I was raped many times; so many that I lost count. The soldier didn't know about the situation I was in, and his mother stopped me from telling him for fear that his reaction would aggravate the situation and I would be killed.

'It was humiliating and painful to be raped while my children watched. That really twisted the knife in my heart. My children remind me of the rape but I am so ashamed to talk about it with them.'

As I spent time speaking to these women, I identified a need among the survivors to speak out about their ordeal. I felt that they wanted to tell their stories, first to validate the unbelievable experiences they had endured and miraculously survived, but also to help them make sense of what they had just come through.

I met Gaudence, who was paralysed in the attacks, and she told me her story. She couldn't believe she had survived while everyone else was allowed to die.

'Before the genocide, I was married and had a baby. We were living at Muhima. On 7 April 1994 at 5.30 in the morning we heard on the radio that President Habyarimana was dead. Immediately my husband became terrified and said that he knew the Tutsis would not survive. He went to hide at our neighbours' house, but I stayed at home. My husband was right, and that morning the worst happened. People were herded into a beautiful new big compound near our house to be killed. We could see the killings through the windows of our house. Men armed with machetes and sticks beat people until they dropped down dead. I began to pack things in a suitcase in order to flee that evening. I bathed my baby and dressed him.

'The next day a directive was issued, through the local defence, telling all men to go on neighbourhood security watch. Before leaving, my husband said, "I am going but I'm not sure I will be coming back." Indeed, they did not take long: the men, including my husband, were immediately attacked and killed. I was frightened to stay at home alone, so I went to a lady who was our neighbour. She told me someone had just been killed: it was my husband.

'Before I could gather the details, a very big group of more than thirty killers came to the house and asked, "Where is Alphonse's wife?" "Here I am," I said. "Take us first to your house and give us money," said one of them. "There is no money at home," I answered. They told me to go with them. I was carrying my baby on my back. When we arrived at that beautiful compound, a group of male killers immediately struck me, still with my baby on my back, with whatever they had to hand: machetes, axes, clubs, sticks, swords and spears. I knew that I was going to die and prayed, asking God to forgive me all my sins.

'Then I heard a voice saying, "And this baby who is shouting must be silenced." They hit him just once, and he died immediately. After killing him and leaving me for dead, they closed the gate of the compound and went to bring other people to kill. I heard people crying out in agony, calling for help until one by one they breathed their last. I was badly injured and covered in my own blood, blood from my baby and blood from other people. In fact I didn't know whether I was alive or dead. I took my baby off my back, made a small bed with the clothing I was carrying him in, and put him to lie near his father. I covered him and felt he was safe with his father. It was then that I realised I was not dead. I was the only person in the compound still moving; everyone else was silent because they had died.

'I left the compound without knowing whether I should go home or elsewhere. People saw me and it was a miracle that no one shouted at me. I was covered with blood and my brain had come out of my skull. I was numb and had not begun to feel pain. Then I saw a lady staring at me and I asked her if she could take me to her house. She was my neighbour and a wife of one of the men who had tried to kill me in the compound. She shouted to her husband to come and finish me off. The husband came and said, "If it is this one, I know that she is going to die very soon. I will not waste my energy on her." He left me.

'I continued walking aimlessly and saw a boy. I asked him to hide me at his house. There were many people hidden there and when they saw me they were afraid. I too was shocked to see them and I fainted. When the boy's father came, he found me in the house and, thinking I was dead, put me in a small building where they kept turkeys.

'I heard people come to the turkey house and debate whether I was dead, but I couldn't move, let alone speak. They forced some tea down my throat, and I swallowed a little. They kept giving me tea and the following day I regained full consciousness. Then they told me that they were planning to leave, and so they had to find another place for me. I was too weak to go anywhere. The boy's grandmother had a house nearby behind their compound, and the next evening they broke down the fence that separated the houses and took me to her. She was poor and there was no light in her house. When she saw me, she was afraid because she said I looked like an animal. I told her I had been asked to come to her and hide because I was too weak to go anywhere else. She took some pieces of wood and made a fire. Then she cleaned me, put me in some of her clothes, and dressed the wound on my head where my brain was exposed with a piece of cloth. When she gave me food, I could not lift my arm to eat. She saw milk coming out of my breast and asked me if I was pregnant or had had a baby. I said, "I have left my baby with his father, where they were killed." She was very sad at this.

'In the morning, she washed my clothes, which were covered with blood, and tried to take me to the dispensary. There were roadblocks everywhere and Tutsis were being killed left, right and centre. People were crying in pain while others were singing and dancing every time a Tutsi fell and died. The old lady waited until evening and asked a soldier who was their neighbour to take me to the dispensary. He came with his car and took me in with the old lady and two of her grandsons. The old woman put clothes over my stomach and pretended I was pregnant and in labour. Whenever we reached a roadblock, the soldier said he was taking his pregnant wife who was about to give birth. We arrived at the dispensary; I was admitted and they covered my wounds. My rescuers left me there, promising to come back to visit me.

'Many people had taken refuge at the dispensary. Then the Interahamwe came to kill the people there. Everyone else left, including the in-patients. I immediately felt as though I had died again; I cannot say that I was sleeping; it was as if I was dead. After some days (I don't know how long I lay in the valley of death), one of the dispensary workers came to me and recognised me. He went and informed my husband's relatives. They didn't come to my rescue, nor did the dispensary worker. I stayed at the hospital and lost count of the days. My body, which had wounds and injuries everywhere, began to rot. There were maggots infesting my head, my face and other places where I had been injured, and I smelt bad. It was at that time that I learnt the difference between body and spirit. The body was completely dead but my spirit was still alive inside that rotting body.

'Then I began to reflect. "I thought I was still alive but I realise I am dead. Is this how all the dead people are? Do they see their bodies?" A miracle had happened to me because I had not eaten for days; I learnt that one can live without eating. I prayed to God to lift my spirit out of my maggot-ridden body. I don't know how, but most of the maggots disappeared, except in my head and on my right hip, where the wounds were exceedingly deep and open. Other dispensary workers came to watch me die, refusing to treat me. They could see my eyes were open, looking at them.

'More maggots surrounded me where I was lying; they had made a trail from my body to the ground. The dispensary workers put on rubber boots and gloves and pulled me outside, so that they could clean the room. They did not lift me up but instead dragged me across the ground like a dead animal. While I was outside, it rained and it was good for me because I found water to drink, although it was painful because I could not move my arms and was forced to drink like an animal.

'When they had finished cleaning the room, they pulled me back in again, but after some time the maggots came back. The workers cleaned the room again and this time shaved my hair with a brand new razor blade. They discovered that my head was full of wounds, which they disinfected, and they tried to give me porridge, saying, "Tutsis are special. They die and come back to life. But let's see what will happen to this person." After I was treated I tried to sit up, but my right side was completely paralysed. It was as if I had no right arm, no right leg and no right side. People, especially children, would come to see me through the glass in the door. They had never seen anything that looked like me locked up in a room.

'I was very thirsty and whenever I heard somebody passing I shouted for them to bring me water, but no one did. Then I heard the sound of many boots, so I shouted loudly, "You people!" One worker came and told me to be quiet because it was soldiers looking for Tutsis to kill and they would shoot me. But I kept shouting. Some soldiers came and saw me, a dead body who could not even move. "How are you?" they asked me. "I have been locked up in this room and they won't let me out," I said. The soldiers ordered the workers to open the room.

'When the soldiers saw me they had pity. But the workers thought that they were going to kill me. "When did this lady come here?" asked the soldiers. "On 9 April," replied one of the workers. "What does she eat?" they asked. I shouted that they had refused to give me water and tried to crawl to them, begging them to kill me. I tried to go out but the soldiers pushed me back into the room and angrily ordered the workers to find me some food. They said that if I died they would be in trouble.

'A dispensary worker brought water in a five-litre jerry can and I drank it as if I had stolen it, fearing that they would stop me drinking. They gave me food once a day but because my arms were not functioning I could only eat with my mouth like an animal. After nearly two weeks I was able to sit despite my injuries, and the dispensary workers said this meant that I would not die. They stopped giving me food and water and I left the dispensary. As I could not walk, I crawled slowly along the ground like a reptile and eventually arrived at a road. I continued and came to a place where aubergines were planted. When I saw children passing, I asked them to give me some aubergines to eat. I continued crawling and when I got to the main road, people came to see me because I was something interesting to watch. Even the Interahamwe came to look at me, but no one could kill me because no one kills a dead person.

'Then one soldier came along, and when he saw me he said, "This thing is making our town dirty. Let me kill and remove this dirt." He took his gun and loaded it, but immediately a colleague of his came running, took his arm and said, "Can't you find people to kill? Is this someone to kill? Do you want to put this one on the list of those you killed?" He left me. Then it started to rain heavily and the people left me alone in the rain. When it stopped they returned and took me back to the dispensary. It was difficult to carry me. When the workers saw me, they insulted me because they hadn't given me the authorisation to discharge myself. They tried forcing me back into my old room, but I didn't want to go in. I wanted them to kill me and end my misery, but they couldn't.

'I crawled back to the main road, hoping to meet angry Interahamwe who would kill me. Some ladies saw me, took pity on me and told me where I was. I saw many cars carrying Red Cross workers, and I hoped one might stop and show mercy towards me, but none did. Some stopped, came to look at me, retched and carried on. From morning to evening I waited by the road, cars passing by and leaving me there. Then late in the evening some policemen passed and one hit me with his gun. I looked at him and recognised him; he used to come to my house because he knew my father. When he hit me for the second time, I asked him why he was beating me if he knew my father. He became afraid and they left me. I decided to cross the road where there was a house and a lady who recognised me from sitting by the road. She took pity on me and gave me a sweet potato. Then she took me into her kitchen and made a fire for me. I lay down by the embers and had a nice sleep.

'The lady's husband came early the next morning and told me to go back to the road because he didn't want anyone to see me in the house. I escaped yet again through their back door onto a rough lane, stones entering my wounds all along the way. When I reached the road, my body was covered in blood. Some people saw me who recognised me from the dispensary. They wondered how I had managed to get there. A man came with his wife, cleaned my wounds, took me to a valley nearby and left me out in the sun. I was like an exhibit and people exclaimed, "That woman who was at the dispensary is now in the valley!" People came to see me.

'Later on that day, the militia came and the good man told them to spare me. In the evening a little girl came and told me her mother said that if I went to their house they would give me food. They lived up the hill, but I could not climb it as I could not walk and my whole body was covered with wounds. I tried to crawl up but it was impossible. I asked people passing by to take me up, explaining that someone there had said she would give me food, but they refused. A soldier who had a Bible in his hand passed and I asked him to carry me. He said he couldn't because the other soldiers would kill him if they saw him doing it. But he did give me 200 francs to give to the children to go and buy me a drink. When he left me, some other soldiers came and asked me what we had been talking about. I was surprised when they all came and helped him carry me. They were frightened in case anyone saw them helping me so they left me near the house. I called the woman's children and told them to tell their mother that I had made it up the hill.

'The mother sent her daughters to bring me in. She heated some water and they washed me and took all the maggots away. The mother gave me some clothes and brought a mattress into a room in a small house behind hers that also had a kitchen. They began to take care of me. They brought me food and after eating I slept.

'It was a very hard time when the remaining Tutsis were aggressively hunted down. The woman's husband was a Hutu but she was a Tutsi and could not go out. The militia came every day to see whether any Tutsis were hidden in houses, but they did not come to the small house where I was for some time. Then one day they did come. I saw them opening the door and entering my room. They looked everywhere but didn't say anything; I don't know whether they saw me or not. The lady hadn't told her husband that I was there, but she thought that now she should. Her husband was sorry for me but was afraid that the militia would come and kill them. He told his wife that she had to take me to another place. She came and told me that she was going to move me but that she would continue to take care of me. She took me to a neighbouring house where the owners had fled. She continued to feed me and to do everything she used to do for me. After some time, I got better and could even get to the toilet outside on my own.

'The RPF had come but we did not know. Then one day, there was an indescribable noise of guns. The following day, I waited for my food as normal but nobody came. After a long time a child came across and said that her mother had told me to come with her. She ran off but when I got outside I could not see her. I went to the family's house but it was closed up and even the curtains were drawn. Nobody was there, not even a bird. I saw many bullets. Then I prayed and asked God where I should go, and at that moment I saw an RPF soldier. He called me and told me to join a group of people down the hill where I would get treatment.'

As I listened to Gaudence, my mind was racing with emotion. I couldn't bring her family back, but I promised myself I would get her treated. Later I raised some money and sent her to South Africa, where she had surgery and, after a year of physiotherapy, began walking normally.

I could to some extent try and address physical injuries, but the invisible injuries were far from my reach. The more stories I heard the more determined I became to help these women rebuild their lives, even if just making them feel valued by listening. So in their numbers they told me the stories of the families they lost when they were escaping, to see if anyone knew where they had fallen or had any information about them. Slowly I became a catalyst for women wanting to share their experiences in a safe environment, among people who shared their views and would not judge them.

'A violent death would have been quicker,' one widow told me. 'At least it would have been over and at least we would have gone with our families. Instead, we are here. But it's as if we do not exist. We are forgotten by everyone, abandoned and extremely lonely. Worse still, we do not feel as if anyone understands our problems, how we feel, our pain and sorrow.'

The more I got involved in AVEGA, the more I noticed how the distinctions between trauma, poverty, ill health and destitution were becoming blurred. AVEGA was providing a facilitating role. The number of widows increased beyond its capacity to meet their needs. I hadn't experienced the genocide; I could only imagine the horror, so I would listen, trying to make sense of, and reflect on, what I was hearing. Being welcome in the circles of AVEGA was a privilege and an honour.

Despite their ordeal the widows were bustling with energy. Within six months they embarked on setting up outstations where widows could meet to find mutual support. Following on from my meeting with Angélique and Jacqueline, an army of volunteers appeared. They all spoke from their hearts about their experiences, expressing their stories powerfully and with authenticity.

AVEGA then started a campaign to encourage widows in different regions to form their own associations. I advised AVEGA to register officially, to give it credibility and to elucidate the shared aims and objectives that would help to forge a common advocacy for widows. I was aware that fundraising would be difficult for a newly formed organisation with no track record, but nonetheless I was determined to solicit support to rebuild their lives.

With my energy and experience, and the drive from the women, AVEGA was registered as a charity. Its headquarters in Kigali acted as a springboard for other AVEGA associations to develop nationwide. It became a national voice and a channel of expression. Its first task was to lobby the government to change the law so women could inherit their husband's property, and it also embarked on a major house-building programme.

But AVEGA's biggest task was to find ways in which the women themselves could own any development initiative, as many were still in shock after the genocide, they were homeless, and they also faced the task of locating if possible and reburying their loved ones. Many had physical injuries that disabled them. Almost all the women I spoke to had been raped and were afraid they had been infected with HIV. I didn't think they had a future and sometimes felt like there was no prospect of recovery.

Listening alone was not enough. I needed to reassure the survivors that I would tell their stories so that I could garner support to meet their needs. I assured them any action I took would be valid because I fully understood their point of view, their pain, fears, aspirations and sometimes helplessness. They gave me their trust to speak on their behalf, to recount their stories to different groups of people including donors in Rwanda, so as to raise awareness, educate and seek financial support for the association's programmes.

In order to give more widows a voice, AVEGA supported an active listening programme run by the widows themselves. At the time the whole of AVEGA had only one counsellor. The actual healing process was provided through these collective therapeutic sessions, which helped to create a missing community network and safety net. Here widows came together to share personal experiences covering a broader spectrum of issues, ranging from psychological problems to material needs. Group therapy relieved the grief and stress of everyday life; a problem shared became a problem halved. It created rapport between survivors, encouraging them to come forward to a one-to-one session if needed.

The genocide aimed to annihilate the entire Tutsi community and to dehumanise them. It was difficult for me to imagine that someone hated them so much that they wanted to get rid of them in this most barbaric way. These widows had no words to express their experiences; they felt that no one would believe them. The group sessions helped validate the fact that they were alive and also helped them to develop new words and expressions – a new language to describe the genocide and its aftermath. For instance, in Kinyarwanda, there was no word for 'genocide', which became *itsembatsemba*, or 'trauma', which became *guhahamuka*.

FIFTEEN

Lives without history

FINDING MY BROTHER'S children alive, spending time with them whenever I could, left me wondering what happened to other children, especially sole survivors of entire families.

During the months of April, May and June 1994, thousands of Rwandan children witnessed unspeakable violence and brutality. Their parents and siblings had their throats slit in front of them, mothers and sisters raped before being killed. Many barely lived before their histories were wiped away.

Fearful of the killers who returned to massacre sites to finish off the wounded, children, often hungry and thirsty, hid under the rotting bodies of their parents and other relatives. They watched as dogs devoured the bodies of the people who had loved and protected them. Many of the murderers were men and women whose children were their playmates. They saw other children among them killing, their peers and friends raising machetes to kill them or their families. Many as young as three were raped and humiliated. They emerged from the genocide frenzy with no support system or family to fall back on, often frightened, needing immediate treatment from stab wounds and infections. The physical scars on their little bodies, legs, arms and fingers missing, ears cut off, spoke for themselves. Some had experienced sexual, mental and physical abuse. The scale of their suffering and the invisible damage was unimaginable.

Yvonne, aged seven, survived with her mother; I met her at one of the meetings I used to attend in the evening after work. She had witnessed the Interahamwe slay her father. Over the hundred days, she saw many people killed in the most brutal way. She became separated from her mother when the Interahamwe smoked them out of a bush where they were hiding. She was taken by a man who claimed she was his daughter. She was grateful because the man looked like her father and she thought he felt pity for her. When he got her home he raped her and told her she would have to do as she was told otherwise he would kill her.

He took her when he wanted and did what he wanted to. She couldn't walk but he didn't stop. When she cried, he mocked her: 'Did you really think I was your father?' For months, Yvonne's ordeal was repeated until this man abandoned her and fled to Zaire.

'I went to find food and met some local boys, and they brought me back to the house and raped me too,' she told me. 'The worst thing is that I didn't even know what they were doing to me.'

She was subject to abuse for several weeks until she was rescued by RPF soldiers. She found her mother after the genocide but it was months later before she could tell her mother about her ordeal. Her mother too had been raped, and she also found it hard to talk about her ordeal to her young daughter.

Sometimes I wanted to ask children more about their stories, but I feared their depiction of the sights, smells, and sounds of human destruction that they had been forced to witness, never mind the descriptions of the deaths of their family and friends.

I can't remember who told me about Valentina, a miracle child who survived in a church where 3,000 people were murdered. One rainy day, a few months after the genocide, I drove for six hours to meet Valentina in her home village in Nyarubuye, south of Kigali.

I set off, stopping first at AVEGA's office to pick up a social worker, and drove for about forty minutes along a smooth tarmac road, before we turned onto a bumpy, steep-sided brown dusty track. The dust filled the car, and as we went along it covered crowds of small barefoot children in blue uniform going to school. After some time the social worker pointed out a group of men to me, about thirty or more, wearing pink uniforms, clearing land. 'Those are our butchers,' she said. 'They have nothing to lose. They work and get some money, receive three meals a day and their wives visit them. The state is looking after them while we survivors are invisible.' A short distance later we came to where Valentina lived. The social worker led the way to the house. Valentina was quick to recognise her, and she ran and embraced her.

Valentina lived with an aunt. She was expecting me and gave me a warm welcome, then introduced me to her new family. She had a beautiful nature, very polite and attentive. She was very excited to have visitors come to see her. She told me an American had visited a few weeks before, and showed me a scrap book which the American had given her, with her photos and testimony.

Valentina spoke with her gaze fixed on the floor, occasionally raising her head slightly and smiling shyly. She was a modest young girl who didn't want to attract attention to herself. We were in a sitting room, where it was quiet and slightly dark, the curtains half drawn. On the wall there was a photo of her aunt's family, taken before the genocide. There were two worn-out brown sofas, some side tables, a bench and a dining table at the rear of the room. The table and chairs were covered with matching multi-coloured crochets. The house was old, but neat.

Sitting on the bench opposite me, she told her cousins to play outside so we could speak in private. 'Sorry, the kids are so fond of me, but I don't want them to hear my story. They are too young to understand,' Valentina apologised.

'How old are they?'

'Four, six and seven. I like them – they keep me busy and amused. I feel like I am a few years older. I just celebrated my birthday, two months ago.'

'Happy belated birthday,' I said. 'Did you make a wish?'

'Yes,' she replied, 'and I got it.'

'Congratulations! Am I allowed to ask—'

Before I could finish the sentence, she raised her left hand and picked up a pen and a pad that were lying on a side table. 'I have finally managed to write using my left hand.'

Valentina had two fingers on her left hand, but I noticed she had none on her right hand. She told me her fingers had been chopped off when she raised her hands to protect her head from machete blows. 'I think I had a mental block,' she said. 'Every time I tried to write and failed, I hated myself. I remembered my fingers and felt angry.'

She paused, and wrote her name on the pad. 'Sometimes, when I am practising writing, my mind goes back to the church. I see machetes, I hear screams and I see blood, then the pencil slips through my fingers.'

As I watched Valentina writing, I couldn't think of what to say. I praised her for being brave, and told her I liked her handwriting. She smiled and kept scribbling something on the pad. I sat quietly, sensing she was relaxed and wanted to tell me her story.

'The killing began on a Friday afternoon. The day after President Habyarimana's death was announced, fires were burning in the neighbourhood. On 12 April we heard that one of our Tutsi neighbours had been attacked and murdered. We knew what this meant for us Tutsis. We fled to the church in Nyarubuye with my family.'

This is where, as her parents told her, Tutsis had found sanctuary in previous attacks in the 1950s, 1960s and 1970s. They arrived to find that the priests had left. They had no food or water but at least they had shelter and they were safe. Or so they thought. There were many refugees arriving with horrific stories of massacres of Tutsis; some had been injured. It was a frightening experience.

Valentina's aunt entered the room, apologised for interrupting and handed me a traditional wooden jug full of warm milk. I politely accepted it and thanked her. As she left the room Valentina continued.

'At three o'clock on the afternoon of 15 April the killers arrived, led by the mayor. I recognised many of our neighbours among the Interahamwe who were surrounding the church. They carried knives and clubs and were supported by soldiers. Soon the church was encircled and the militia were shooting at everyone. Inside the church it was chaos as everyone ran around screaming, trying to find a place to hide. Originally I had been with my mother and brother but we became separated in the hysteria that ensued.'

She stopped speaking for a while and apologised because she still missed her brother, who was four years old.

'I heard the sound of gunshots. Some people ran as soon as they heard the fighting but they were immediately gunned down and killed by the Interahamwe. First they asked people to hand over their money, saying they would spare those who paid. But after taking the money they killed them anyway. They took off their clothes, leaving them naked, and then they started to throw grenades. I saw a man blown up into the air, in pieces, by a grenade. The leader of the Interahamwe said we were snakes and to kill snakes you have to smash their heads. The killers then entered the church, hacking and clubbing as they entered. If they found someone alive they would smash their heads with stones.'

Valentina's expression changed, she moved her hands restlessly and lowered her voice, her breathing getting faster and faster. I asked her if she wanted to stop. 'You don't have to tell me anything.

I came to see you and to tell you how sorry I am, for your family and your experience.'

'I want to tell you about this young boy,' she said, raising her voice slightly. 'The mayor called out, "If anyone is hiding in this church because of a mistake, because he or she is a Hutu, they should tell me now." After a few seconds a boy of about seven or eight stood up. "I am a Hutu," he said. Of course everyone knew he wasn't, and two Interahamwe soldiers ran forward and beat him with machetes so fiercely that his body went flying up in the air and came down in several pieces. I saw the killers take little children and smash their heads together until they were dead.'

I could tell she was at the scene in the church, replaying the killing and massacres she witnessed. She fixed her gaze in one place and spoke with great concentration, as if she was speaking to someone other than me. I had seen similar expressions with other survivors, when they would lower their voice and sometimes fall into a spasm or collapse in the middle of a story.

Three days into the killing, Valentina was still unharmed. She had managed to slip under a pile of dead bodies and had been left for dead. On this day another group of killers and soldiers came, led by neighbour and a friend of her family. She knew one of the soldiers, whom she begged, 'Can you find it in your heart to forgive me for being a Tutsi?'

He spat at her and said, 'I'm not going to smear myself with your blood. I'm going to ask someone else to kill you.' He gestured to another neighbour.

'I'm going to kill you,' this neighbour said, and Valentina put up her hands to protect her head from his machete. Then he began smashing her hands with a clubbed stick, so that her fingers were broken and her skull bled. The pain was terrible. After that he beat her some more on the shoulders and then again on her head, which was agonising. Soon the pain was so great that she knew no more.

When she awoke, still lying in a pool of blood in the compound, Valentina saw some soldiers dragging out people who were still alive. She saw her sister among them, who was badly hurt. They only looked at each other and couldn't speak. The soldiers hit her with machetes and clubs until she lay still. That was the last time Valentina saw her alive.

Later that evening when the Interahamwe had gone home, she crawled back into the church to hide among the dead bodies. She found her mother's body and lay next to it for some time – she didn't know how long. During the course of the killing she had seen the militia kill her father, her mother, her sister and her younger brother.

She had been speaking to me for nearly two hours, giving a detailed account of the smell, the colour and the horrifying images of this scene from hell. I sat silently, holding back tears of pain and grief.

The memory of this tragedy was too raw and painful; Valentina excused herself and left the room. I stole a moment to let my tears flow. I felt helpless and angry. I had to do something but I couldn't think what. Her story was so painful that I developed a headache and mental strain as I listened.

Valentina returned, forcing a smile. 'I'm OK now, we can continue.'

She had left the room to weep for her brother. She didn't have to tell me. I could see she had been crying – her eyes were red. She didn't seem to notice I had been crying too and had suppressed my tears when she entered the room.

Valentina told me she watched as the dead bodies changed colour to greenish yellow and then dark blue, turning into skeletons. She lay among the rotting corpses for forty-three days without food and only holy water or rainwater to drink. She became too weak to stand up, convinced that the world had come to an end.

When we met, Valentina had just turned twelve, but she felt much older, she told me. I couldn't agree more; no twelve-year-old could tell a story so horrific with dignity and calm. As I listened to her, lost for words, silently tormented by her painful memories, she buried her head under a maroon cardigan she was wearing and blew her nose so hard that I thought she had cracked the veins in her head.

It was getting late in the afternoon. I told her I had to leave before it got dark.

'Please come back to see me,' she said. Then she began to tell me about a dream that she often had.

'I see my mother dressed up in white like an angel. She visits every night. I show her my injuries and tell her my younger brother is dead. But what disturbs me is, every day I promise myself to ask her where she is, yet I don't. I would like to know where she is, I miss her so much,' she told me. 'I like to sleep so I can see my mother.'

One thing that keeps this young girl from a daily reminder of the horrors she went through is a chance to see her mother.

'She is a guardian angel and lives in heaven,' I told her. With a shy girlish smile, she thanked me and told me I reminded her of her mother. There was an answer for me: I would be a mother to Valentina, give her love and support her, I thought as I bid her goodbye.

On my way home, I let streams of tears flow freely; I felt exhausted, hungry and thirsty. I even forgot my original reason for travelling there, why I was so keen to see her. I don't know if I wanted to hear her story so I could help her, or just so that I could believe that children were not spared. I wanted to scream and ask God, why let children go through this ordeal? I had no answers and I needed help to do something, otherwise their stories and their lives would have no meaning. As time went on, I felt a need to live these children's lives, to remember their pain and draw energy from it, so that it would enable me to make sure that they and their stories are never forgotten.

They told me how they had survived the genocide, pulled alive from heaps of corpses, or how they had been found wandering alone through deserted streets. Stories of how they had survived by hiding in cupboards or in bushes, unable to do anything when their families were massacred. Their stories were filled with fear and suffering, both emotionally and physically. Every child had been marked for destruction simply because he or she was a Tutsi.

For many children, revisiting memories was a big challenge. They preferred the solitude of silence, to protect themselves from the pain and grief that they carried every day. Some didn't know how to describe or interpret what they had gone through. They hadn't mastered the art of description or speech; their world had collapsed when they had barely lived.

SIXTEEN

Lost a family, gained a daughter

WHILE STILL WORKING with the Ministry of Rehabilitation, I began to meet some of the parents who were looking for and registering missing children in their thousands every day. Children looking for missing parents registered too, in the hope that their families would find them. Many of the children then in Rwanda's orphanages needed to be reunited with any surviving relatives or families. Sometimes there were success stories, children reunited with a mother who had survived. In many cases, though, there was no news of loved ones.

I had registered some NGOs that were involved in family tracing; they were overwhelmed by the numbers of children involved. Not all younger children, babies in particular, benefited from family reunification, yet they were the most vulnerable. Many had changed tremendously in appearance, some completely malnourished, and they were dying fast. Of course, babies could not identify their parents, and no one knew their names or where they came from. Within six months of the genocide, more children were dead than reunited.

Groups of social workers were sent out to communities to look for missing parents. Relatives and families were transported in large numbers to the seventy orphanages spread across the country in a bid to find their children. This was a lengthy and costly process. Meanwhile there were four major international humanitarian organisations involved in tracing but they acted independently of one another, often having the same list of children and reuniting one child with more than one set of relatives. Sometimes they showed little understanding of the nature of genocide, leaving children in the care of neighbours who had killed their families.

I had a chance to visit an orphanage with one of the agencies and that altered my life forever. It was heartbreaking for me to meet these children, and leave them in these overcrowded institutions, unloved, waiting to see someone they recognised come through the gates. I made several more visits and every time I would witness the anguish, the wish for a miracle to find even one relative alive. I had seen children come to register who could not make sense of when and where they separated from their families. Some were too young even to know their parents' names; they just called them Mama and Papa.

There was an announcement on the radio asking any Rwandan in a position to help to take care of orphans. The government was appealing to Rwandan citizens to act as guardians to these children, either by providing support at the orphanage or by temporarily placing children in the care of able families. Many people responded to this call, myself among them.

One of the conditions was to make the child available in case a family member gave a description that fitted the child you were looking after, or in case the organisations tracing families found someone who recognised the child among the many photos they had displayed for identification. These organisations recorded names of parents, location where the child lived before the genocide, and where they last saw their parents. Every two weeks the photographs of these children would be retaken and centrally displayed for anyone to check if their child was among those posted.

I spoke to the charity that was hosting me, also involved in family tracing; I needed to know the process of placement and family identification. I also wanted to know what the chances were that anyone would recognise a baby after six months. I was told that babies develop fast in the first nine months, and apart from its mother, it would be difficult for anyone, even siblings, to remember the baby if it was less than three months old at the time of the genocide. Many of the babies were undernourished and sick, which reduced the chances even further. Another difficulty was the use of photos. Some parents were likely to find it difficult to recognise their baby in a photo because of the way it was clothed, or because they might never have had a chance to take their baby's photo and would not recognise it in that form.

I resolved to visit an orphanage and support a baby, giving any help needed, albeit on a temporary basis, but without considering adoption. I discussed the placement with my husband Richard, who was very supportive, and he sent me some money.

I approached the Foyers des Hirondelles orphanage to see if they had a child who needed special attention and whose parents or relatives could not be traced. I was taken to see a little boy, possibly five months old, who had a high fever and was slipping in and out of a coma. I filled a huge number of forms about myself, and I was assigned a social worker who checked my records. I asked if I could take the baby for treatment, due to the bureaucracy involved, but the orphanage would not release him into my care. I left to wait for the personal checks to be carried out. A few days later I was informed, a day after the baby had been buried, that he had died of pneumonia.

I blamed myself for the baby's death. I was distraught with grief and visited the orphanage to find out what had happened. The staff took me to his small grave at Kigali cemetery. I stood gazing across the valley, covered with grey and white gravestones. There were many new graves, and some people nearby were digging yet another grave for another victim. The little boy lay among strangers, surrounded by people unknown to me. I felt sick to my stomach. How could I not have protected him? What was I to do to give him a good send-off? I paid for a headstone to be put on his grave, but what would be written on it? 'Name, not known; born, not known; son of, not known.' The only accurate information was his gender and his death record. I never got to know the little boy; I never saw the details about him that would have been released when I was ready to take him home. I don't even remember his name; if I was told it, I must have blocked my brain from registering the fact – with the pain of losing him, his name must have disappeared somewhere deep in my memory. All I could remember was his light skin, a large head that didn't seem to match his small body and the light blue jumper he was dressed in even though he had high temperature.

On his tiny grave I laid a heart-shaped wreath with a central white rose, surrounded by rich eucalyptus foliage. A red ribbon read, 'RIP, from my heart, Mary.' I wished he were safe somewhere; I could not save him now. Meanwhile other children were dying and I needed to save one. I went back to the orphanage and asked to support another child who they thought would not make it. The director told me he had five critical cases. How was I to choose?

It took two weeks to get an approval letter and referrals from the Ministry of Social Affairs allowing me to take a child home for treatment. The procedure was relatively easy for me because I was already known to the ministry. I was aware how difficult it would be to temporarily take on a child, but I prayed that the parents of these children had survived and the family would be reunited.

I didn't want to choose a child myself, so I asked for the baby who was most at risk of dying of hunger or one who was sick and needed immediate help. It didn't matter whether it was a boy or a girl. I felt the need to help one child at least, even if I couldn't reunite them with their families. But first, I had to spend a day at an orphanage, a day in the life of an orphan. This was not a requirement for the placement, but I wanted to learn the routine a child was accustomed to, so as to minimise the disruption and make the transition stable for him or her.

It was a Monday in May. I struggled to contain my anxiety as, through the early morning mist, the spring sun shone on Kimihurura English School, where some 200 or more orphans were getting ready for breakfast. The orphanage was housed, as the name suggests, in an old school in the middle of Kigali. Rectangular blocks faced each other, separated by a bare compound with beds of withering flowers. The compound was dotted with large eucalyptus trees that provided shade for children escaping the burning rays of the sun.

There were hundreds of children, in different age groups, dressed in old but clean dresses or multi-coloured shirts, but with bare feet. Many wore oversized sweaters, not entirely appropriate for a hot sunny day. They stood and stared, snot falling from their little noses, or with some dried white greasy substance stuck on their cheeks. The older orphans were paired with younger ones. There were not enough adults around – only a handful of carers or matrons, as they were called by the children. So older and younger orphans looked after each other. Some of the older girls were carrying young babies, carefully knotted with an African cloth, on their bent backs.

There were children everywhere, some playing, chasing each other around, others standing and watching, unable to decide which group to join. They were speaking at the tops of their voices, sometimes all at once. They seemed no different from any other children, except they were orphans and some had just seen things no children should see, their safe world shattered. They had escaped the violence and brutal murders, but they had been subjected to the trauma of witnessing the torture and murder of family and friends, and the vengeful and sadistic systematic rape of half a million girls and young women.

In a far corner, a group of young girls were bathing some smaller children with plastic buckets under the hot sun, scooping up water in their hands and splashing it over their little bodies. They jumped up in fright, but laughed and came back for more. It was obvious they were enjoying the coolness of the water against their warm bodies.

Then a boy of about fifteen years seized a chain attached to a bell, which was dangling from a tree. Another boy joined him and as they tugged rhythmically at it the bell begun pealing. Instantly the jostling, hubbub, racing and fighting stopped. The children rushed in different directions around the compound, the smaller ones making their way towards the front of one of the buildings, where an aroma of maize porridge was coming from. It was a dining room and it overlooked the director's office.

The children ate in shifts because there were not enough plates and utensils to go round and not enough seating places either. The younger ones went first, lining up in an orderly manner not normally seen in such small children. There was no pushing; they were hungry and were focused on getting their share for the day. Some of them noticed me and I smiled or winked. Some shyly looked away, others remained expressionless and occasionally one winked back.

I could hear sounds of singing in an adjacent room where some of the other children were waiting their turn to eat. The children had split up into several groups, each under the watchful eye of a matron, and were waiting in their dormitories. These rooms, converted from the original classrooms, had large windows and the matrons passed in and out of vision, chants breaking out from different parts of each building, or what sounded like poems.

I was standing next to the director's office; he was running late but had sent a message to say he was on his way.

Each child was handed a bowl of maize porridge and three small sweet bananas. They sat in rows on benches, quickly eating before the next group lined up to be served. I watched their hungry mouths, their tongues licking the plates clean. I felt they needed bigger portions, but they knew they couldn't have more. They moved on and the next group went through the same routine. There were around fifteen sittings, possibly more.

I noticed one little boy, about four years old, crying for his mother. His sister, aged six or so, was trying to comfort him. 'Don't cry, Manzi ["brave soldier", a Kinyarwanda word]. Mama will come back.' She pulled him up and with her small hand she wiped away his tears. I wanted to take them home with me. But there were more like him.

Among all the children was a woman rocking back and forth, her face puffy, her eyes red, stricken with grief. She tightened an African wrap firmly around her waist, which was so small it seemed like she hadn't eaten for days. I couldn't tell how old she was – in her thirties, perhaps, or even her forties. I stopped to listen to her. She said she was weeping for her three children, because she couldn't find them. She had been visiting all the orphanages hoping to find her children, but they were not here, just as they hadn't been at any of the others.

Drowning in a morass of pain and helplessness, I silently looked away to avoid eye contact. Here was a mother mourning her children among children waiting for their mothers.

The director of the orphanage eventually invited me to his office. He spoke to me about the condition of the children at his orphanage, saying that he couldn't get enough food for the children. He had just been speaking to the World Food Programme (WFP) but they did not have enough supplies. A UK-based charity had donated sweaters knitted by volunteers in Britain. That explained why most children were dressed in winter woollies on a hot sunny day.

He told me about a baby girl aged between four and six months, who had been very ill. He was not sure she would survive. He said a young girl had brought her to the International Committee of the Red Cross (ICRC) in Kigali during the genocide and left her there, claiming the baby was an orphan. She was then brought to this orphanage after the genocide; there was no record of her origins. They knew neither her name nor her age. I was ready to love and keep her with me, away from the orphanage. I wanted her better.

I told him I would take her and get her treated; if she died, she would die with my love. I would mourn her as my own and give her a decent send-off.

The director summoned a matron, who walked me to a room full of babies, some crying, others staring up at the ceiling, their tiny eyes wide open as though trying to make sense of what was going on. I couldn't look at the little faces buried in baby cots, like animals in cages. I fixed my eyes on the back of the matron's head, now walking ahead of me. I feared remembering the babies' faces, and leaving them to their fate.

We passed about twelve wooden cots; they were in rows on both sides of the room. The matron stopped at one baby, who was crying at the top of her voice. When we approached, she tried to turn but couldn't; she seemed too weak to move. But she kept crying, her voice getting louder and louder as we got closer to her cot. Matron called out, 'Nyiragasazi' ('little crazy one', another Kinyarwanda word). The little girl tried to turn again but could not move.

It was difficult to tell her age. Her skin was dry, scaly and wrinkled. Her head was bare, with sunken temples and the back of her head had a big wound, I thought from lying in the cot for days and days. Her nails were brittle and overgrown, but she had beautiful big eyes, the only part of her that seemed alive.

When I picked her up, I couldn't let go of her. She gazed motionless into my eyes as if to say 'Why me?' She stopped crying and stared directly into my eyes. I thought for just a second that she seemed to be communicating her world to me. I could not interpret her gesture, her gaze, but I felt a deep connection.

I sat through the matron's explanations of what she liked or didn't like, her daily routine, bath time, eating habits and ill health. Nyiragasazi had been poorly for months and had lost her appetite. She woke up at five o'clock in the morning, earlier than all the other babies, and yelled until someone picked her up. If she was not picked up quickly, she woke the whole dormitory and soon all of them would join her cry for attention. She didn't like eating anything at all, and meal time was battle time. To get her to eat, you had to distract her and shove some food down her month with a small spoon. If you were lucky she would swallow some but most likely she would spit it all back. Her breakfast was rice with milk. She looked as though she could be as young as three months and I wondered if she would not do better with pureed food, but I didn't say anything. The matron said she would miss Nyiragasazi. Apparently when she felt better she made wheezing noises and she squeezed her nose in a gesture that made everyone laugh.

Meanwhile, breakfast was over. The sun beat down and the children had split into different groups, some playing games and racing around the compound, others picking up litter, sweeping the paths, clipping the lawns and weeding the flower beds.

I visited the orphanage twice more and spent time with Nyiragasazi. Later that week, I was ready to take her. I agreed to keep the orphanage informed of her health. I also had to take photos, which they displayed at the orphanage in case someone, a family member, came looking for her.

First of all I took Nyiragasazi to a private doctor, a renowned paediatrician in the city. My best friend Joe gave me a lift. It was a depressing afternoon when we arrived, worsened by my state of mind and the sickly hospital environment. I wished I could help all the babies I had left behind. I also wished Richard was around to help me take care of her. I had no direct communication with him, because there were no phones. Once in a while he called through to the charity that was hosting me, but I had no chance to update him on what I was going through. How was I going to manage alone with a very sick baby in Rwanda? It consoled me to know that Richard junior was lucky to have love and care, back in Ethiopia. I wished I could call them to tell them about Nyiragasazi.

Anxious to see the doctor, all the patients were crowded around the door to his room. I sat on a bench with my back firmly pressed against the wall, the baby on my lap. The room was quite cold, I remember clearly. Before me in a disorganised queue were women standing alongside their children, with sunken or swollen cheeks, and some were also sitting on a bench in the corridor. There were a handful of male and female doctors and nurses.

Nyiragasazi was now asleep, peacefully purring like a cat on my lap. Judging by the length of the queue it would be a while before I saw a doctor. I gazed outside through a large window at some purple flowers, blowing freely in the wind, and wondered about the baby's family. Who was her mother, her father? Did she have sisters and brothers somewhere?

I was lost in my thoughts when my name was called. The doctor, a short middle-aged man wearing thick glasses and a white coat, stood and examined the baby. He turned to me with a worried look on his face. 'Do you have children?' he asked.

'Yes, I have a son.'

'Good luck. You'll need it to turn this beautiful girl around. She needs more than drugs and food.'

I had never seen such an undernourished child before. The matron at the orphanage had already dressed Nyiragasazi when I picked her up. With her clothes off, I saw that her skin was pale and cracked. She was covered in blisters and her stomach was virtually glued to her back. Steadying my nerves, I asked the doctor what was wrong with the baby.

'Everything,' he said, 'but she will need love and warmth first.'

She had malaria parasites and her ears were highly inflamed. He prescribed medication that was not available in Rwanda, so I had to send for it from Uganda. For the first few weeks, Nyiragasazi was as anxious as I was. She tested my endurance because she couldn't stop crying. I had sleepless nights and looked like a zombie. She was too weak to move, so she curled up and stayed still, staring at me without even attempting to move. One could see the trauma and distrust that this little girl had.

I was now living with Jeanne d'Arc. There were relatives and other people staying with us. Nyiragasazi wouldn't let anyone except my sister and me carry her, feed her or bath her. I bought a baby sling and sometimes took her with me to work. She loved being held in the sling with her little legs dangling around. She would gaze at me patiently, until she caught my eye, and make silly faces. She was most comfortable when she had physical contact. I moved her into my bed to give her reassurance and security. She was still unwell, though; I needed to give her time to get to know me properly and to recover from her traumas of hunger and lack of love.

It took nearly two months to get her to settle into some kind of routine. Meal times became less painful once I discovered she liked pureed meat. At bath time, which I enjoyed, she would splash water over me, kicking her thin little legs and smiling cheekily. When I picked her up out of the water, she would scream loudly and have a tantrum, but I would settle her on my knees and wrap her in a warm towel. It was during these moments that I thought I should either adopt her or try and trace her family.

Slowly but surely, Nyiragasazi started to form her first word, 'ndai-i-i'. At first we couldn't make out what she was saying, as she only used it when she was agitated or clearly didn't want to do as she was told. Unlike other babies, she never spoke in baby talk – 'gaga', 'mama', 'papa'. Soon we worked out she meant 'ndaze', which means 'I don't want'. I enrolled her in a private crèche so that she could meet other children and develop her speech and play skills.

For seven months, I tried desperately to locate the baby's family, sending photos and visiting the orphanages. I gave up my voluntary work with the Ministry of Rehabilitation to give her more time and to focus on finding her family, but my efforts were to no avail. By November 1994, the government was becoming worried that no one had claimed her or sought any child of her description, so I was given the go-ahead to start the process of adoption. As Nyiragasazi was Rwandan the condition for adopting her was to bring her up in Rwandan culture and to bring her back to the country often in case someone had claimed a child of her description. There was a hope that the young girl that had brought her to the ICRC might come forward to claim her.

I was due to go back to Ethiopia soon to join the two Richards. I agonised over giving up my baby. I had grown fond of her and she of me. So I discussed the possibility of adopting her with Richard senior and with his blessing I started the adoption process in earnest, which lasted for five months.

When I left Rwanda, I weighed just 45 kilograms, having lost 30 kilograms. Richard was shocked when he first saw me and he put me on a fattening diet. All the money that he had been sending me for food while in Rwanda I had been spending on survivors.

Thinking back now, one of the reasons I adopted the baby, who we named Christine after an old friend I had studied with in Uganda, was so that through her I could better understand what other children had lost. While I had lost almost my entire family, I was old enough to fend for myself. Nyiragasazi had not been so lucky. However, we found each other, and Richard and I gained a daughter and Richard junior a sister. The time I had spent in Rwanda with the survivors, listening to their testimonies, and now living with Christine as my daughter was most rewarding, but turning my back on the many widows and orphans I had met was not possible.

SEVENTEEN

A second-generation burden

I WAS PREPARING to return to the UK with Christine. While in Rwanda I had met many patriotic Rwandans whose paths had crossed with mine either at school or within the Rwandan community in Uganda. It was a confusing period; I was shocked to see classmates who I regarded as Ugandans now claiming to be Rwandans and even speaking Kinyarwanda, which they had never dared speak while in Uganda. The young convent girls that I had danced with when we went to the boys' school were now older. We had grown apart; many were holding ministerial and other high-level jobs, making up in passion for what they lacked in experience. The only common factor, at least from what I could see, was the confidence that the school had instilled in us and the Catholic ethos that drove our moral obligation to serve our country.

I also met other friends with whom I had shared my childhood. They reminded me of the good times and the bad; we embraced each other because we shared a common destiny: being a Rwandan in exile. We understood survival; our parents were strict and instilled in us discipline, respect and education; and our culture was paramount. Our parents slowly passed onto us a second-generation burden to fight for the rights denied them and – so far – us. When the Rwandan refugees were forcefully returned to Rwanda, President Habyarimana said, 'The glass is full.' We suffered anger and frustration when young that toughened us up; we grew up before our time.

For some reason I never did take to Rwanda, despite being among friends, especially in higher places. I suppose I felt little inclination to love a country where my own race's annihilation was planned and executed. Living with survivors and working with them reinforced my dislike for the place. Right from the start, people were cold and aloof, and hung around in different camps. Although we were all Rwandans, the divisions were pronounced.

There were the minority Tutsis, marked and hunted by extremist Hutus for extermination, and those who had survived sheltering under IBUKA ('Remember'), the national umbrella of survivors' organisations. They were the people I had come to know and had empathy with. Then there were Hutu genocidaires, the bulk of them in prison but some still in the community and others hiding in refugee camps; and there were the Hutu bystanders, some of whom may have saved survivors' lives and who did not support or get involved in the genocide, but who nonetheless, by being Hutus, in whose name a million people were murdered, held the collective guilt of genocide.

Once I visited a Christian organisation that supported survivors. One of its staff asked to speak to me in private after a meeting. I assumed he needed money for a project or other needs. He apologised for being a Hutu, telling me he was ashamed of how the Hutus had become cold-hearted animals. I was suspicious of Hutus. I could never trust them, because I could not know which of them to trust. I avoided this man as long as I worked in Rwanda. I couldn't work out why he didn't apologise while in the meeting with his colleagues, who were survivors themselves. He didn't owe *me* an apology; I wasn't in Rwanda during the genocide. I wasn't sure if his intentions were sincere or whether he had something to hide. Many of the people I met testified to a deep suspicion of the latter.

Then there were the returnees, mainly Tutsis, who had lived in exile, each group's characteristics and loyalty defined by their country of exile. Ugandan Tutsis spoke more English, Luganda and Runyankole than Kinyarwanda, and they couldn't put together a ten-minute presentation without slipping in a vague reminder of where they came from. Once a top Rwandan official, addressing a meeting at Westminster, said, 'The people of Uganda are ready for change.' The MPs present turned to each other, possibly confused as to whether they were in the right meeting room.

The Tutsis from both Burundi and Congo spoke French, but you could tell the difference between them from hearing them speaking Lingala (Congo) or Kirundi (Burundi). They were mainly involved in business and seemed more enthusiastic about being back in Rwanda. They were easy to talk to, relaxed and laid back even when times were tough. My paternal uncle had returned from exile in Burundi; he was known to take a nap, a siesta, after lunch, which usually lasted over an hour, before returning to work for the afternoon. He would not run to catch a taxi or be hurried by anything at all. In a way I envied his chilled attitude to life.

Then there were the Tutsis like me, from as far afield as Europe, the Americas and Asia, each one of us with different experiences and languages. Many of us were professionals, eager to give something back to the mother country. We brought a culture of work, work, work and no play, and we were used to putting more time in, working overtime with the pressure to deliver and meet deadlines. This was not possible in Rwanda, where time waits for you. People are always up to three hours late with no apologies, while everyone else waits patiently for them to eventually trickle in.

Then there were the minority Twas, of whom I probably met one during the time I worked in Rwanda. But the real minorities for me were the survivors, the widow and orphan heads of household who had just lost entire families and a sense of humanity, and who were faced with a new trend of Rwandans, each with different opinions, backgrounds and priorities. Sometimes they spoke with resentment and suspicion about Tutsis from exile. I secretly agreed, because for me Rwanda was a foreign land to which I did not fully belong. I could not force myself to be a full Rwandan in a country I didn't know, but by virtue of it being my ancestral land, I had an attachment and a duty to support my people.

I also identified with the Ugandan returnees. In my family we shared hard times when the Ugandan regimes were prosecuting foreigners, from Obote to Amin, Bazilio Olara-Okello and Obote again, who, in his second term in office, forcibly returned Rwandan refugees to Rwanda.

One misty morning in my second year at Makerere University, I got a call from my mother. She was in hiding, escaping deportation to Rwanda. She had arranged for my siblings to hide at a friend's house. She called because she needed me to get them out of our village safely to a place where no one knew we were Rwandans. Rumours about forcing refugees from southern Uganda back to Rwanda had been circulating for some time, but even then the sudden turn of events took me by surprise.

My mother had been tipped off weeks before by a friend who worked for the ruling party, the Uganda People's Congress, that the Ugandan armed forces were planning to remove all Rwandans in refugee camps and those residing in southern Uganda and put them on trucks for the Rwandan border. For days her neighbours were talking about it, and the air was charged with gossip and anticipation.

Mother had contacted her cousins who lived in Lukaya, about 20 kilometres south of Kampala, to find an alternative place to settle, and prepared my siblings for the inevitable event. Mother had chosen to relocate from Mbarara to Lukaya because it was a safer place. The area is occupied by the Baganda tribe, who supported the opposition party and were more sympathetic to Rwandans and other foreigners.

Milton Obote's government persistently targeted us Rwandans living in the south of Uganda and planned a hasty and bungled operation to deport Rwandan refugees back to Rwanda. Those that were unlucky enough to be caught and deported were denied the right of citizenship and many were pushed back to Uganda by the government of Rwanda, President Habyarimana claiming that the 'glass was full', in other words that he had no room for refugees returning to their motherland.

For these and other reasons, and because of the lack of response from the government of Rwanda, some Rwandans in exile took to the bush and started a guerrilla force, the Rwanda Patriotic Army, to compel the government of Rwanda to recognise exiled Rwandans as citizens and grant them a right to return. After thirty years of living under hostile circumstances, unprotected by the UNHCR, which had settled Rwandans in Uganda many years before, the harassment of young Rwandans culminated in anger, despair and a collective demand from all Rwandans living in exile for intervention by the international community.

Mother had been in Lukaya for two days when the deportation order was issued. Her best friend, Aunt Janet, not really a blood relative, called her. She had heard that the deportation was going to start at the crack of dawn and she had managed to remove my siblings, who were staying with her.

Mother's call to me sounded desperate. There was none of the usual 'How are you and are you eating well?' Instead I could detect fear in my her abrupt voice. 'Mary, neighbours have stormed the hiding place.'

'What hiding place?' I asked.

'They are demanding to have the children handed over, threatening to dig a grave and bury them alive.'

'What?' I held my breath and listened, not wanting to interrupt. Mother was trembling; I could almost hear her heartbeat down the phone.

'Fortunately she hid them in a shallow pit and covered them with banana leaves. They searched the house and left without them,' Mother said.

'Who hid them? Where are they hiding?'

'At Aunt Janet's house.'

'Don't worry, Mum, I'll sort something out.' But I was left wondering how I was going to sort anything out. The news of my family filled me with anxiety and fear of the unknown. I took a deep breath and headed for the taxi rank.

I walked down the hill from the university campus, my eyes fixed on the beautiful valley below, to distract myself from the terror that was tearing me apart inside. The tall buildings below were hugging the skies, and couples in love, possibly university students, were strolling by, arms around each other's waists, without a care in the world. I felt trapped in an emotional turmoil, with no one to turn to and Mother hoping I could find a solution.

I knew I had to get my siblings out of the village, but, like all university students, I didn't have much money, just 500 Ugandan shillings, and that wouldn't take me far. I had a part-time voluntary job, marketing for an import and export firm. My boss, Josy, sometimes gave me money to cover travel expenses or a small bonus when business was good, which I always saved in case Mother came on days when she had no food for the family, which was often.

I went to ask Josy to lend me some money to go and find my family. She knew our circumstances, and was always friendly to my mother. She too was a widow with two young children. While explaining to her my desperate situation, I spotted a man out of the corner of my eye, standing parallel to me, listening.

'Wait here,' Josy said and disappeared into the back room.

I turned around to walk out of Josy's office, and I could now see the man, possibly in his late fifties, stockily built, clean shaven and wearing clean shiny shoes. I could tell he wasn't from here by the way he carried himself. He held himself high.

He smiled at me. 'I am Gerrard. Call me Gerry.' He politely extended his arm to shake hands.

'Mary.'

'Sorry for eavesdropping. I heard about your family. I am here on business from the United Kingdom and am travelling to Kabale today. I pass your home town and would be happy to give you a lift.'

'Thank you.' I was grateful and relieved. I didn't stop to think that this man was a stranger; I was only thinking about my siblings. In Africa it was commonplace to take a lift from anyone.

'I see you two have met,' Josy interrupted; she was holding a khaki envelope which she handed over to me. 'Gerry lives in London. He is a good friend who I met when we were both exiled in Nairobi.' She assured me Gerry would look after me. But there was still business to discuss and he wouldn't be ready to leave for the next few hours. 'You'll have to wait,' Josy said.

Gerry then asked if I wanted to go back to the university to get ready. He would pass by and pick me up. Get ready? What did he mean? I couldn't wait to go.

I excused myself and went out to wait on the crowded pavement. I lost myself in the traffic crawling up and down the street, windows covered in red dust, threading through pedestrians, honking at children and the odd cow that wouldn't move from the road; the traffic wardens blowing their whistles frantically; pedestrians crossing the road almost walking into each other; noises everywhere. I wished I could stop time and have a moment to think. I was worried about my family and what lay ahead. The thoughts of my mother and siblings came back to me. I wondered where my siblings were.

I had no idea how I was going to get them out of the village, but I understood how risky the operation was going to be. I feared that I might be arrested and forced back to Rwanda with everyone else. I was nervous; there were many questions without any answers. All I wanted to do now was to get home and, with luck, rescue my siblings.

I must have been waiting for nearly an hour when a woman carrying a baby on her back passed me. The baby was crying in distress. An empty milk bottle fell from the hand luggage she was carrying. I picked it up to hand it to her and our eyes met. She opened her mouth, I think to thank me, but instead burst into tears. It took her a few minutes to compose herself, drying her face with the palm of her hand. She told me that her husband had sent her away. He had taken a young woman and was now living with her in a small house they rented. She had nowhere to go. She hadn't eaten for days, and her baby was also hungry. She had no money to buy milk.

I felt her pain and pulled out a hundred shilling bill from my purse and gave it to her. She bade me 'God's blessings' and left, the baby still crying.

Yes, I need God's blessings right now. For a moment I felt good: I had temporarily relieved a small problem; I had given hope to a stranger. But the distress in the woman's voice stayed with me, filling me with sadness. Tears started to fall from my eyes. I dried my face and looked to make sure no one had noticed me. I knew this was not about the woman. I was worried I didn't have enough money; I knew there was no one else who could help. Mother was depending on me to save my siblings.

Mother always said, we should never cry about a situation because it's a bad omen. Just what I didn't need, right now. I dried my tears and forced a smile as I walked back to the shop, only to meet Gerry coming out of Josy's office.

'Sorry to keep you waiting. The meeting took more than an hour, longer than I expected,' he said politely. 'I am ready to leave now.'

His car, a silver Citroën, was parked nearby. He opened the passenger door and motioned to me to sit down. The inside was spotless, with leather-covered seats and dashboard, a sunroof and many buttons for the radio, cassette player, air conditioning and electric windows. It smelt of an expensive air freshener. The ride home took well over five hours; Gerry and I hardly spoke as we snaked our way over the high and low plateaux between Kampala and Mbarara.

He told me he was a supplier and acted as a middleman between businesses in Europe and Africa, specifically Uganda and Kenya. Josy was one of his clients. He explained that his visits tended to be brief, so there was always a lot to discuss. He was trying to explain why it took him so long and apologised for the anxiety I was feeling towards my family. Josy had told him about my mother, 'a single parent with not much money, and no relatives to help us.'

'It must be a big responsibility on your shoulders, especially being a student,' he said sympathetically.

I could feel where the conversation was leading; I didn't want charity from a stranger. I remembered my mother's honour and pride, and I could not accept handouts. I changed the subject to avoid commenting on his statement.

At this time my family were living at the trading centre. We had lived there for nine years, peacefully until now, since escaping the harassment of Amin's state bureau in the village where Mother had built her house, but being foreigners was something we could not escape, and now we were again being haunted and hunted by our neighbours. I spent all my childhood as a fugitive, always moving to new locations to escape insecurity or so that Mother could find work.

I felt uncertain and betrayed by people we had known and lived with for a long time. Suddenly, the lady in the drugstore, whose daughters I had gone to school with and who had invited me to her home; the old man in the corner grocery where I had shopped for many years; the market guard with his blue uniform and a rifle on his shoulder who would always smile or leer at me when I passed – they were now our enemies and dangerous. We had shared weddings and funerals, had sung and danced together in church and at communal gatherings, had walked together when I was a child. How could these neighbours threaten to bury my siblings alive or return them by force to Rwanda? I imagined someone waking me, telling me this was all a nightmare. But it was not. I couldn't escape reality.

Late that afternoon, we approached the a house that a few days ago had been my rented home, a place I came back to as though I had never left. The house was deserted, broken furniture, odd pieces of clothes and plastic bags scattered around. Gerry drove past slowly, but he didn't stop for fear of attracting attention. As he drove past I lowered my head, not looking at anything or anybody. I could hear a dull, monotonous throbbing in my ears over the noise of passing traffic. If anyone had called out to me at that moment, I wouldn't have been able to hear them. At this moment I felt utter terror, as if I was waiting for someone to pounce on me. I tensed my muscles, and bowed my head down so low that my back ached.

We drove on to Aunt Janet's village, taking a rutted, uphill dirt track that branched off the main road, a mile away from the trading centre. I hoped the neighbours wouldn't notice a strange car driving into the village.

Aunt Janet was not expecting us. As we approached her house a dog barked. I saw a movement behind a curtain, but no one came out. I looked around, quickly got out of the car and hurried to the front door. Just as I was about to knock, the door flew open and Aunt Janet pulled me in, quickly closing it behind me. I gasped for breath as she hugged me so close that my tender breasts hurt.

'Thank goodness you're here,' she said. 'Your siblings are safe for now, but you have to leave at once.'

Aunt Janet didn't want to keep us long in case the neighbours spotted us. She told me she had transported my siblings away under cover of darkness. My sister Riisa was a midwife at a hospital in the town centre and she had hidden them in the hospital, disguising them as patients. The town centre, and especially the hospital, had not been too badly affected overall by the deportations. Gerry kindly drove me to my sister's hostel. I arrived to find that she had arranged for a friend to smuggle my siblings out of the hospital and drive them over 100 miles to Lukaya, where they joined my mother.

My siblings were safe! My adrenalin levels dropped, the day's anxiety, fear and distress over at least for now.

It was now getting late and Gerry had to continue his journey. 'I will be coming back in the next two days. Would you like a lift back to Kampala?' he asked. He gave me some money to help resettle my family, saying, 'That will tide you over.'

'I would be grateful, thank you, Gerry. Have a safe journey.' I could not believe his kindness, nor the emotional rollercoaster that had swept over me during the past ten hours.

I spent the night at my sister's hostel and the next day took a taxi to Lukaya. I found my family safe, and with the money Gerry and Josy gave me I paid a year's rent and bought them food. Mother had no source of income now, but at least everyone had escaped the carnage of being returned to Rwanda.

With my mother displaced and my sister, a newly qualified midwife, earning just enough to keep herself, I had to find a way of supporting my family. I became preoccupied with this and I could hardly concentrate on my studies. I returned to Lukaya almost every weekend and in the evenings went from one hall of residence to another selling merchandise. That year I had to retake my sociology paper.

It took me nearly seven months for my mother to settle down. Once my siblings were back in school, and Mother's medical practice back on track, money started coming in, but Lukaya was expensive. Obote's men had no collaborators in Lukaya so it was easy for my family to settle unnoticed or harassed. The whole deportation incident had left many Rwanda refugees displaced in different locations in Uganda.

Our new home was in a middle of a dynamic trading centre, a hub of illegal trade. It was a stopover town for long-distance truck drivers and their assistants and mechanics, carrying goods from Mombasa to Rwanda, Burundi and Congo. There was plenty of wheeling and dealing going on, especially at night. The place was polluted with the smell of petrol and diesel, which were offloaded every night and sold to the illegal traders.

Dense and vibrant, Lukaya had sprung up spontaneously without much in the way of planning or forethought. The streets were unpaved, some just dusty red earth. From the crack of dawn until dusk it was alive – full of people, rich and poor, going about their daily business. In the chaotic early morning, the city woke to the call to prayer from the mosque, the rumble of traffic and lorries warming up their engines. Their broken exhaust pipes belched out layers of carbon monoxide that almost choked you in your sleep; sometimes the only way you knew you were still alive was when you heard a rooster's crow cutting through the morning racket.

I began looking forward to visiting Lukaya whenever I could get away from the university. It was only a two-hour drive away and offered a total contrast to my old home. Soon I forgot about losing my previous home, as Lukaya offered anonymity and economic opportunities. I took the chance to set up a small business. I made a deal with an Asian wholesaler in Kampala, who loaned me merchandise which I took to Lukaya, and I set up a partnership with a friend of my mother's who would sell it for me in her shop. Soon my business was doing well and I was able to subsidise my family's income.

I divided my time between studying and taking supplies to Lukaya. My business took a turn for the better when Gerry returned from the UK. He was impressed with my initiative, providing for my family and yet staying focused on my studies. He offered to help by sending bales of secondhand clothes over from Europe, which I sold and increased my turnover. Money problems well over, I could concentrate on graduating. I was in my third academic year now; soon I would be out and running the business.

Increasingly, though, Rwandans were being fished out and imprisoned or intimidated. Many of my friends disappeared, joining Museveni's army to escape; others, less convinced about serving in the army, left the country. I lost so many friends when I left Uganda and came to the UK.

I never thought I would meet any of my Ugandan friends in our motherland; we never spoke about returning to Rwanda. When Museveni came to power, a number of his high-ranking army officers were Rwandans, and they led the campaign to allow me and others the right to citizenship. Many people I knew died during the liberation – they paid for my freedom. Those that survived also carried invisible psychological wounds, every one of them paying a price for our freedom. The campaign needed money to keep it alive, and those that could not make the frontline, like me, contributed funds to support it.

EIGHTEEN

Why I set up the Survivors Fund

THE TIME I spent with survivors inspired me to think about what else I could do to help. I wanted desperately to do something constructive, to positively channel my anger and negative energy. The survivors were ready to share their memories with me, memories of their loved ones. They trusted me, with no guarantee that I would make their lives better. They had only one thing they asked of me: 'Please don't let the world ever forget what happened to us.'

Each survivor would tell me the same thing I felt: that they had survived only to serve as witnesses, for the world to draw lessons from their experiences and to try to ensure that this would never happen to anyone in the world again. I felt a call to support my people, to use their pain to educate others about the suffering that should, and could, have been so easily prevented. Only by doing so would I be able to make sense of my life.

While in Rwanda I documented the experience of the survivors. I then helped the widows to share their experiences with donors to secure support. The greatest needs to be addressed were not trauma but a wide range of social and economic effects and HIV/ AIDS, with which many women had been infected after being raped during the genocide.

When I was finally due to return to the UK, I asked the women who had become part of my family how I could help. 'Please tell people to remember,' they said. Everyone was concerned with preserving the memory of the genocide, and I was to carry this heavy burden, to tell the story of the survivors, to make people remember. But what good would this be if the same people abandoned them again as before? What benefit would they get from people thousands of miles away from Rwanda remembering them?

I had to tell their story. I had been entrusted with many stories, and I could not keep them to myself. I recounted how lucky I was. How guilty I felt for not sharing their pain or experiences, living to tell the tale. I had experienced the power of their testimony, and had became more aware of the genocide and what the survivors had endured. That is why on my return to the UK I set up the Survivors Fund (SURF), to help me to help survivors and to make the world realise what humanity is capable of. For me it was not just the machetes or the guns that killed; the indifference of the world contributed to the human suffering in Rwanda.

Setting up SURF was a relief, because I could finally do something to help survivors, orphans, widows and widowers, and rebuild a sense of humanity. I convinced myself that the grief and pain I had experienced from listening to survivors should not be wasted, that their tragedy provided an opportunity to do good. I had become the survivors' sponge, absorbing much of their pain. Their trust in me became my strength.

I should have been happy after setting up SURF, but there were more challenges waiting for me. I felt like I was standing on the sidelines, survivors' voices lingering in my mind. The words of one of them, Clémentine, went round and round in my head like a record that wouldn't stop: 'If you didn't manage to protect me in 1994, at least stop me from dying.' My mind replayed the horrors I had witnessed in Rwanda. Those that survived the genocide were now dying of grief, hunger, destitution, and from the effects of HIV and AIDS.

Rwanda was virtually unknown in the UK until the genocide, and the horrific scenes of 1994 were soon replaced by other disasters. I felt isolated, desperate and trapped. I seemed to be the only person who understood what had happened in Rwanda, but no one wanted to hear me. I visited NGOs working in Rwanda and the UK Department for International Development (DfID), pleading for funds to be channelled to survivors. As had happened in Rwanda, I was informed politely that funds were already committed to the country, and with the emergency period coming to an end, there were no more earmarked for it. I invited myself to meetings of humanitarian agencies, the European Union and the United Nations. For two years, the response was the same. Everyone was sorry for my loss, but they would not help.

Every day I remembered during my early days in Rwanda the many women I met who told me confidentially how they had been raped and deliberately infected with HIV during the genocide. I could hear the voices of thousands of women who had been put through the same dehumanising and degrading experience, many in front of their own families, who were then killed while they were allowed to live, being told by their rapists, 'You alone may live, only so that you will die of sadness.' I would remember the women I knew who had slipped through my fingers and died from AIDS-related illnesses.

I visualised little children at night, huddled up on the floor, quietly shedding tears and feeling very, very lonely, while the bigger ones did their best to cheer them up and comfort them, and tried with all their might not to think bad thoughts. My daughter Christine's laughter and cheekiness reminded me every day what would have happened to her in the orphanage, and what a little love can bring back to humanity.

Despite all the odds, I began to see that the survivors were able to come to terms with their experiences and, incredibly, get on with their lives. I was fascinated by what memories came back to me, the past seeming so near that I could remember particular phrases and the faces of the people who had told me their stories. I faced daily obstacles, and led an often intensive and stressful existence, in order to give them a voice, and their trust overcame these obstacles.

I found motivation in my background. I would cast my mind back to when I was growing up, to find a source of resilience. I would think of my childhood, the hurdles I jumped, the bridges I built, the pain and hardship that became part of my existence. I would think of how my parents protected me from the pain of sharing their horrific experiences: their flight from Rwanda during the 1959 revolution; my father's tragic death while in exile in Burundi; my grandfather after the funeral taking my siblings with him back to Rwanda, and remaining separated for years; my mother's separation from my stepfather; my mother's and brother's deaths; and the rest of the family that were slaughtered in cold blood. Here I was, just like my mother, focusing on the task at hand, pushing the agony deep into the back of my mind, and building an armour of strength around me to protect me from the pain of existence.

It was not until I met the Jewish community and the survivors of the Holocaust that my pain was at last validated. My first call was to the Medical Foundation for the Care of Victims of Torture, to meet its founder, Helen Bamber. A beautiful petite woman sat opposite me in her modest office and listened to me without interrupting. My burden of genocide had at last found a home, somewhere I could unburden my soul. I was then taken under the wings of Alex Sklan of the Medical Foundation, Judith Hassan of Jewish Care, Karen Pollock of the Holocaust Education Trust and the Chief Rabbi, Lord Sacks. They became my mentors, at every opportunity raising awareness and endorsing my work with survivors. There is no way in the world I could have survived the journey without them.

The Jewish community identified with my cause. They too had seen indifference and those who had survived became my heroes. For decades they lit candles to remember the victims that fell and bore witness to the Holocaust, so that the world would not repeat the same mistakes, and yet 'Never Again' proved only to be rhetoric. I was among friends who had empathy, who reminded me that what I was feeling was real and that we shared a common aim: to educate the world about crimes against humanity that should not be allowed to happen. I regained the confidence and strength to fight for the Rwandan survivors.

Clémentine's words stopped haunting me. I had a bigger task to deal with: to access medical support for women raped and deliberately infected with HIV.

On a return visit to Rwanda, I met again with Clémentine. She had lost weight from her face, causing her cheekbones to stick out, and her eyes, sunken but still bright, were a sign of what the deadly HIV was doing to her body. Twenty-five years old, she looked fifty. She held my gaze for a minute, until I looked away, afraid to remember her like that when she died, her eyes the only sign of life. She wasn't the only one; many widows I met were succumbing to the virus.

Clémentine's family was hacked to death with machetes, while she was spared by the Interahamwe and taken to a house with other women, where she was raped repeatedly. Everyone who wanted to have her, and could stand the blood and dirt that covered her, did. She lost count of how many soldiers and Interahamwe raped her. For three months that was her routine. She hoped she would die but she didn't. She lost her entire family except for a twelve-year-old niece, who she later found in an orphanage.

Many women recounted experiences like Clémentine's; they had been told they were infected with HIV and would die a slow painful death. AVEGA was encouraging women to take an HIV test, and 70 per cent of those who did were found to be HIV positive, an alarming statistic. I was given the task of raising awareness about the plight of survivors and galvanising resources to secure antiretroviral drugs, which could save their lives.

I convinced a major donor in the UK to film Clémentine and other widows and tell their stories as part of the fundraising campaign. This film was a matter of life and death, covering the stories of women dying of AIDS, which raised the curtain on the world's indifference to the plight of women survivors. The public was deeply moved and donated well over £55 million pounds, doubling the size of the donor's fund. The fourteen women who appeared in the film were the first ones to receive antiretroviral drugs. But no further funding was allocated to women survivors with HIV and AIDS; instead the donor built homes and memorial sites.

At a cost of £75 a day, the task of accessing further funding for the life-saving drugs still needed by the 7,000 widows, who were now at risk of dying, fell back on me. All the donors were shying away from the responsibility, so I settled to raising the £15 needed to buy a coffin for each of the women that slipped through the net.

SURF took campaigning for free access to antiretroviral treatment to another level, organising a readathon, which attracted women from all walks of life in UK. Lawmakers, celebrities, professionals, housewives and activists joined the actress and television host Josie D'Arby and lined up in Trafalgar Square from six o'clock in the morning to six o'clock at night to read the stories of widows and girls who were raped and infected with HIV during the hundred days of the 1994 genocide. A large platform under Nelson's column attracted an itinerant group of keen listeners while tourists sitting around the fountain paused occasionally in their chatter to tune in. Among the speakers were Baroness Williams of Crosby; Lady Jakobovits, a survivor of the

Holocaust; the president of the League of Jewish Women, Penny Conway; the founder of the Charities Advisory Trust, Dame Hilary Blume; the singers Beverley Knight and Kym Mazelle; the actresses Helen Baxendale and Hanna Waterman; the actors Danny John-Jules, David Harewood and Paul Bradley; and the journalists Lindsey Hilsum and Polly Toynbee.

I was desperate to save the women, while the international community was providing healthcare for murderers and rapists in prison while their victims died. I knew that if SURF succeeded, not only would the lives of these women be prolonged, but they would be able to carry on caring for the orphans of genocide. If I didn't get treatment for them, they would die one by one. Once again, just as in 1994, the world would have watched and done nothing.

SURF gained the support of an increasing number of British MPs. In April 2004, to coincide with the tenth anniversary of the genocide, Brian Cotter, a SURF patron, tabled an early day motion in the House of Commons and received cross-party support from over 100 Members of Parliament. SURF also collected 7,000 signatures and delivered them to 10 Downing Street with a petition calling on the British government to do more to pressure pharmaceutical companies into making antiretroviral treatment more affordable and accessible in Rwanda.

This was not the first time I had been invited to Number 10. Cherie Blair was a committed supporter of SURF and she hosted a dinner in honour of its work, and even visited SURF projects while on an official visit to Rwanda, where she named a testimony centre built with the support of the British public.

SURF's campaign was also supported by the First Lady of Rwanda, Mrs Jeannette Kagame, who is passionate about the plight of the survivors; she added her voice to the campaign to lobby the government and the international community to provide women with the necessary drugs.

The three-year campaign paid off. The DfID eventually pledged to support 2,500 women survivors with access to antiretroviral drugs, committing nearly £5 million over a five-year period. Supporting widows alone, though, was inadequate, when many children in Rwanda found themselves suddenly assuming adult roles and responsibilities when they themselves needed parental care.

On the night of 20 December 2001, I couldn't sleep. That morning Richard junior and Christine had sat on the floor and emptied onto the carpet all the pennies they had saved over the year in their piggy banks. It came to £16. Unaware of how little that was, they asked me to buy all the orphans in Rwanda a Christmas present with the money. I promised I would.

Keeping my promise wasn't why I couldn't sleep. I was thinking of the widows who could not afford food for their children at Christmas, and the child heads of households who could not look their siblings straight in the face for fear of seeing hunger and disappointment in their eyes. Among all that, Christine was also worrying me. A few days before, we had watched *Harry Potter and the Philosopher's Stone* and she sobbed all the way through. She asked me to hold her hand because she was so sad. Afterwards, I asked her why she was crying and what had made her sad.

She replied, 'I'm like Harry Potter, except my family doesn't mistreat me, but I have no magic to see my real mum and dad. Why did they have to die, Mum?' I don't remember what my answer was. I always found it hard to discuss Christine's family with her because she was too young to understand the details. This was the first time my daughter, aged seven, had made me aware that she was not too young to know what had happened to her, but I had no answers for her.

Some time before, I had written an abstract poem for her summarising the children's stories I'd heard in Rwanda after the genocide. I hoped to share the stories with her in order to reconstruct what her family may have gone through, the family for whom justice will never be achieved.

Uyisenga 1994

I do not cry for justice, because it is beyond my reach; the horrors of genocide have been reduced to mere manslaughter. . . not even justice in totality can bring back my sanity and life. I was there when the madness struck; I was a child, and yet not really – I was only fourteen years of age. I don't know how I became separated from my family, all I know is that wherever they lie, they have more peace than I can ever achieve. Pain and sorrow can never reach them. I ran with different people in search for safety – children, men, women, grandmothers, grandfathers, struck with machetes, clubs and pangas. As they fell, those with the energy continued their journey, surrounded by heaps of mutilated and rotting bodies.

I don't know why I was being chased, but it felt the right decision to run. Now I know I should have stayed put, and joined the fate of my family. I was struck in several places with sticks and machetes, but I still ran on; I was raped and abused, but still had the courage to keep running. You may say that I am brave and courageous. Yes, I have looked death in the face, and courageously paid a shocking price to survive.

I didn't see my family get killed; I don't know whether they were tortured. Seeing babies shot at like targets and killed – this should never happen to anybody. Then the day of judgement came: I dug up and reburied some of my family, but I don't know where the others lie. I am among the many dead and yet I am not buried. I remain as a statement of what happened to a million others, for you and for the world to see. History has a way of repeating itself. Don't allow it.

By remembering me, you remember all those innocent victims.
Moving forward and forgetting what happened is forgetting me,
then, and there will be no reason for me to live since I will cease
to bear witness.

I thought this was the right time to tell Christine that I had no
idea who her family was, whether she had sisters or not, whether
they were alive or dead, whether 'she alone might live'. I did not
have the courage to burden her with feelings beyond those which
she already had. I prayed that she would forget, at least for now.

Her words lingered in my head for days. My daughter was a
baby when the genocide occurred. I wanted her to grow up feeling
that she had survived for a reason. I knew many children lived
alone, some the sole survivors of entire families, many with ill
health, suffering from wounds sustained when machetes hacked
at their small bodies, others HIV positive or dying of hunger.

I had, a few months back, received the first-ever grant to support
young people raped and infected with HIV/AIDS from the Diana
Princess of Wales Memorial Fund. After speaking to Christine, I
could see how important it was to set up a centre where children
could find space to talk about their fears. A donor from the City
was organising an adventure for his staff to climb the Rwenzori
mountains in Kenya to raise funds for SURF. I arranged to see two
members of the staff, Talal and Tracey, shortly before Christmas. I
was relieved when I met them and explained that I wanted to set
up a centre in my daughter's name to help children like her but
who had no love or care. I had already managed to raise funds
from CAFOD to buy a centre for AVEGA widows, which had
become a refuge for many, but children had no place to go.

The year 2002 started with my dream coming true. A centre
was bought and an organisation called Uyisenga N'Manzi was set
up in my daughter's honour to support lone children infected with

or affected by HIV/AIDS. SURF's role was to help with setting up programmes in the hope that Rwandans would take over and work with young people. SURF raised 100 per cent of the funding for the programmes.

These were challenging times, working with the most vulnerable. Sometimes partner organisations would compete for funds from SURF. We had many success stories working with and supporting these organisations, but given SURF's size and capacity, with only two staff members in the London office, there were also many nights when I hardly slept, worrying where I would get funds to support the many competing causes. There were hard times ahead for me, particularly as I was on the front line, trusted by survivors, giving unconditional commitment to their cause. I had become the iron lady who would solve all the survivors' needs.

The phenomenon of child heads of households was new, emerging as the orphanages were closed down. SURF responded by supporting L'Association des Orphelins Chefs de Ménages (AOCM, the Association of Orphan Heads of Households). Most of its members were still at university, some educated through a SURF sponsorship scheme. The needs of these children were more pressing than even those of the widows. They had no adult love, nurture or supervision. SURF raised funds to help these children learn to speak for themselves, and to collectively assess the immediate needs of AOCM's members.

Efforts to enable these children to go to school met several challenges. The more grown-up were expected to be at school for more than ten hours a day, but had young ones to take care of at home. They needed food and clothing, scholastic materials and shelter. Although the Rwandan government set up an institution called FARG to facilitate orphans to study, its contribution covered tuition only and many children were unable to obtain additional support from FARG.

A good number of orphans were supported through their education with direct assistance from SURF. SURF was also able to facilitate the twinning of a school attended by many survivors in Rwanda, Don Bosco, with the London Oratory School, whose chaplain, Fr George Bowen, is a SURF patron. SURF also set up a hardship fund to meet sudden emergencies encountered from time to time by the survivors, such as funeral costs for the death of loved ones, house repairs and sickness, especially opportunistic infections. With SURF's support, all the organisations assisted were able to respond and help survivors in times of emergency.

Perhaps besides fundraising, the other most important contribution from SURF has been its work in the UK to advocate for the rights of survivors in Rwanda, and to improve the conditions in which they are living post-genocide. Right from the start the involvement of Fergal Keane OBE, a SURF patron, played a major role in educating the international community on the plight of the survivors. Fergal's films for the BBC on Rwanda straight after the genocide were a testimony to the horrors the survivors went through and the lack of justice they suffered.

SURF paid particular attention to raising awareness among MPs of reports that survivors were being intimidated and assaulted as a result of giving evidence against alleged perpetrators at local *gacaca* trials. The term *gacaca* ('flattened grass') was adopted from Kinyarwanda, where it describes the traditional way of addressing conflict resolution at a local level. MPs demanded that the government should report on what was being done. Andrew Mitchell MP, another SURF patron, took a leading role and supported witness protection initiatives.

SURF also organised trips to Rwanda for key donors and supporters, enabling participants to get a firsthand impression of life for survivors, through meeting partner organisations and beneficiaries. All participants found the trips moving and highly informative and many on their return stepped up their networking and advocacy work on behalf of SURF in the UK.

Thousands of the survivors who ended up in the UK literally lived in my sitting room. When times were hard many would be lonely and my home become their home. I treated them like my children, and gave them time and support whenever it was needed. Whenever their coping mechanism would slip, I had the Medical Foundation to fall back on. Like my mother before me, who had welcomed many Rwandans who came to Uganda to study, here I was welcoming Rwandans to my home. Some of them were demanding, never happy whatever I did for them, but a counsellor at the Medical Foundation once said to me, 'If you ever feel that they are hurtful and you want to give up, ask yourself how much genocide hurt them. If it's too much for you that will be the time for you to let go of them.' I then gave up expecting gratitude and focused on making them manage alone, for example organising trips to Butlins and other places in the summer to help them network and establish friendships among themselves, which helped to divert some of them from me to each other.

Not only did the genocide claim human life, but the killers effectively destroyed their victims' property. By 1995, shelter was the single most important basic necessity at stake in Rwanda (for survivors and returnees from exile alike). The problem has lessened, but not surprisingly many genocide survivors still lack shelter. Even the houses which were not totally destroyed in 1994 were vandalised and require serious repair.

A number of organisations were uninterested in supporting shelter programmes for the widows, claiming it was not a priority. Nevertheless, SURF's work was appreciated in advocating for survivors who did not have a home of their own. As one of them, Mugeni, testified, 'When I realised I had to take care of my three siblings after the genocide, my worst nightmare was where I would bring them up. Our home was destroyed in 1994. We became street kids, sleeping rough but always looking out for each other until four years ago, when Uyisenga welcomed us into their home and found us a small room to let. The landlord evicted us because she had tenants who could afford to pay more rent and we were back on the street, but only for a short time. We were happy to be among the first children to be selected for houses in Niboyi village. We are now back together living as one family; the fear of losing my siblings is over. We get time to thank God and pray for other orphans to be helped.'

The building of simple low-cost homes was more than just about improving the condition of shelter for the survivors – it was also a catalyst for the further development of communities by helping survivors create local jobs and by lobbying the government to provide materials and infrastructure that benefited everyone.

Despite all the successes of the interventions, healing was difficult for many who could not find their dead relatives and for those who could not give them a decent burial. Unlike them, I was lucky to have found my brother and the rest of my family. However, every time I visited Rwanda, I found it hard to visit my family's memorial, because I felt guilt for not burying all the dead that had greeted me when I first came to the country. I didn't need to be reminded of the dead; I wanted to be associated with the living. However, five years into my work, I could not ignore them any more.

Despite all my trips to Rwanda, I had not yet been to Jean Baptiste's gravesite. I asked Valencia to come with me. I was winding up work in Rwanda, leaving for London that evening. There was no time to buy a wreath. Before we arrived at his marital home, where he was buried, Valencia reminded me that we needed flowers. I could see beautiful yellow, purple and brown blooms dotted everywhere. I stopped the car and suggested we pick some. I wandered around, picking and arranging the flowers that blessed Rwanda's rolling hills, the killing fields. The reality of my denial hit me. I remembered so many dead that had no resting place. I remembered that I had brought many visitors to Rwanda but had not yet plucked up the courage to visit the Gisozi national memorial site.

My sister-in-law looked disappointed and helped me arrange the wild flowers. She opened a small building to the left side of her house and there he lay, with half-burnt candles and dried flowers, a few black ants marching in an orderly procession over his grave. There were cards neatly arranged on top. 'Your family will never forget you,' said one, the words beginning to fade.

I stood there, numb, indifferent. I didn't feel any emotion. Since I started visiting Rwanda, there was less and less for me to smile about. My love of music and dance had slowly evaporated. I had lost all sense of fun; everything in my life had become serious and driven by a tension and urgency to support the survivors. You cannot imagine having to go through life finding something horrible and sad in everyone you meet or work with. I could not see hope, only despair and pain. It is extraordinary that the human spirit keeps going, despite the unimaginable horror.

After visiting my brother I focused on raising awareness of the need to give the victims a decent resting place. I had not visited my village, where my family was buried in a mass grave in a school playground. A survivor had taken me to Butare stadium, where thousands perished, and showed me a pit in a field nearby where her family lay. Cows and goats were grazing over the dead. He was visibly upset as he tried to chase the animals away. For the next two years I raised funds to build more than twenty memorial sites for the victims, ensuring that they had at least a peaceful resting place. I later returned to visit the dead of Butare at the Isimbi and Mbazi memorial sites, which I had built.

Mucyo, a chief prosecutor for Rwanda and a survivor who has since dedicated his life to finding the dead and giving them a decent burial, told me the value of giving his family a resting place. His home is in Butare, but in 1994 he was living in Kigali. In the beginning, straight after the genocide, he was left wondering: what really happened? Where were his people buried, if at all?

'I remember when I arrived home, people ran away from me. My main preoccupation was: where were all the bodies of our people?' he told me. 'The only possible place was a pit into which the local butchers throw their rubbish, near the Mbazi Stadium. The pit was purposely built for dumping rubbish. Many of our people were killed at the stadium and dumped in this pit.

'We had to remove them,' he continued, 'and this included my family. We dug a big grave, lined it with plastic sheeting and then dug out the remains from the rubbish pit. It was a long, difficult journey,' he said, pausing to compose himself, 'because we hoped to identify our relatives. All the survivors came to search for the bodies of their families. We dug people out, very many people. My family was among them. But at least we buried the rest in dignity.'

After receiving support from SURF, Mucyo and his associates built a cellar under a house, where they exhumed the bodies, cleaned them and reburied them. 'At least this time we had coffins. At last they were protected, safe from the rain,' he told me. This helped many people, especially survivors, who always wanted their families to have a dignified burial.

Bodies still lie unidentified here and there. There are people who are beginning to tell what happened, with recently released prisoners confessing to killings at *gacacas* and revealing where they hid the bodies. Sometimes people have found bodies when building or farming. They are brought to a collection point until they can be buried.

'Nearby there is the Isimbi Memorial site, which you helped us build,' Mucyo reminded me, 'where even more people are buried. We have now a total of 41,000 victims buried in both sites.' I could only imagine the enormity of his burden to provide a decent resting place for the people of Butare.

'The burial site is a home to our family. It helps, especially near April. At least you are comforted to know your family is resting in peace. People have a place to hold remembrance events, and to visit every day. I bring my children to see where our family lies. There are many places with unburied remains.' He spoke with his voice subdued, looking at the floor and nodding his head.

In Cyangugu, SURF built the Nyamasheke memorial site, which today holds the remains of 45,000 victims. The government of Rwanda selected this site for the national event to commemorate the twelfth anniversary of the genocide. A young man, a survivor of Nyamasheke, whose family lie in this site, shocked me when he approached me in London and said, 'Thank you for giving my mother dignity. I feel I can now start to rebuild my life. Here is her photo.' He showed me a picture of her remains decently laid on a sheet; the body had no face but nonetheless I could visualise his mother and I was grateful. I was able to do one decent thing for this young man: give him a place he can visit and put flowers on his family's grave.

Every year I visited more memorial sites, including Gitarama (200), where I laid flowers for my family, Bitsibo, Shorongi (3,600) and Kamonyi Never Again (12,000). I stopped for a minute's silence for the victims of Mugina-Ruyemba (40,000) and Nteyo (4,027). In Kibungo, where I helped build an AVEGA Eastern Region centre, many widows could not move on with thousands and thousands of bodies unburied. SURF built memorials at Kaduha (550), Sovu (350), Rutonde (5,500), Mukarange (3,500) and Rukamberi-Sake (2,800). There were many more memorial sites elsewhere, such as at Ruganda (3,000) and Birambo (5,000) in Kibuye province; at Humure (250) in Byumba province; at Cyanika (2,000) in Gikongoro province; and at Musha (7,000) and Nteyo (4,027) in Kigali province. In all, including individual burials, SURF has laid to rest 229,322 people deserving of dignity and respect in designated memorial sites.

Despite the success of the work, revisiting the memories and experiences of fifteen years working with survivors was now finally taking its toll. Speaking about my anxieties had been very difficult; because of the successful way I had run SURF, even my own family saw me as an iron lady. I couldn't fail; intelligent and driven, I had what it took to tackle the world, but who knew me when I felt down or sometimes unable to move on?

The load of other people's memories was a great burden to carry. I felt unwell and grieved. I began to lose control of my emotions: every presentation or speech about the survivors triggered buckets of tears. I cried because I could not think how to escape the grime that I had been trapped in since the day I started SURF.

My husband's support was wearing thin. He repeated all the time that he wanted a normal life. I sometimes couldn't even understand what a normal life was. But every day I went to work and life went on. I was alone on this journey into the future. I had been made an OBE; how could I fail everyone? I was thinking a lot and wanted to stop, but I was doing it more for others than for myself. I couldn't let my family, friends and others down, and the disclosure of my feelings remained a personal burden.

I took a journey back in time, reminding myself that I started working when I was just thirteen years old to support my family, mostly during school holidays, and since then I had never stopped. The stress and exhaustion of running SURF and being the custodian of the genocide was catching up with me. Deadlines for reports, proposals and evaluations, networking with the wide range of stakeholders that I had met over the past few years, listening to individual survivors' needs as well as wholesale organisational challenges: the tasks were endless.

I began to feel less superhuman and needed to scream out for help, but there was so much work to do. I was building a Testimony Centre, a space for survivors to archive their memories. It was a big project, the last piece of intervention for the survivors, and I had to stay focused and committed to making this project a reality for them.

Then one winter's day my life changed. What began as a reminiscence of my childhood love of music became my refuge and healing power. As the stress increased, it became a way of life for me.

A writer who had been patiently waiting for an interview with me finally got a slot. I am not usually keen to speak about myself, unless the interview is about the survivors. But this writer was so persistent that in the end I gave in. We sat in SURF's small office, with no privacy. I wasn't comfortable praising myself for the work I did at SURF. The writer was researching 'forty of the world's most influential women, whose powerful voices fight for change'.

She had read about my work and I featured among the women she wanted to interview. What an honour, I thought, that despite the fatigue and tough times I am going through, at last I can see my name in print, among women I have modelled my work on, and whose contribution to humanity ranks high in my books, including Maya Angelou, Mary Robinson and Benazir Bhutto.

One of the writer's ten questions, however, threw me off balance. 'Do you have a favourite work of art, book, poem or piece of music that has personal significance for you?'

Very easy question, I thought. Our house is wired up with speakers and media stations in every room, even in the garden, and we have a great collection of music from different countries. My children and my husband love music; there are always different types playing. I was pleased it was the one question that I didn't need to think hard about. I opened my mouth, expecting a title or an artist to pop out. . . and I couldn't remember any. I couldn't think of anything of significance other than my work with the survivors. Somehow so many tunes were competing in my head that it was difficult to choose or remember one.

I paused and thought for a minute; still I couldn't remember any specific song, music or artists. I then realised I had been listening to music for fifteen years without hearing it. I replied, 'Anything that makes my head move is nice. Anything that brings joy, however small it is, I absorb it.'

What am I talking about? What a lot of rubbish this is! Then I continued, 'Music is actually very therapeutic for me. I like to listen to classical music.' What? I never listened to classical music – in fact when my husband did I took refuge downstairs and listened to old school or R&B. I had no idea where that came from.

I wanted to end the interview, because it was embarrassing that I could not remember any significant piece of musical pleasure that ticked my passion box.

Come the evening after the interview, I went through all my favourite music memorising titles and artists. I stayed up into the early hours of the following morning, dancing to music and remembering the lyrics that had once meant so much to me. Despite little sleep, at work I felt lighter and happier the next day.

Christine uploaded some tracks onto my iPod. I listened and sometimes moved my head in between meetings, on the train, anywhere. I had found something I could do to block any worries and pending deadlines even for a few minutes.

The following weekend, I told my husband and children I wanted to go to a nightclub. This was out of character, at least when the children were growing up. But they were now fifteen and twelve, and I felt liberated from 24-hour care.

Weekend walks to the cemetery, trips to the gym or films were over. I never really did like films, first because I never decided what to watch – my husband and kids made that choice – but also because I couldn't stand blood and killing even in a movie. In some cases happy films made me sad, especially if they touched family lives. I decided I had had enough hurt in my life and therefore didn't need to pay to get hurt.

When Richard was abroad working, the children and I would sometimes dance at home, and invite their cousins; my brother and sisters and sister-in-law joined in too. I felt alive again, getting in touch with my childhood days, my history, the memories of the songs and dances that brightened our gloomy days when mother could not afford food, the days we would dance and sing, pulling out our last ounce of strength to keep happy.

I was nervous going to the club for the first time. I listened to Choice FM, which recommended a night at Cameo, and Richard came along. The dancefloor was small, full of people half my age, but the music was good. Then we went on to Le Palais. It wasn't so much the young audience as the kind of music, techno and garage, which left us exhausted.

During the week, I would feel lighter and able to focus at work better. Richard started missing some weekends and eventually declared he didn't want to dance at all any more. But I looked forward to Fridays, to dance and do something that made me alive. I investigated several clubs and, thank God, the dancers were pretty much as I expected: many older, some younger, a few thin, most average to generous. It was different from the gym or an aerobics class, thin trendy girls half my size who frankly didn't need to be there, working out like there was no tomorrow. Hey, the chicks in these clubs looked like me! I thought I could hang here.

I even took dance lessons, enrolling in a salsa club to brush up my moves. My instructor was great, rebuilding my confidence in dancing. For a forty-something I felt so fit and good, young girls would ask, '*How* old did you say you are?'

As I approached SURF's tenth anniversary in 2007, I knew that without dancing I could not get through the year. The pressure from the survivors to fulfil all their needs, the quickness to blame and their passive-aggressive behaviour were becoming unbearable. I knew that I had to find ways of shielding myself from a new wave of self-destruction. I took the brave decision to step down and reflect on my work, while continuing my commitment to support the survivors in a different role.

I reconnected with the only place where being myself was acceptable or didn't matter – the dancefloor. It could have been purely psychological but it's what I needed to stay sane. I don't know anyone who would understand what dancing brought to me except my siblings. We had shared the same coping mechanism for years, and it worked.

Every day at work, during the last year of my service, I struggled to stay motivated. At night the silence made me want to scream. I cried most nights, sometimes not even sure why. I turned on the music to drown out my stress, as hate mail both from survivors and from families of the genocidaires flooded my inbox.

Nights without music and a bottle of red, red wine became unbearable. Life is supposed to be normal – hanging around with friends, laughing and drinking, or sharing the odd glass of wine with your husband. But even Richard made a song and dance about a bottle a night. He was worried. He didn't understand that without it, coping with the witch hunt going on around me and running SURF under duress would have been unendurable. It took SURF nine months to find a replacement for me. I was emotionally drained and I could only feel the turmoil churning up my life.

The only way I could get through the day was to focus on work, which was increasingly stressful and causing me panic attacks and high anxiety. In my last days, as I stared at myself in the mirror, a wave of that awful lonely terror so deep it almost made me sick came over me and I had to hang onto the door to stay on my feet, even as everyone around me was singing of my iron lady strengths.

Suddenly a feeling of emptiness, drowning and extreme fear swept through me. I had never felt such terror. I visited the doctor, who diagnosed an anxiety attack. I was prescribed sleeping tablets, which knocked me out for three days.

But no one had any idea what it was like during those months of tearful nights. I would come home from work, drop my keys and handbag on the table, open the mail. Go to the kitchen, grab a bottle of red wine, have a warm sip, and another. Go to my bedroom, change out of my office clothes, carry my wine back to the kitchen, turn the cooker on, make dinner. Take the wine through to the sitting room, talk to the children about their homework, ignore phone calls, check mail. Sip from my glass, the bottle emptying slowly but surely. Carry it back to the kitchen, where dinner would be ready, then into the sitting room, sit and watch television, as the children go to bed. Take the last glass to the bathroom, run a bath, sip more wine, settle in the tub, cry alone all night.

My husband was either away or asleep. I'd go back to the sitting room, lie down on the sofa and close my eyes. Wake up in the dark, stumble to my bed and fall into a deep sleep for three or four hours.

On the worst nights, I couldn't sleep at all. I turned on a music channel on the TV and danced nearly all night. There was no other way to ride my emotional rollercoaster, a lone journey. I closed my eyes, filled my lungs as far as I could and exhaled, turned on the treadmill and ran for 5 kilometres, sweating out all the toxins and bad energy trapped in my veins. Sometimes I went through the whole night without closing my eyes.

Before I finally left SURF, I had one more moving act to perform – literally. I needed to rebury my brother. I made a trip to Rwanda to face my demons and the denial of my loss for the last time.

NINETEEN

My brother reinterred

IT WAS SATURDAY 21 July 2007 when I finally closed the book on my family's loss in Rwanda's genocide thirteen years earlier. It marked the end of my long journey and the beginning of a new one.

At three o'clock in the afternoon, I stood at the gravesite at Gisozi, Kigali's national memorial and mass grave for 250,000 victims of the genocide. I was here to rebury Jean Baptiste.

The Gisozi Memorial Centre is a modern whitewashed building strategically placed on a stunning hilltop in central Kigali. I had visited the site before, when it was empty. The mayor of Kigali had conducted a tour of the building, for which funds were still required to turn it into a memorial site. To the right of the building there was a pile of thousands of remains, shabbily placed together waiting to be laid to rest. In front of the building were the official mass graves, giant concrete vaults covered with slats where thousands would be buried.

The covers were pulled off to reveal deep graves that could take up to 500 coffins. Further down was another vault, with the belongings of the dead: black and brown handbags, identity cards, clothes, unmatched shoes. The smell of death still lingered in the air. On returning to the UK, I raised money to pay for a caretaker who could give tours of the site.

For my second visit, the weather was beautiful. The entrance, a grand gate, was manned by three armed security guards. A gardener was mowing the grass in the memorial gardens. Scented beds of roses surrounded the building, and the walkways were covered in evergreen creepers. Tall eucalyptus trees and wild flowers adorned the hill opposite, which was bustling with a lively market. There was a petrol station in the distance, where cars could be seen pulling in and out, kicking up dust; in the main street there were delivery vans, 4x4s, motorbikes and bicycle taxis. It was really no different from any other summer day in my country.

It was business as usual at Gisozi. Tourists of many nationalities were registering to visit the museum. I arrived ahead of the other members of my surviving family, to ensure I could locate the grave in which Jean Baptiste was to be buried. The receptionist told me to wait and went off to find the person in charge of the allocation of gravesites.

After a while a pleasant young man approached me. 'Please sign here. I will take you to the grave,' he said.

I wondered why he was coming to my brother's funeral. I didn't know the young man, and I wasn't expecting anyone.

'I am here to accompany you,' he explained. 'Just let me know if you have any problems. I am here personally to help you.'

I ask him if he knew Jean Baptiste.

'No, I didn't know him. But I know you,' he replied, offering me his arms. I extended mine to his shoulders, in the traditional Rwandan greeting called *guhobera*. 'I am one of the children you helped. I am a member of AOCM. You paid for my education. I want to be here for you. It is the least I can do.'

He walked me down the stairs towards the concrete grounds of pain that house thousands of innocent victims. We passed about a dozen graves all covered over, the young man telling me they were full to capacity. Jean Baptiste was to be buried in a gravesite on the left of the grounds towards the bottom of the valley, where most of the vaults were still half empty. The young man hesitantly encouraged me to get closer to the grave, which was half open. I could not see what was inside from where I was standing. He called a caretaker and asked him to open the cover fully and lower a ladder into the grave because remains of my brother were being brought here.

'That's where your brother will be buried at three o'clock. Please try and get everyone here on time, because we have another funeral at five o'clock.'

I had some time to spare. My guide asked me if I wanted to go back to the museum and wait there. I gave him a warm hug and thanked him. 'You must have work to do,' I said. 'Please leave me here. I will see you when the funeral starts.'

Alone at the grave, I had a moment to take it all in, to reflect on the enduring consequences of genocide. Sadness engulfed me.

Nearby was another half-full grave and another family burying their loved one. Two people came up to me and asked me if I was here for Saverina's funeral. 'No,' I said, 'I am here for my brother, Jean Baptiste.'

We looked at each other; we exchanged no other words. But I felt as though I could read their minds. We were in this together. The genocide was not yet over for us. We were still burying the victims who fell in 1994. Our grief united us.

As they quietly moved back to their gravesite, I begun to wonder about Saverina. Who was she? How were they related to her? Was Saverina a baby, a child, a mother, a grandmother? Why was Saverina only being buried now? Had they just found Saverina's body, perhaps located through the confession of a released prisoner? Where had Saverina been lying since 1994? What was her story? What was their story? These thoughts swarmed around my mind. I cast my eyes around me, remembering why I was here now, standing alone at the site.

My phone rang and brought my thoughts back to the grave. It was my younger brother, Francis. 'Maria, can you see the pick-up? We're here.'

I went to the gate and calmly directed the driver to the gravesite. We picked up the coffin and took it to the half-filled grave. The cover had been fully drawn back by now and there were more than a hundred coffins inside, neatly stacked together in rows. Ladders on either side led down to the floor. Many flowers lay around, some fresh, others withering, an indication of how many people had been there before us. The smell of death mingled with the dust and seemed to settle on my shoulders. Strangely, it gave me the balance, the strength, I needed.

I looked out across the valley. I could see lots of people moving around, but seemingly in slow motion. Children were skipping outside their houses. I tried to focus on what they were doing. I thought I could hear the song they were singing, as some swung the rope around, and others tried to dodge it. There were vans and cars of many colours – blue, red, brown, black. Bicycles carrying food and people were flowing in all directions. Women were walking barefoot, carrying baskets on their heads, babies slung on their backs.

The priest pulled out a bible from his briefcase. 'Dear brothers and sisters,' he said. 'We are gathered here to remember our beloved brother and father whose life was taken in the genocide.'

My uncle moved closer to us, Jean Baptiste's immediate family. He whispered, 'Courage.' I turned to nod and acknowledge his support.

I saw many people I didn't recognise. Many were dressed in black or purple, the colours associated with death. I was dressed in pale pink, though, with black and white high heels – not entirely appropriate for a funeral. But I was happy with myself. I had not kept to the tradition or upheld community expectations. I don't think that anyone who knew me would have been surprised. I always do my own thing. But this was not the reason I had chosen colourful clothes. I was celebrating my brother's life. What I was burying was ashes, his body not his spirit. His presence with me was real and overwhelming. It filled me with both happy and sad memories. I wanted to keep the good memories with me from now onwards.

Suddenly, in my mind, I was dancing in a nightclub. A warm thought crept over me. After the funeral, I would invite everyone attending to join me for a dance. I smiled to myself as I imagined what people would think. Would they laugh and break the pain and concentration, or would they think I was wild and unruly, I wondered. But it didn't matter at this point what anyone thought. I would dance tonight to celebrate my brother's life. As a child I always loved dancing, just as Jean Baptiste loved music and playing the guitar, and tonight I was going to dance in his honour. He had always wanted me to be happy, for life to go on.

I was brought back to reality as the priest invited the family to say something. People turned to me, as the eldest. But it was my niece, Jean Baptiste's daughter Gigi, who finally spoke.

She was seventeen. She held a photo of Jean Baptiste tightly to herself. 'Dad, we love you. We will always remember you. We were just children when you were murdered. We didn't get a chance to know you. But rest assured, you are always in our hearts and our prayers.'

My nephew, standing close to his sister, sobbed deeply.

When my father died in 1964, I was only five years old. I can barely remember him, just as Jean Baptiste's children can barely remember him. The pattern is repeated.

Then Francis began his last words. 'As you all know, we are here to give our beloved brother a decent send-off, for the second time.'

My mind returned to the previous evening, when we had exhumed his remains. A crowd gathered round the burial site and I couldn't help wondering if they had known Jean Baptiste, if they too had committed genocide. I asked them politely but firmly to move away, and they did, but not before a man and an old woman muttered something to each other and giggled. Gigi told me that they were neighbours. The thought of these neighbours chuckling as they left disturbed me.

Francis continued: 'Those who joined us to bury him the first time remember that he was found clutching a bible under his arm, with which we buried him. Jean was a man of God. . .'

I remembered the whole ordeal: finding his remains, his skull, carefully sieving through the soil and finding his shoes and the leather cover of his bible, a few pages still attached. I was far away in a different world. Despite the family around me, I felt selfishly alone and deeply sad. Thirteen years after the genocide, I again had to disturb my brother's soul. I missed the rest of Francis's speech.

When I came to, my two brothers, a cousin and Jean Baptiste's old friend were lowering themselves down the ladders into the grave. This would be Jean Baptiste's final resting place, with thousands of other victims of the genocide. As he took his place on top of another coffin, with more room for perhaps eight more on top of his, a chilling thought ran through my heart. There were many victims sharing the grave with my brother whose stories and lives I didn't know. Would I ever find out who they are? I thought of asking the caretaker if they had a list of everyone in this gravesite. Of course they did, but did they know the story of each individual buried here?

I thought of the twenty-two mass graves and the 229,322 other victims provided with a decent burial through SURF: 45,000 at Nyamasheke, 25,000 at Insimbi – the list goes on. The scale of the horror became a reality. At long last, after thirteen years of work, I had stopped and was now considering the magnitude of death. There were so many victims that I couldn't restrict my pain to just my brother. Overwhelmed by sadness, I couldn't help but wonder about the many other bodies still lying in unmarked sites, as yet undiscovered. The need was so vast, I couldn't but stay determined to find a solution, which was now more urgent than ever.

My uncle Discore closed the ceremony and asked everyone to meet at a nearby restaurant to wash our hands, a Rwandan way of inviting friends for a drink and thanking them for joining us. As people left, my aunt Laurence, standing a short distance away, looked across to me, but she made no effort to persuade me to join them. Since the genocide, I had only attended one family event – the funeral of an aunt, and even then I stayed only for the burial, leaving before the traditional mourning began. I was always too busy working, so everyone knew not to bother me or get angry when I did not attend. I politely said to Aunt Laurence that I need time to think about my brother. Resigned, she headed off with everyone else.

I stood here alone again, feeling numb, thinking of my brother and wishing I had treasured more all the days I spent with him, remembering the last time I saw him alive and his last words: 'Big Sister, you always worry too much! The UN Blue Berets are here, no harm will come to us. Take care of yourself.' It haunted me. Jean Baptiste was really dead. In my mind I couldn't see him properly. I couldn't reconstruct him into his original image. I slowly submitted to the fact that Jean Baptiste was no more.

Still quietly standing by the gravesite, I was joined by another family coming to bury their loved one. I joined them and listened. The deceased was a woman in her mid-thirties called Domitilla. Her relatives had recently found her remains when one of the released prisoners, given amnesty at a *gacaca*, confessed to killing her and identified the location of her body. I dared not ask or I would disturb the funeral ceremony, but I promised myself to get to know this person now joining Jean Baptiste. Suddenly, I felt less alone. There were others still hurting and dealing with post-genocide challenges.

Standing watching another grief-stricken family, I realised that until now I had denied Jean Baptiste's death. I had never actually mourned him; the stresses of working with survivors kept me occupied. I felt his strength and presence, just as for many years, I felt my late mother's presence around me. After my mother's death, I blocked all my emotions. I threw myself into work, work to support my siblings who were now orphans. I thought she was lucky not to have witnessed the murder of her family. Wherever she was now, her spirit was resting in peace. I couldn't say the same for me.

I was relieved because in a few days I would fly to Uganda to visit my mother's grave and then back to the UK – far away from Rwanda. How lucky I was. Many would remain in Rwanda with no chance of escape, even for a few seconds, from the reality of genocide. Most would have to stay and face the perpetrators that killed their families, that they witnessed killing their families. Many would have the funerals of friends and family to attend for a long time to come.

I look down into the grave where Jean Baptiste was now resting peacefully. I whispered a final parting: 'Goodbye, my beloved brother. I will always remember you. Rest in peace.' I picked up one of the bouquets of flowers that we had placed on top of the grave and threw it down into the abyss. It landed on Jean Baptiste's coffin. I knew that he had accepted this last gift. I could walk away. I quietly said my parting prayers and left.

Godfrey, my driver, was waiting for me in the car. 'Where do you want to go?' he asked. I didn't reply. He drove towards town, sensing my anguish. He had driven me everywhere.

Godfrey was a polite young man whom I had known for six years. He drove me everywhere when I was in Kigali. 'Where should I take you?' he softly asked me again.

'Home, please,' I replied.

Feeling exhausted, I put my iPod on full blast to drown out the thoughts of my brother in my head, as we made the short twenty-minute journey. Half way there, I changed my mind. I had to get on with business as usual. The next day I was due to take a group of Conservative MPs and supporters to the Murambi memorial site. I headed to town to remind them of the trip, and to say that I would be going ahead of the team. I invited them to join me later at the Cadillac, a local nightclub, to celebrate my brother's life.

By eleven o'clock that evening, my younger sister Rose and I had hit the floor and were dancing like crazy. We danced to every record from when we got to the club to when we left, at four in the morning.

I took time to reflect on my brother, and turned to my sister. 'Jean Baptiste should have been here with us.'

'Maybe he is,' she replied.

'Let's dance to him,' I said, and we laughed. Soon I felt uplifted, absorbed in a world far from the graveyard, far from my troubles, so unimportant and invisible that nobody even noticed me. I shook off all the week's stresses, anxiety and exhaustion.

Rose and I left the club as the bright yellow shades of dawn opened in the distance. A blue sky began to appear, and the birds spread their wings and sang. Kigali was still asleep. Ours was the only car on the road, driving across the hills of this most undulating of cities.

I slept for two hours, and then the alarm unkindly woke me up. I covered my face and ignored it. My brother Louis, who had travelled with me from the UK, knocked on my door. 'You have a mission to accomplish. The Tories await your presence at Murambi, remember?' He was coming with me to visit the memorial site. I crawled out of bed, my eyes half closed, and stumbled into the bathroom to get ready. I would catch up with my sleep on the road, I consoled myself.

TWENTY

Keepers of memories

IT WAS 22 July 2007, Sunday morning, and the Conservative MPs and volunteers were waiting for me. We had hired a seventy-seat bus, but I had to leave ahead of the party, to make sure that everything was ready ahead of the group's arrival. The plan was that the local mayor and the director of the site would receive the guests, take them through the history of the site and guide them through the twelve classrooms full of mummified bodies.

Godfrey, Louis and I set off in the misty morning. I put in my iPod earphones and drifted into oblivion. Bob Marley sang, 'Don't worry about a thing, 'cos every little thing's gonna be alright.' I shut my eyes and dozed off. The sleep was a godsend.

The driver wanted directions to Murambi and woke me up. I had no idea where we were. He had turned off the main road and driven towards the site. Our car was flanked on either side by very tall eucalyptus trees, hiding the rolling hills, one of which could be Murambi. I decided we should drive on until we saw someone who might give us directions. After fifteen minutes a small trading centre came into sight. We had to be careful who we asked for directions, as I had been told there were hardly any Tutsis still living in this area. We were treading on a scarred landscape, where friends and neighbours had turned into killers.

I told the driver to keep going until I saw someone I could trust. Having spent years reading expressions and body language and listening to survivors, I could easily tell who was a survivor. Suddenly I spotted an old man walking ahead of us. I couldn't see his face, as he was going in the same direction we were. He was wearing a brick-coloured cowboy hat and was carrying a cudgel over his left shoulder.

I look back to catch sight of his face as we drove past him. There was something about him. He could pass for the grandfather I never had. I asked Godfrey to stop and got out of the car.

'*Muzeyi, muraho?*' ('Old man, how are you?') I extended my arms to him in a *guhobera*. He was calm and very handsome, despite deep lines on his face that seemed to tell a thousand stories. He looked very thoughtful, intelligent and dignified, and returned my greeting with an air of authority. He welcomed me as if he was meeting someone he was comfortable with. I felt a connection straight away.

'*Muraho mwana wange? Mumeze mute iyo muvuye?*' ('How are you, my child? Where are you coming from?')

I explained that I was visiting the Murambi memorial site and that we had lost our bearings. The man started to give us directions, and then stopped. 'I am actually walking there myself. You can give me a lift and I will show you the way,' he said. I opened the front door for him and he sat down, half turning round to speak to me and my brother in the back seat.

'Where do you come from?' he asked.

I explained that I was a Rwandan who now lived in London and I was bringing visitors to see what happened to our people in the genocide. I introduced Louis to him.

Just seeing him take interest in us, and watching his facial expressions, I felt sad for him and for myself. I wondered what his story was. I felt the loss and emptiness which I often experienced when I thought of my dead family. As I was about to ask him what had happened to him during the genocide, he pointed to a whitewashed building. 'There is the Murambi memorial site.'

The memorial appeared unannounced through the trees. Like Gisozi, the building was situated on top of a hill, a beautiful site against the spectacular backdrop of the interweaving green hills. As we walked up to the building after parking the car, the old man showed me where the reception was and said goodbye before I could find out about him and his story. I thanked him and proceeded to speak to the receptionist about the visit and to organise tour guides for the impending party.

The man who directed us to Murambi reminded me of my hero, Simeon, a survivor of Bisesero who fought against the genocidaires and survived to tell a remarkable story of resistance. While I waited for the receptionist to locate the mayor and the tour guides, my thoughts wandered to the Bisesero memorial site, which houses 45,000 victims. Its beautiful setting is similar to Murambi's, and it was here that Simeon had told me his story with great dignity and pride. It was no surprise as he is a *musesero*, a clan known for the bravery of its warriors. They managed to fight off attacks during the genocide for nearly two months, until it became too difficult to defend themselves against the guns and their hunger.

Simeon called his survival a miracle with no purpose. He lost his entire family. Sometimes he found it hard to make sense of why he was still here. I loved Simeon. He was the most genuine person I had ever met. Unknown to him, for years after I met him he was my inspiration, my motivation, a model of dignity. How could I possibly feel fatigue and despair when he soldiered on?

I had driven from Kigali to meet this astounding old man the previous year. I had never initiated or sustained a dialogue with older people, but nonetheless always held them in the highest regard.

When I first met Simeon I felt like becoming his adopted daughter or granddaughter. As I never knew my grandparents I wanted to adopt one, but Simeon was not up for adoption. I always wondered what kind of relationship I would have had with my grandparents. Meeting Simeon, despite having prepared by speaking to his granddaughter, I didn't find the answers or clues that I was after. Neither did it prepare me for the aura that Simeon commanded.

Simeon had lived in Rwanda all his life. He represented something cultural, something real that I had missed for many years: the wisdom that comes with age. Mother always told us to respect adults because their experience and wisdom was worth learning from.

I met Simeon at his home, a traditional round house thatched with grass, set in a compound among modern brick houses and evergreen trees. Simeon shared his home with a local woman less than a third his age: he was seventy-seven and she was twenty-four. He didn't introduce her, and she sat cleaning utensils at the back of the house. I had come with two widows from the neighbouring village and a cameraman. He greeted us and, picking up his coat that was hanging on the branch of a mango tree and his stick, led us to Bisesero, where other survivors were waiting for us.

On the way, he told me that his family had been killed by the local people, so he was not ashamed to live with a local woman who cooked and took care of his needs. 'I wouldn't call her a wife,' he told me. 'She is a representation of everything that was taken away from me. She is a maid; they took away my family so one of their own has to look after me.' I sensed his hatred and resentment.

At the memorial site Simeon gave us a tour of the victims, some buried, others still lying on an open iron sheet. Then he got ready to tell me his full story.

We sat on two stones that seemed to have been positioned deliberately for this meeting. I sat facing him, pulling down my skirt to cover my legs as a sign of respect. He put down his cudgel and sat facing the camera, but he could still see me out of the corner of his eye.

I cast my eyes across the beautiful gentle slopes of Bisesero, and took in the most astonishing view. The dark and silvery leaves of the evergreen trees seem to provide a cloud of protection, only letting the faintest amount of light through. I was lost in this heavenly setting for a moment, escaping the fact that I needed to speak to Simeon about the betrayal of these remarkable people that had resisted the genocide. I could sense his enthusiasm to begin, but he patiently gave me time to absorb the beautiful countryside he had known from his childhood.

Andrew Sutton, the photographer, was equally distracted. He was spoilt for choice, trying sensitively to get all the scenery in shot. Andrew had voluntarily filmed all the work that I did for the survivors through SURF over the years. He sat through every conversation in Kinyarwanda, though he had no greater idea of what was being said now than he'd ever had.

Six feet tall and handsome, Andrew is patient and gentle, a very down-to-earth and unassuming man. He has a way of reading body language and facial expressions, and always knew when to stop taking pictures when I was interviewing survivors. He never interrupted or asked questions. He only filmed. We spoke about the content of the interviews during breaks, or sometimes months later when we returned to the UK.

Neither of us knew what to expect from Simeon but we knew this was not going to be easy. Andrew was buying time to get the best photo, one that would tell a thousand stories to the many who would never make it to Bisesero.

Simeon's patience was wearing thin. He had probably told the story a thousand times before. He shifted his sitting position, crossing and uncrossing his feet. He cleared his throat to get our attention. In a gentle but commanding voice, he said, 'Can we begin?'

'On 13 May 1994, a large number of militiamen and soldiers from Gitarama, Gisenyi and practically the whole country arrived in Bisesero by bus and truck. They surrounded us and shot at us persistently. If you escaped a bullet, you got struck with a machete. We were decimated that day; many of the women and children were killed as they were unable to run away. My wife, Marthe Nyirahategeka, my seven children and my grandchildren were all killed that day.

'Those who survived gathered in the evening and walked past heaps of bodies, one heap after another. From then on we hid in bushes on a hill. We couldn't fight back. Every day they continued killing us in the hundreds. They would smoke us out of hiding places like animals, chase us down and kill us. They would surround groups of us. Out of fear we threw spears, sometimes managing to hit some of them, and they would scatter, giving us a chance to run. A few, maybe five, would escape. The others would be killed as more Interahamwe advanced. We would gather back at the hill in the evening. Those who didn't come back we were sure were dead.

'We fought for two months, based in the same location. We hid our families in the bushes. They would find us and try to drive us towards Lake Kivu. There was nowhere to escape. We had to fight. We hoped that we would be killed first, before our children and families. Though we fought hard, they had reinforcements coming every day with guns and grenades. All we had to defend ourselves were spears and clubs. In the end we were overrun.

'There were too many of us on this particular hill, Muyira. We decided to elect a person who would be able to lead us, someone who was not afraid and who would be able to spur us on. Someone who had experience in battle. We chose Aminadabu Birara. He was a wise man and as old as I. He laid out a plan for us to follow, so that we would be able to repel the militia. Birara had

288

taken part in the revolution of 1959 and had lived to fight again. Unfortunately, he did not survive the genocide.

'I was appointed his deputy and I was in charge of my own brigade. The militia were always dressed in white and they wore green foliage on their heads when they launched an attack. When we saw them coming, I would lead the charge. Commander Birara would bring up the rear, urging on any who were too afraid. He would hit those who refused to advance.'

At this point I couldn't help laughing at the thought of being hit because you were retreating from danger. The men were caught between the machetes ahead and Birara's stick behind. Even Simeon stopped and laughed at the thought. 'I'd never considered it that way,' he said.

'As time passed, a small number of us hid in a hole. It was difficult to organise ourselves and we were hungry since we had had nothing at all to eat. We had suffered a lot. At night we saw dogs and other animals come to devour the bodies. During the day crows would come and eat the bodies as well.

'In the hole, we had radios and we heard that French soldiers had come to Rwanda and, more specifically, that they had arrived in Cyangugu, Kibuye and Gikongoro. Some of them arrived with us at the end of June. They were accompanied by a neighbour, a teacher whom I knew. He is now in Gisovu prison. He has confessed to his role in the genocide.

'When we saw their white cars arriving, we all emerged from our hiding place. At this time there were still many survivors. One of them, Eric, who could speak French, explained who we were. They took photos of us. The militia were there with them, carrying their weapons. The soldiers then left and said that they would return on Monday. It was then Thursday.

'It was a whole week before they returned. When the French left, the militia came in to kill. They killed a lot of us that day because many people had come out of their hiding places, thinking the French had come to liberate them. But in their place they found a sea of buses and lorries, all carrying more people, there to kill us. By the time the French returned, many people had died. We were gathered together on the hill. We found it in ourselves to sing to the glory of God "*Nyemerera ngendane nawe Mwami*", which means "Lord, let me walk by your side".

'After the genocide I donated this hill, which is family land, to bury our dead. I take care of the site to protect our families from further humiliation. Forty-five thousand families lie here at Bisesero,' he said, lowering his voice as if this was his last breath.

Simeon's courage was an inspiration to me. That year I built twenty-two memorial sites. I had connected with men who were the guardians of memories. I vowed to keep my strength up, because people like Simeon, with nothing left to live for, were living for those who were not there to speak for themselves.

My thoughts returned to Murambi. I thought about the thousands of people lying at this site, mummified bodies of children and adults. I thought of wasted lives, killed in cold blood because they were Tutsis.

The telephone rang, and I felt my stomach freeze. I stayed still, holding my breath, as if my silence might change the course of what had befallen thousands of victims I was about to visit. It continued to ring, and I finally gathered my thoughts and answered it. It was Gabo, the director of my office in Kigali. The visitors' bus would arrive in thirty minutes. He asked if I could wait at the front entrance.

The receptionist was now tapping me on my shoulder. She handed me a visitor's book to sign and said, 'Your guide is here.' I turned around and who should appear in view? The old man who had directed us.

He smiled at me and led the way. His name was Emmanuel. He told me it was his pleasure to show me around. I told him my name, delighted to see him again and curious to hear more of his story. He walked ahead of us, every now and then leaning against a thin but strong stick, about 5 feet tall, that he carried with him. He took me around the main block, revealing rows of classrooms, looking a bit run down, surrounded by well-cut grass.

Suddenly, after a lengthy silence, he explained, 'I was at this school during the genocide. I survived, by the grace of God. But my family did not.'

I listened intently. I wanted to know more, and I prepared my mind to take it all in.

'My family died here at Murambi: my wife and my five children, two boys and three girls. They all died here. The oldest was only thirteen. I cannot find words to describe the horrors they went through.'

He told me how Tutsis and their families were lured to Murambi Technical School. Women, men and children were kept in classrooms where they would supposedly find safety. Just like my family, they were told to gather at the school by the local mayor and herded into a classroom until the Interahamwe were trucked in. In both cases the Tutsi refugees were denied water and food, to make them weak so they would not try to defend themselves and their families.

We walked into the first classroom. Up close, the faces of the corpses were more expressive than I had ever imagined. Some of their faces were quite clearly contorted in a final scream. Bodies were spread on tables side by side. Emmanuel then led me to another classroom and showed me the bodies of his family. 'This is my wife and this is my son. These are all my children. I decided to take on this job to keep them company. At least I know where they lie,' he told me.

I held my hands on my stomach, to stop it from churning. There was no smell of human flesh, just corpses that were once his family. I saw before me a little boy with his arms aloft, in a desperate effort to ward off inevitable death.

'I felt the need to take care of my family until they are buried. So I am protecting them,' he said with deep sadness on his face. 'I visit them every day and lock the site safely. It will be the greatest relief if we can give them a decent burial. But given that there are thousands of bodies resting here, it is not likely to happen in my lifetime.' He sighed deeply.

Panic hit me without warning, and it was very different from the cold terror I had been feeling up to now. I had just buried my brother, whose remains had no resemblance to the person I knew. Here was Emmanuel able to identify his family, with no means of burying them with dignity. This put the pain of burying Jean Baptiste in perspective. I felt I was able to move on, but for many, like Emmanuel, there was no hope in sight of rebuilding their lives. Given his age, he had resigned himself to not seeing his family buried. I thought of Simeon, how both old men would die in sadness, bearing witness to the memories of loved ones. Genocide could not break their spirit to protect the remains of their families until they could afford them a decent burial.

I remembered all the people who I had managed to help give a decent burial. But Murambi was beyond my capacity to contemplate. I knew that it was one of the national memorials, now serving as a tourist attraction, where the reality of the genocide is kept alive for the world to see. Emmanuel would not, even if he wanted to, remove his family in isolation and bury them. I felt lucky that I had freedom and the means to bury my dead.

Emmanuel told me how every time visitors came to the site, he experienced the pain of reliving the memory of the genocide. But he took comfort from knowing that he spoke for the thousands who were not there to speak for themselves. He said he was a witness and their voice, and no one would ever deny that the genocide happened.

I knew that by hearing Emmanuel's story I would validate my determination to speak for the survivors, but I was also aware that the genocide was far from over, that each one of us was still struggling to make sense of it, to find peace and move on. I listened to the story of Murambi as Emmanuel continued.

'For two days, from 19 April, we were able to hold off against the infiltrators. Then on 21 April, at 3 a.m., a truck arrived full of militia and soldiers. They offloaded at the roadblock, surrounded the area and started shooting, throwing grenades into the crowd.'

He gave a look so long and silent that I feared our conversation would end right here. He seemed to have transported himself to the scene of massacres, his deeply wrinkled face showing the extreme strain and the pain. I stood in silence as the first tear escaped down my cheek. I felt pathetic. If he wasn't crying, what right did I have to cry? None. Yet this feeling built up inside, minute by minute. For fifteen years I had suppressed tears and grief, but today, I felt my heart couldn't take any more pain. I thought of the children with their feet cut off to stop them escaping while the adults were murdered. Once the adults died, then the militia came back to finish off the children. I felt a pain that had no name. I didn't even begin to wonder how Emmanuel felt.

He turned towards the rain pelting against the window, and carried on. 'It was mayhem, children clinging on to their parents, people scattered, all trying to escape. Those who did were either shot or clubbed to death by the Interahamwe, who had joined the killing spree.'

I thought of my family's last day, escaping only to be macheted by neighbours and Hutu killers waiting outside the classroom.

Emmanuel shut the classroom door quietly and gently led me to another room. It was as if he was walking silently so as not to disturb those resting peacefully. Room after room revealed more horrors. He gave a deep sigh and continued to narrate the story, the experiences he encountered and his miraculous escape.

'I was shot in the head. I was stripped naked and left for dead. Their mission was to kill every last one of us – if there was no one left to tell what happened, they could deny it all later. After they left, I made my way to Nzega forest nearby.' He took his cowboy hat off and leant against his cudgel for support. 'Next day, they brought tractors to bury the bodies, and they killed whoever was still alive. I watched them bury the people and when I realised that my family had all died there, I decided to leave. I walked through the night and rested during the day, until I made it to Burundi. It took me three days to cross the border, because there was no place to pass safely during the day. By that time, my head was badly swollen, but I was saved by the soldiers I found there.'

He had survived to be a witness to genocide, a keeper of memories for his family and for the thousands still lying at the Murambi memorial site.

As Emmanuel shut the door of the last classroom, the image of the white mummified bodies so closely resembling the people they once were, with skins and clothes intact over their bones, stayed with me. They looked like people, recognisable, some with machete wounds on their limbs and their heads, others showing the signs of the agony that had gripped them in their last moments of despair. There were children still clinging to their mother's backs, and women who had fallen with their legs open, stripped and raped before being killed.

I wished that I could forget what I had just experienced. Instead I only needed to close my eyes to see the dead bodies, imagining the people they once were, each with a name, hope, aspirations. The stories that the survivors had told me over the years crept back into my memory – the description of the killings, rape and mutilation; the smell of death; the shock and the horror that marked their last days.

As I replayed Emmanuel's testimonies in my head, I started to reflect on what happened to my brother and family. A lump rose in my throat and my breathing got tighter and tighter. I wanted to scream at the top of my voice to release the lump, but I didn't dare. Who was I to cry and make a scene, while Emmanuel remained so composed? Soon the bus arrived with the group from the Conservative Party; that was a good excuse to suppress the tears. I had to focus on business as usual, pull myself together and take them to the site. The mayor took a few minutes to welcome the visitors, which was followed by the usual speeches from the dignitaries and a brief history of the site.

The tour ended shortly before two in the afternoon. The bus journey back to Kigali was sombre. Everyone was lost for words, totally exhausted both mentally and physically. I began to think about Emmanuel and Simeon, keepers of memories and victims. Suddenly I had so many questions to ask Emmanuel. How did he cope? Did he ever cry and get angry? How did he sleep at night? Did he see his family in his dreams, his children playing? Could he still remember the good times? Had he any emotion left or were his memories frozen?

And then I thought: How have I coped with these stories and working with the survivors? Why me? Who am I really, and how have I dealt with the responsibility to give survivors of the genocide a voice to help them build a sense of humanity?

Some tasks were too big for me to take on, even as an iron lady. After fifteen years working with survivors, I could feel that I wasn't going to solve every single problem, that I needed to reflect on my own life and the burden of others that was now starting to overwhelm me beyond my normal capacity to cope or find solutions. The armour that had protected and suppressed the pain and held me together for years was splitting at the seams.

I had met Emmanuel in the hope that he would energise me, just as Simeon had done before him. But the pressures of my life and the burden of my work made it feel like I was carrying a nation on my shoulders. Emmanuel had unleashed a pack of untold stories of grief, from broken hearts. There were too many painful memories to contain.

Every night when my family was asleep, I used to recite this poem by Martin Niemöller:

First they came for the Communists, and I did not speak out –
because I was not a Communist.
Then they came for the Jews, and I did not speak out – because I was
not a Jew.
Then they came for the trade unionists, and I did not speak out –
because I was not a trade unionist.
Then they came for the Catholics, and I did not speak out – because I
was a Protestant.
Then they came for me – and by that time there was no one left to
speak out for me.

I had trusted my instincts, and made a moral choice which over the years enabled me to listen to survivors of the genocide and to dedicate my life to their cause, despite the challenges this posed for me. But these years were nearly at an end. Leaving Rwanda would be seen as betrayal to the survivors, but I longed to be normal.

I was about to open Pandora's box, stuffed full of repressed memories. I knew it wasn't going to be easy. For years I had cried at night or alone, because I didn't want my family to see me sad. My husband would be asleep or preparing for another trip; there was no point pulling him into my memories. My children would also be sleeping safely. I would be crying for my mother, wondering if she too waited for us to sleep safely, stealing time to reflect on her life. She had protected me from pain and I had been doing exactly the same with my family.

I was finally beginning to face my own challenges post-genocide. Jean-Baptiste was resting peacefully. But after reburying him I had to fly to Uganda, to make the pilgrimage to my mother's gravesite to confront her death. Then, I felt, I could finally focus on my own life.

TWENTY-ONE

Forgiveness or delayed justice: Rwanda's post-genocide moral dilemma

LETTING GO OF SURF was the most difficult choice I had ever made. Many people associated me with the pain and memory of genocide, so the idea that I should be happy and have fun or even take a break from work was increasingly unacceptable. I had no right to my own life because the memories were still raw and I must continue to be the sponge that wiped away the painful tears. I was wedded to SURF, as one of the donors commented when I mentioned I was stepping down as director.

My vision of SURF was shared by many of my colleagues. It had been nearly a year since I announced, in February 2008, I was planning to step down, but SURF could not find a replacement. I was getting increasingly anxious and very tired, but today I was excited. It was past midnight and I had spoken to David, the new director. David was eagerly waiting to take forward the legacy of SURF. I had known him since 2004, when he first joined SURF. He had been particularly supportive of me, a very committed individual with so much energy and a belief in SURF.

I enjoyed working with David and saw him as part of the generation which would take SURF to the next level. I congratulated him and pledged my help and guidance. One hour on the phone to him was time well spent and I felt ready to move on.

The next morning I went to the office as usual, had a look around and collected my personal files. Though I felt relieved, I was also filled with sadness, knowing that I had built a legacy, given all my heart and soul, to speak for the survivors, yet this sealed the end – the end of my chapter in SURF's story, if not the end of the post-genocide challenges ahead.

I was reminded every day of what Uwase, a 21-year-old survivor had told me, on my last trip to Rwanda in 2008 as director of SURF: 'Those that have not experienced the anger, animosity and brutality of our killers have forgiven them, but I am not fooled. I live with the truth that has not come to bear. I know the speed with which my neighbours turned against my family. To keep the peace I utter forgiveness and engage in community reconciliation. What other chance have I got of surviving with no family, living on the hills where my family was killed, next door to the killers? To buy peace among the killing fields, the most vulnerable community of widows and orphans give forgiveness.'

I learnt during my work with survivors that the weight of memory of the genocide obscures an important reality. For most survivors, the collective therapy of national healing and reconstruction available elsewhere is not an option. Unlike the survivors of the Holocaust, who built a Jewish cultural homeland and independent state in Palestine, and created a framework in which post-Holocaust Jewry could heal itself and thrive (despite the conflict with Palestinian Arabs, which was not probably anticipated), the survivors of the Rwandan genocide do not typically enjoy ancestral homelands far from the site of their agonies to which they can return. All are fated to remain in, and forced to come to terms with, the country in which their extinction was intended, planned and to a large extent executed. Such is the fate of the

Tutsi survivors; they must remain in Rwanda, continuously seeing the sites of their nightmares, forever risking encounters with the murderers of their loved ones. In brief, the Tutsi survivors have no sanctuary.

I prepared to let go of SURF knowing full well that there is a major dilemma confronting the survivors: they remain the minority in a society populated on the one hand by erstwhile enemies and collaborators, and on the other by sympathetic returnees, whose recent experiences and current preoccupations differ from their own. For while the survivors demand justice in post-genocide Rwanda, the perpetrators, bystanders and returnees struggle towards reconstruction and reconciliation.

The pursuit of justice is complicated by the existence of two parallel judicial systems, one national, and the other international, both trying accused genocidaires. There are different procedures of trials, standards of proof, punishments and levels of resources. In the years after the genocide, the rights of the survivors were overshadowed by the importance placed upon the rights of the prisoners – many getting food and medical insurance, an opportunity to work, contact with their families and international solicitude. Given the wretched physical and financial state of many survivors, such treatment of the accused genocidaires was a slap in the face to the survivors and their healing.

Meanwhile Rwanda was becoming a new nation, where 'there are no Tutsis or Hutus any more, only Rwandans'. Our history, written in our blood, was easily washed away; the survivors' memories were erased. The beautiful green hills laden with ghosts whose unburied remains scream from inside the many mass graves, those displayed on tables in churches and schools for the world to see, and those unidentified remains in fields, ditches, latrines, dotted all across the nation, lie still and silent, with no justice – their deaths in vain.

Rwanda has healed its people. There is no problem. Rwanda is at peace, on the mend and outwardly serene. Forgiveness is easily obtained when the killers confess. The achievement is astounding given what the country suffered. That is what the world sees. But having worked and spoken to so many survivors over the past fifteen years, I know that their views about justice and reconciliation differ, but they have no voice. Most survivors endure poverty and economic hardship, and their three greatest problems as they see them are insecurity, mistrust and lack of justice. These are not the responses of people optimistically building a new future for themselves in a redemptive society.

When the outside world first became aware of the genocide, many assumed it was a spontaneous outburst of hatred, a terrible expression of tribal passions. The truth of the genocide was only known through the testimonies of survivors, and the reality of its impact was only measured by the Hutu killers and those they sought to annihilate. Today they live side by side, with barely a whisper of trouble. Even when the released killers eventually manage to finish off a survivor, life must go on. Has the nation healed the minds and the hearts, of the survivors and their fear of those who butchered their families?

Many people have recently written about the shortcomings of the alternative indigenous solution to the post-genocide justice dilemma, the *gacaca*. The *gacaca* trials started in 2002, and aimed to ensure that the truth about the genocide emerged, that justice was done for the victims, and that those who had participated in the genocide and related massacres were justly punished. To the survivors, though, there has remained apprehension that the *gacaca* is first and foremost an expeditious mechanism that has resulted in ultimate impunity to the genocidaires. A goal of any genocide is to leave no innocent, living witnesses. How then could local communities that turned against each other a mere fifteen years ago reconstruct faithfully their murderous past and assign guilt truthfully? Many who have written about the *gacaca* have emphasised the judges' lack of impartiality. Survivors, meanwhile, see the *gacaca* as maintaining a post-genocide reality in which they continue to live in grief, pain and fear, their loss reduced to only a single piece of an imponderable vast suffering.

The survivors have been able to continue with their lives, accepting the inescapability of death, while mutual suspicion and inner tension gnaw at the edges. Whereas the world sees reconciliation between Hutus and Tutsis as the only solution, the international community has never called for reconciliation between Jewish survivors of the Holocaust and their German persecutors. This was never imagined. Although some Jewish–German goodwill encounters have taken place, this does not translate to asking former Nazis to sit down with, or to make public confessions of their guilt to, Jewish survivors.

It's not difficult to see why survivors can't speak from their hearts. Their tight-lippedness has a number of reasons. They are a minority community, mostly poor, with no family safety nets, homes or assets. Many are physically and emotionally unable to hold down jobs, trapped between Hutus who killed their families and targeted them, the bystanders, and other Tutsis like me returning from exile to a country we barely knew. But above all, all Rwandans share the same culture of total compliance.

Years back, my mother sent me to a school made up of children like me, refugees from Rwanda. She hoped I would learn the vulnerability of my people, but also the culture that distinguishes us from other races. I understood my background and built up a resilience to any form of difficulty. I became proud of my culture, my origins and my identity. I learnt that Rwandans are good-natured people, very good at putting up a front, able to handle concealment and ambiguity with remarkable skill. Working in

Rwanda since the genocide, I could see this culture at play in everything and everyone I met.

One survivor opened my eyes to the notion of reconciliation and forgiveness. Cyondo lost his entire family in the genocide. Their few remains – skulls, skeletons, fingers, legs – are displayed on tables, all separated out. He can just about make up a single skeleton from the bones on display. He spends time looking at each bone, in the hope that he can at least speak to his family in the school where they lie. 'We sing collectively to reconciliation and forgiveness, even though we may not totally agree. What would happen if one million skeletons of the dead whose lives were taken away, and whose rights we have not upheld, walked down the street of Kigali? Would they comply, forgive and forget? Would we imprison them or kill them again?' he asked me firmly.

I could not find the words to respond. His image of ordinary Rwandans, once people like ourselves, many still unburied, in the middle of a nation that is building peace and moving forward, became a visual answer for me. 'Justice delayed is justice denied.'

Cyondo told me that, during the genocide, there was a collective pressure to kill. Afterwards, the survivors are still invisible, poor, haunted by their memories and living in extreme fear. The collective pressure now is to forgive and reconcile, without due justice. Cyondo believes that those who did not face the killers can forgive, but he would never forgive without justice for his family.

Cyondo's sentiments are discussed by many of the survivors, among those who are trusted friends, sometimes with anger and emotion. They speak of fighting for their rights. But sadly, it's not only their rights that are cause for a fight. Because of their trauma and the many years of bottling up pain and grief, they seem to fight themselves. Generalised aggression and frustration are ever present as they target the people who listen to and support them. Like a storm they blow up ferociously, sweeping up everything that touches their lives. The survivors lack trust, and blame is inescapable.

Once I sought an explanation from a counsellor for the explosive anger I was experiencing from survivors. He said, 'Mary, torture does not make for good people.'

It is not difficult to see the trauma and torment that gnaws at their existence. They live with the hope that one day justice will be served. Struck with daily challenges of survival, many are still destitute, homeless, unemployed, downtrodden, suffering ill health and fighting HIV and AIDS. Battling for retributive justice has become irrelevant without social and political justice. One survivor asked me, 'If you had a pound, where would you spend it? Burying the dead, seeking justice or feeding a survivor?'

Right from the start of my work with the survivors, my burning anger and need for revenge were absorbed by providing them with social justice: giving them a voice, building homes, giving them access to education and healthcare, preserving the memory of the genocide, burying their dead and listening to their needs and their stories. When, with time, I saw signs of hope, smiles on survivors' faces, I knew I had defeated the killers' goal of exterminating all the Tutsi people. But I didn't defeat their intent to kill the witnesses. Still today there remains no trace of guilt among the killers. They want no one to face justice, they want no one left to tell.

As I prepared to leave SURF, I felt I was walking away with a responsibility to remind the world that, strictly speaking, the genocide may have stopped when the men wielding machetes were stopped, but that it is still going on in many other forms – homelessness, lack of education, lack of protection and total destitution. Genocide is an ever-present reality in Rwanda, not just during the anniversaries, but in the remains displayed everywhere of Tutsis that were once human beings with aspirations and hopes and who are no more.

I have been credited for my work with the survivors despite my constant personal struggle to address such horrendous crimes committed against my own family. I cannot be expected to simply forgive and reconcile myself with my brother's killers so that Rwanda can rebuild itself, without justice for his murder. Is the forgiveness I am asked to give for the nation or for me? I personally will never forgive the killers of my family. Forgiveness is a Christian notion I subscribe to, but in this case, forgiveness without justice is a betrayal of my family. Forgiveness is between me and my God; it's not a matter of national policy. Individuals should not feel pressure and live under scrutiny because they don't want to forgive. Through SURF, I felt I could reach survivors and raise awareness of their plight, and in that way an element of justice would be achieved. Without SURF, the wall of silence would have become impenetrable in later years.

I attempted to know and understand their survival mechanisms, after witnessing death and evil inflicted by fellow human beings. How many of one's family – children, spouses, parents – must be murdered before losing a sense of humanity? Like hunted animals, the perpetrators tried to hide. Some were found. Others died. But the survivors, despite their heavy scars and injuries, were left to live with the legacy of the murderers' crimes: mothers being told to choose which child to save or kill; children being told to deny their mother, so they could be saved, and seeing the fear in her eyes as they were chopped to death; many raped and stripped naked and left by the roadside to be raped again; old women tied upside down to tree trunks and raped by drunken and cheering youths; thousands thrown into the river with their families, hearing the helpless voices of their children as they drowned, swallowed by angry rivers and lakes; men watching as their daughters and wives were raped and killed. How much guilt and pain do the perpetrators bear? How do they survive?

Rwanda has done much to rebuild internally, but remains scarred. Whereas national reconciliation may be possible, expecting individual survivors to reconcile is unfair. Survivors are mindful of years of abandonment, stemming back to 1994, and global indifference. The memories of such atrocities may be wearing away, but to the survivors, these events are still fresh. Their survival depends on bearing witness and making sure such crimes should never happen again.

'Genocide marked the end of my life. I am a shadow of the person I used to be. I am alive to the world but my soul is dead,' Félix told me. Early in the morning of 7 April 1994, he heard the news that the President was dead. He suspected the worst, but had no idea of the scale of atrocities that was to follow. He gave me a detailed account of his experience.

Félix lived in Nyarubuye. On 13 April he went with his family to the church, seeking refuge, only to suffer the ferocious attack that Valentina had so vividly described. His family managed to escape through a door into the back yard of the church. Along with other refugees they held the door shut to stop the Interahamwe and the soldiers getting to them. They did this for some time, but the shooting continued and grenades were being thrown over into the yard. Félix was lucky to be near the door. The grenades didn't get him, nor did any shrapnel hit him. His family managed to reach the priest's lodgings, and soon he let go of the door and ran to join them and other refugees. He knew this place very well; he always prayed here and knew the priests too.

The priests tried to console them and asked them to pray. 'My family was sitting in a corner of the house. The shooting continued non-stop around us. The bullets were too much to bear. I tried to climb over the fence, fearing that we would eventually be overrun by the Interahamwe, who were now harassing the priests to hand us over to them. Unfortunately the Interahamwe spotted us. I saw them coming and I ran and hid among the dead bodies. There were many bodies so I pushed my way under them but my wife and children were caught and taken to a tree,' he told me, tears streaming down his face.

'As for my wife, she had no choice. Before they killed her, they raped her. I saw it all. They gang-raped her. I managed only to see five men. After a while my concentration failed and I passed out. My youngest child, who my wife was breastfeeding, was torn off her and smashed against a wall and died straight away. My other child rubbed his fingers, begging for mercy and pardon, as if he had done something wrong. A group of Interahamwe hacked him to pieces with machetes and he died. After debating who should take my wife home with them, they decided that they should all have a piece of her. One man cut one arm off, and one the other. They tore her to pieces so that none of them could have her for himself.

'It was a miracle that I survived. The shooting usually stopped at night, when the Interahamwe went home. I would emerge from under the dead bodies to see if there were any survivors. Apart from my immediate family, all my relatives were in that church. Over 200 of them. They were all killed, one by one. I thought, well, they have killed all my family, what is keeping me?

'Days passed. The Interahamwe would find people to kill, but here I was still alive. Bodies were beginning to rot and the smell was unbearable. The Interahamwe could not bear the stench, and they stopped coming to the church. I stayed with a handful of survivors, living among thousands of dead bodies. So many were killed here.'

Félix identified all his relative's bodies, but the grief was too much to bear and he became hysterical. He wanted to die to stop the pain. He left the churchyard and ventured out hoping that he would be lucky enough to find someone to kill him. He wondered from one roadblock to another, asking people to kill him, but they refused. 'He alone might live.'

Hutu refugees were now fleeing to Tanzania in large numbers, apparently escaping the RPF soldiers who had arrived in Kibungo, the province in which Nyarubuye was located. He was rescued by these soldiers, whom he had approached asking them to shoot him.

Reconciliation and forgiveness involve revisiting memories. The pain of such memories can't be erased easily. As Félix told me his story, I wondered what forgiveness had to do with his painful existence. Would forgiving the gang rapists take away the pain he felt about men raping his wife, and those that killed his children and wife? Some atrocities are so evil that the unbearable truth cannot be erased that easily.

Félix told me that telling the truth in *gacacas* didn't translate into forgiveness. The truth has empowered him, helped him to control his feelings, so that with time his soul has not been poisoned and in his own time he can move on, without the pressure to be seen to forgive. Forgiveness is voluntary, and no one can coerce another to forgive.

I have spent time counting my losses and those of the survivors I came to know. The pressure to heal and move on is a burden for many. The international agenda demanding reconciliation from them continues to grow. However, it fails to protect the memories of the victims, and in the case of survivors in Rwanda, they still have too many reminders of their past to be able to do so. No nation has come forward to truly help. Without due process for social, as well as political, justice, any reconciliation is delayed justice for survivors.

Justice may mean different things to different people. The world should not impinge on the rights of survivors to think independently. Because the international community has failed to punish those that committed the genocide, in some cases even providing more support to them than the survivors receive, any

307

call for reconciliation only serves to cement the past horrific memories and anger.

The best revenge is survival, I was told by Jean-Pierre. 'I will not let Hutus triumph over my failure, because they would win again. We will overcome even them. I will not give them any excuse to rebuke my family. I will always remember them, as part of my revenge. I will celebrate their lives. We have witnessed Hutus throwing grenades at memorial sites during the April commemoration of the genocide, and heard the complaints that it is time to move beyond genocide. There are many killers still angry to see us here. They left us for dead. But though injured, we are still here. The anger eats them up and they anticipate further violence.'

I have come to learn that even those who have forgiven their killers lose their strength when they meet them face to face. For a few seconds, it drives them back to the days of the massacres, when they were smoked out of their hiding places, herded as animals to the slaughter. Then there was no help and many died. Today the survivors know they have no protection, so they tremble anxiously when they meet the killers.

Revenge for the majority of survivors was to bear witness in courts. So they have waited patiently. First the world acknowledged the genocide. It accepted only diminished responsibility. It offered an apology but no reparation. It asked the survivors to forgive the killers and move beyond genocide. Is this justice? Or is it a compromise, the consequence of which will be endured by the second generation?

INDEX